Mesa

Jude Stringfellow

MESA

Mesa

MESA

By Jude Stringfellow

Mesa

Jude Stringfellow

Copyright © 2024 by Jude Stringfellow.

All rights reserved. No part of this book may be reproduced or transmitted in any form or by any means, electronic or mechanical, including photocopying, recording, or by any information storage and retrieval system, without permission in writing from the copyright owner.

This is a work of fiction. Names, characters, places, and incidents either are the product of the author's imagination or are used fictitiously, and any resemblance to any actual persons, living or dead, events, or locales is entirely coincidental.

Mesa

DEDICATION

When I knew I would write "*Mesa*" I knew I would include in that writing, a brief (very brief) description and understanding of the American Mustang. I wanted the world to have a taste, just a nibble of knowledge about these amazingly formidable animals of the American frontier. There is no one better to dedicate this book to than my own daughter Laura, who for years has been not only a horse trainer, but has been intimately involved in the process of gentling, taming, and training wild Mustangs. She has owned a few herself and has worked with those belonging both to the United States Government and to individuals who took upon themselves the privilege and challenge of owning such a powerfully majestic creature.

To Laura, you are the horsewoman of my life. I have watched you, and I have learned from you. I wish I could set you free within the canyons of the Sierra Northwest so that you could be as free and as wild as the horses I know you love with every pulse of your beating heart.

Jude Stringfellow

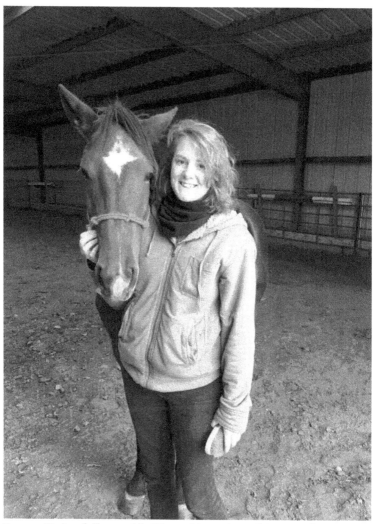

Laura Stringfellow with Nova (American Mustang) 2018

Mesa

Jude Stringfellow

THANK YOU PAGE

The *"Thank You"* page is a fun one. I like to thank my friends and family for sharing words with me that they think will enhance my book(s) and/or stories.

Thank you, Penny Makington, for suggesting the word *"quixotic"*.

Thank you, Jeannie Clarke, for suggesting the word *"conundrum"*.

Thank you, Yvonne Espinosa Ramirez, for suggesting the word *"cataclysmic"*.

Thank you, Ellin Daum, for suggesting the word *"irrefutable"*.

Thank you, Marty Kapp, for suggesting the words *"Navy Pier"*.

Thank you, Gordon Dean Flick, for suggesting the word *"lugubrious"*.

Thank you, Lorna Pratt, for suggesting the word *"fractounatious"*. *(Which isn't a word)*

Thank you, Laura Stringfellow, for suggesting the words *"heterochromia iridium"*

Thank you, Caiti Stringfellow, for suggesting the word *"vindicated"*.

Thank you, Reuben Stringfellow, for suggesting the word *"flexed"*

Thank you, Julie Szabolcsi-Anderson for suggesting the word *"Latrodectus"*

Thank you, Tex, for continuing to face the stampedes in your life with grace and prayer.

Mesa

DISCLAIMER

There will always be a reason to write a disclaimer as long as words are being published in print or eBook form. I will be the first to stand in line to write such a disclaimer as I believe in them. I am a true fan of all things disclaiming; since fiction writing is not to be taken literally. It is not to be believed. It is not to be held to any form of standard other than for what it is – which is fiction.

Like all of my fiction books, this book should not be held to any measure of worthiness; if you like it, you like it. If you don't, please stop reading it and use it for toilet tissue or something you find useful. I am a writer who writes, an author who auths. I hope that you find the book entertaining, and so much so that you'll share it with those you trust, love, and admire. Share it with anyone really, I'm not picky.

You will find mistakes in this book. You will find errors. You will see that I did not do as good of a job as I could have when it came to editing. The reason is simple; I am not an editor. I write. If I paid for editing I wouldn't feel as human as I do when I do it myself. We all make mistakes. I can live with mine. I hope you can too.

Mesa

Jude Stringfellow

ONE

A dry hot breeze blew in from the Southwest, dragging with it the loose red clay sand from the newly graded street. Oklahoma City Police Chief Ian Moore pulled the loose chain of his pocket watch, opening the thing he checked it before entering the street-side door of the downtown precinct. At 7:17 a.m., it seemed unnatural for the outside temperatures to be as high as it was; yet, there he was, wiping his brow for what would be the first of many times that bright June morning.

As he opened the heavy front door of the precinct and passed the front desk clerk, Moore made some sort of off-handed comment about the weather under his breath, only to have it returned with an equally unintelligible remark about the two of them choosing to spend their time and lives in the southwestern state of Oklahoma when Hawaii was sitting pretty out in the middle of the drink.

Some people wake up in the morning already hating their day and themselves. Still, others think of new ways to make it worse; some try their best to face the day with an attitude of gratitude and hope. This was the way Chief Ian Moore chose to live his life each and every day. By the time he reached his second-floor office, Moore had passed a half dozen open windows. Another half dozen electric fans blew simultaneously with enough noise to drown out a herd of elephants charging if there was one.

Mesa

"Thank God, we have the fans", shouted Moore to an uninterested and unresponsive detective whose partner was crossing the room with a fresh pot of coffee. *"I've never understood why or even how we can all drink that stuff when it's this hot,"* Moore stated to no one in particular. Drawing the last drop into his cup, he turned to face veteran Detective Sean MacArthur, asking him if he had any news about their last discussion. Moore wanted to know if his senior detective had made up his mind about possibly leaving the Sooner State to search for the killer of the last Governor's niece and possibly her best friend several months back.

"We couldn't catch the bastard; he's left the state. Governor Pate could use your help, Sean. You're the only one with federal jurisdiction. This case isn't going to go away. Pate may not be our governor now, but he was and he may be again, and the people still want to bring the thing to a close." Moore pleaded without specifically doing so. MacArthur looked Moore in the eyes before turning his head to not give away what he was truly feeling about the past governor's woes.

"Hold your horses Chief; I'm not inclined to do it. The case is closed as far as I'm concerned. It may be something J. Edgar Hoover may want to take up since the guy fled to the desert, but no, I have enough trouble surviving this damned heat in our state, why would I want to put myself through even more of it out West?", he answered.

Chief Moore pivoted on his heel. Looking down he noticed the detective's shoes had been freshly polished. He couldn't help himself and he gave a bit of a muted chuckle. *"It's the heat, is it? Maybe you just don't want to have to*

Jude Stringfellow

run a brush over your new Derbies. What did those things set you back?", Moore laughed. *"People either make things happen or watch things happen, sometimes they ask themselves what the hell happened. Know what I mean Mac?"* He asked.

"No, I don't think it's the heat. You don't want to push the envelope. Maybe you're afraid this Ken Burke is still alive; maybe he's not dead like all the papers said he was. He's out there Mac. He's out there living and killing, and he took our own governor's niece in the mix of it. Damn sure of it. If he didn't marry the friend, he killed her too. Dorothy...her name was...Dorothy something."

Turning to MacArthur's lanky young partner, Moore questioned him silently by raising his chin into a nod while squinting his eyes. The man picked up on the gesture and reacted. *"Say, I don't want to take the rap on this one. I could look it up for you, Chief. I know her name is all over the files they took back into the ground floor store room."* Not wanting to seem inconsiderate or uncompassionate, the younger man gave his own silent signal to MacArthur letting him know he'd handle the Chief and get him off their backs long enough so they could leave the building for the day, maybe making their way onto the streets to pursue the cases on their desk before having to add another one to the already unmanageable stack.

MacArthur sat down, pushing a shorter pile of files to the side before giving Chief Moore the look men give to others when they want them to understand what they have to say. Like the Chief, Detective MacArthur had been in the uniform in one capacity or the other for over a quarter century. He had been the guy to chase the impossible leads. He wasn't about to push himself now; not if it wasn't in his wheelhouse to begin with.

"I work for the City now, Chief. I'm not a rank-and-file man. You can put in a request if you want, but I don't think the department is going to want me to go out into the Mojave Desert to traipse around looking for a man who may or may not be dead. The papers said they found him. You don't think it's him.

"You didn't see the port stain birthmark in the pictures they posted. I get it, you think he's still out there. Let's say he is. Let's say he's out there living and killing like you said; he's not in Oklahoma and he's certainly not in Oklahoma City." MacArthur continued. *"He's not Ken Burke anymore either. He's Russell or Russo; wait – Rushby. I don't want to seem like I'm hard on this one, but he's not my problem. He's not any of our problems really. He's a dead man who did a bad thing. Case closed."*

When the partner came back he handed a rather thick and well-organized file to Chief Moore but before he let it go completely he had an idea that may solve the situation for everyone.

"Chief, I know I'm just a dumb kid. I've been a detective only a few weeks, but when I was on the beat, on the streets with you, I respected your opinion and I still do. I think you're right; I don't agree with my own partner on this one, but he is my partner, and I have to follow his lead or be washed up for good.

"Maybe you can get Nick Posh to do it. He's not under our payroll. He's not likely to have the same restraints Mac and I have about going out there and dying in the smothering heat trying to catch a ghost just to settle some score that may not even be a score." He

said. *"I mean, it may be an election year, but Pate hasn't even thrown his hat back into the ring yet, has he?"*

"You're not half wrong Koch," Moore said, *"...you're not half wrong."* Moore took the file into his office to review knowing the name of the dame who had been with Asta Pate, the governor's niece, was Dorothy Ellen Eischer. Her initials spelled out the word *"Dee",* a nickname she went by; one that was noted in the file as well.

Dee had recently inherited quite a bit of money from her father's estate. Splitting the money with her kid sister, a half-sister from a romantic affair, she hadn't been too easy or too quiet about letting the kid know how she felt about having to give up more than eighty thousand dollars to someone who shouldn't have been hanging around the family in the first place. Maybe, thought Moore, if only for a split second in his mind, the half-sister had something to do with it. Maybe she could have hired Burke to do her sister in and they could split the money. It was a thought; albeit a fleeting one.

Moore read through the file with the interest of a bloodhound on a scent. He tried to find something to hang his hat on, something that would give him the authority to make the calls he would need to make in order to bring about a true end to the case; not just hanging it up for lack of evidence. That sort of thing always stuck in his craw.

If it wasn't solved it was unsolved. That was his hardline motto if he had one. Every crime had to start somewhere. They don't fall out of the sky and happen. They were either planned or unplanned. They were either organized or not. He gave Koch's suggestion another mulling-over in his head before lifting the receiver of his desk phone.

Mesa

When the call rang through on the other end, it wasn't the Commissioner's office secretary answering it. Chief Ian Moore had placed the call to the one man he believed could do what he needed to be done. Private investigator, Detective Nick Posh's voice rang strong for such an early hour. Chief Moore drew his breath and stared into the distance hoping the next few words he spoke would hit their mark.

"Posh? Chief Moore of Oklahoma City Police, how are you this morning?" he asked. Smiling, Posh set his morning coffee cup down and reached instinctively for the pad and paper he kept by the telephone book; he knew he would need it.

"Fine, this morning Chief. It's gonna be another hot one. I tell you; this Oklahoma heat is something I did not miss when I lived overseas. I think the hottest it ever got in the United Kingdom was just around eighty degrees, and we have that now before the sun rises."

When Moore relaxed, he drew another breath and put his plea out into the universe, hoping for a positive response from the pay-on-demand investigator who could not only be counted on to take strange or unusual cases, he was fair about his fees. Having been passed over a few months back for a permanent spot on the force as Detective First Grade based on political and office seniority issues reasons, Posh knew he'd need to take a case now and again if he wanted to keep himself in the good graces of the city he lived in and had decided to remain permanently. A few bumps in the road wouldn't make much of a difference to a man who had already been up and down those roads for most of his adult life.

Jude Stringfellow

"OK, so to clarify, you want me to drive out to Las Vegas, or maybe around that area, and find a man who may be dead, but if he's not dead, you want me to bring him back so he can be tried for murder? Maybe I should just shoot him in the head and be done with it. I don't want to have to feed him all the way back to Oklahoma", joked Posh.

"You've got most of it, Posh. I want you to find out if he's dead or not, and if he's not I do need you to apprehend him. You can turn him over to the local police out that way and we can then extradite him properly. We can even transfer the caseload to them if they will have it. I'd need to check Nevada law to see if they'll even play ball with us." Moore replied leaning back in his chair.

"I'd say a rope is an even cheaper route to go, but finding a tall enough tree in the desert may prove impossible." Nick speculated before adding, *"...I could drag him behind my Buick."* With more sarcasm and good-natured bantering being shared, Moore felt confident that the man had all but accepted his request.

Assuming the close of the offer, Chief Moore indicated that he would call back in an hour or so after he had time to talk to the Commissioner about the budget. The end of June was the end of the City's fiscal year; if he was going to ask for an extra bounty, now would be the time. Any extra money left over from the year could be used to apprehend a suspect; especially one of such high profile.

"It's settled then," Posh added, but then there was a pause. The kind of pause that sent a cold sweat down the back of the police Chief because he felt he hadn't quite made the sale. *"Chief, I won't be able to go it alone. I'll need to take a man with me, and by taking a man, I don't*

Mesa

mean MacArthur or any of the men there in the precinct. I have a friend in Chicago who would pretty much cotton to tag along with me on this one. He hasn't been let out of his cage for a while." Nick laughed.

"He and I went through the Battle of Somme in the war, and a few other unnamed attacks. I trust him. He'd be a good soul to bring with me and keep me company, and he's had my back more than once since we got back stateside. If he can go, if you can pay him what you pay me, I'll do it."

Posh's counteroffer could have been a deal breaker, but Moore wasn't going to let him think it was. *"I'll get back to you. Will you be around in about an hour so I can call?"* he asked. *"I'll do you one better, Chief, I'll call my man and then come up to the station to tell you what he says,"* Posh promised. Posh's newly purchased modest home sat probably less than three miles from the heart of downtown; he could drive or catch the street car straight down Classen Boulevard if he thought he needed to. The two men respectively hung up their phones only to pick them back up and make their next calls; one for permission, the other for interest.

TWO

Ralph Ferguson's response to his good friend was not only unexpected, it was quick. *"Posh, you must have been sitting over there in some sort of a meditative stupor to come up with such an idea. I was just about to call you to ask you if you wanted to help me go out that way to catch up on why the Las Vegas syndicate is making heads and tails over what the organization is making up this way.*

"There's a battle about to brew between these families and not a week ago I mentioned to the Stateville Senior Warden that I'd like to go undercover to hone in on what I can." Fergy's enthusiasm caught his good friend Nick Posh off guard for one of only a few times it had ever happened.

"I gotta tell you, Ferg, I'm usually the one to get your goat, but I'm speechless on this one. You've been undercover before, so I'll not give you any hell on that, but are you sure you want to deal with the underground that deeply seated? I mean, the St. Valentine's thing sort of rang my bell for wanting to get too close to those guys again." Posh admitted.

"It had the opposite effect on me, Nick. I was that close to nailing that thug Moran and them, I wanted to be the one to cuff 'em, read them their rights, and maybe knock a head or two before they found their way into the cage." He added. *"If you want me to help you, and you're*

willing to help me, we can kill a whole flock of birds with two stones. I'm in if you are." Ralph stated.

Nick thought for a moment before asking. *"What about Stella? You're just barely married and having a baby. Will she be able to let you go for a few weeks not knowing if you'll even return?"* Posh questioned. *"If she's not she shouldn't have married a Chicago cop"* was Ralph's answer.

They continued their phone conversation both taking notes, asking questions, and listening as the other gave details of what they knew about their individual missions. Posh had the idea that there would be one mission with both men achieving it, while Ralph Ferguson could see a way of separating the two, splitting up their priorities into two pieces. First, he imagined they would want to research and do a bit of recon on the killer Posh was chasing, to find out if he was actually dead or not. If he was dead, there would be less money coming in from Oklahoma City, and the Chief would want the case tied up, paid, and closed.

If on the other hand, this Burke fella was in fact alive, the payroll from the City of Oklahoma City could keep them afloat until the end of the month when Ralph received funds from his side of things; with enough to pay not only his share of expenses but hopefully add to the totality of both of their earnings. A win-win.

"I'll get my side to pay me and you both Posh. You get your side to pay you and me, and we'll be sitting pretty on top of the whole thing. If either side talks to the other, we could be questioned, but both sides want something done, and both sides are willing to pay for two

to make it happen. I don't see a downside to this one," Ralph said.

"Let me work my magic, Posh. I'll call you this afternoon to let you know what the verdict is, but I suspect I'll be catching the Santa Fe Chicagoan Express to Oklahoma City in a day or so."

With the confidence of having his best friend and comrade excited about making the next few weeks their own, Posh felt certain that Moore could convince whomever he needed to convince that whatever needed to be paid could and would be paid to close the Asta Pate and Dee Eischer murder cases. Bodies would need to be recovered if possible as well. The last word on either of the women was a vague description from a Lake Mead, Nevada police secretary describing an out-of-towner, a woman who was found decomposing in the desert. She was found alone – no one with her. No promises it was one of theirs.

The body they found had been so badly affected by the elements of the harsh dry semiarid weather and the mauling of wildlife that she was recognized as being a woman only by the loose torn clothing she wore and what appeared to be breasts under a mostly intact brassiere. She had been left alone in the open to rot away.

The county coroner set the closest estimated time for her death was between six to ten months; give or take. With no one to claim her, she was surrendered to an *"interested party"* was all the secretary would say. There was another possibility of a female victim being found near the Calico Cliffs, but with its steep ridges to maneuver through, and it being too far from the jurisdiction of the area, no one had bothered to try and recover the remains.

Mesa

The woman at the bottom of the ravine had been found a few weeks after the first and was identifiable in that she was clearly female; they could make that determination with a pair of binoculars. Her supposed age, height, weight, and general description matched Dorothy Eischer. It was believed she could have met her demise from falling. No other women that age had been reported to have been found in the same general location over the past two years.

Aged twenty-two at the time Asta was last seen in Oklahoma City's downtown district, the former debutante had made quite a name for herself, at least as far as the Society Pages were concerned. She stood nearly six feet tall. Her lean almost waif stature gave her the look of a magazine model. Blond as her good friend, the two girls could be considered sisters themselves, if it weren't for their vast differences in height, and the color of their eyes.

Dorothy bore a strong resemblance in some ways to her friend, but being nearly half a foot shorter, she was often called the "*little one*" though she was a full two years older than Asta. Both women had celebrated late into the night of December 26, 1930, with several close friends at the very swank Skirvin Plaza Hotel on Broadway in the city. Champagne flowed and small sandwiches filled their plates as did various cakes, fruits, and sundaes.

It would be a night they would both remember. Asta Pate had been introduced publicly as one of the city's most eligible bachelorettes a few years earlier; an honor which had afforded her college tuition as part of the award package. Dorothy had been an honor student in high school, with her own paid scholarships; both women were clearly marketable and smart enough to know it. They were both exceptionally talented in their own right; for someone to take this and everything from them was unthinkable to anyone.

Wanting to spend the next few years of their young lives striking out on their own rather than finding husbands and settling down; both women had haughty plans after graduating from the very private and prestigious Oklahoma City College with Business degrees. Flying high on her father's money, Dee Eischer had hopes of becoming an accounts receivable employee for one of the smaller circus units currently crisscrossing the country. She had read their advertisements in the local newspapers, calling for young and excited entrepreneurs whose minimal investments now could bring them a lifetime of steady and passive income. Dee wanted this and more for herself.

Because she could invest some of her money into the struggling entertainment corporation, she was accepted via correspondence and through several telephone conversations with the Operations Manager, a man known as Titus Rushby; working directly for the owner of The Bollen Group; Aldo "*Buster*" Restani. The Bollen Group, though unknown to Eischer, was apparently an up-and-coming circus corporation of the Southwest vying for its piece of the enterprising pie in the world of family entertainment. It had, according to Rushby, traveled throughout Mexico, Texas, Arizona, and California and was making its way through the great Sierra Northwest currently.

At Dorothy's own assertiveness, the two became acquainted when Dee answered the classified ad in the paper. Not satisfied with simply becoming a part of the company as a paid employee, it was Dee who had suggested the investment of her own money to both secure her position and that of Asta's, but also to begin what she hoped would be a life-long income maker as well.

Titus Rushby, through Aldo Restani, had hired Dee and promised to interview Asta to be her assistant, believing he could pay Asta Pate less, and she would be dutifully trained by her closest friend. Two birds, one stone. Dee's enthusiasm on the night of their celebration was over the top, strong and boisterous even; at one point she had mentioned that her new position would help her not only see the entire country first-hand but that the percentage she would make from her investment into the company could afford her anything she could ever imagine. For her part, Asta was thinking the same thing.

She would use her family's influence to gain access to the business end of it, and upon her twenty-fifth birthday, when she received her own inheritance from a family trust, she too could invest in the circus futures for a percentage. Everyone loved the circus. It was a glorious dream for the two entrepreneur-minded women. Degrees and money in hand, they found themselves giddy from all their hopes. Rushby by her side that night, Dee felt comfortably confident in her new position; enough so, to bid farewell to the city of her youth for what she hoped would be a lifelong triumph of success.

As it was an election year in Chicago, the Senior Warden looked forward to sending Ferguson out as an undercover officer in his pursuit of becoming a detective in the department. Apprehending or gathering intel on the syndicate families of Las Vegas could only pump up and boost the all-but-tarnished reputation of the police force in Chi-town. Having another bright feather in their cap could

Jude Stringfellow

prove to be useful in more than one way; those who were on the take in the department would be less apt to speak up and their silence could out them.

Ferguson saw the other side of the coin as being equally advantageous; perhaps they really could put an end to the rising rivalry between the two factions, allowing the Chicago crime families a shorter leash which could benefit law enforcement and make the side-smiling politicians happy for a while. It couldn't hurt to try and come back with more undercover experience under his belt. Besides, the buttons on his double-breasted blue cop's uniform were beginning to squeeze a little; married life had taken its toll.

On the one hand, politically, a newly organized Democrat party was on the rise, making their move against the Republican incumbent. A switch in parties would mean more power for their personal and professional agenda; the fact that Ralph Ferguson himself was a staunch card-carrying Republican didn't stop the new Police Commissioner from using his unique talents and perspective to solve another piece of the unending puzzle by convincing the Senior Warden that Ferguson would be a hit out in the field.

If Ferguson uncovered intel that would benefit the force or the new government, more power to him. If he was killed in the line of duty making his point, he would be given a hero's send-off; Commissioner Dougherty would certainly see to that. Immediate plans were put into place to send the man undercover and with whatever resources he needed to bring home the win for the City and the people of Chicago.

With the contract for hire signed and filed securely in his credenza, Commissioner Dougherty handed

Mesa

Ferguson his train ticket, leaving his return open and his expense account unlimited with the caveat that he'd rather not see booze and brothels on any line of the weekly expense report he was expected to telegraph into Stateville every Friday by noon. He cautioned Ferguson to use discretion when filling out the forms as well. He'd be reimbursed of course, but only if the details made sense to the billing department.

"You won't have to worry about me, Commissioner. My wife put an end to any and all of my shenanigans about a year ago. We're having a baby close to Thanksgiving. I wouldn't even know a whore if I saw one. She'd have to be on top of me before I had a clue anything a foul was going on." Ralph's way of turning a word kept the head of the department on his toes at least; his smile and slight cough to compose himself said it all.

"Ferguson, you just come back in one piece, and with the information, we need to keep our fine citizens safe from all that we know is already going on right up under our noses. This mess stinks to high Heaven.

" If we can get a grip on it, and maybe curtail it a bit that would be great. Having these small upheavals popping up now and again makes me think the boys in Las Vegas are getting antsy. They want more than what the desert can offer them. I'm thinking if they could they'd take over the families here in Chicago, turning a tighter crank on the necks of the business owners who have it pretty rough as it is." Doughtery continued.

"We simply don't have the wits or manpower to stop who and what we have. Families have a way of growing. Each criminal in the business produces three or

four sons and maybe in these more modern times, even their daughters will get involved in the family business.

"By the '50s we're looking at an entirely outrageous amount of criminal activity in Chicago; much worse than we can even imagine; it'll make prohibition look like a party. Keeping the Vegas boys out of it will help; do what you can." With that, Ferguson was driven to the train depot to catch the late train to Oklahoma City.

Mesa

THREE

Nick Posh kissed his mother goodbye before taking off for the desert in his trusty blue Buick. Another smothering hot day had passed over the Sooner State without much in the way of relief for anyone who wasn't willing to open their icebox door and stick their head and shoulders into it for at least a few minutes.

Ama Posh, untangled her emotions to comment to her son that she was a bit nervous about putting out the good dinner candles for fear they had already melted in their box. It was her way of coping with the hard fact that her son would be away on another dangerous mission with no guarantees he would return. She knew it would only be a few weeks, but a few hours is too long for a mother; no matter how old or independent the son may be.

She had already found herself chuckling over the fact that the small milk chocolate bar she had purchased at the corner store had to be cooled before she could even unwrap it; she had almost made a habit of walking the six blocks from her small modest home in Military Estates to Mr. Ho's general store every Wednesday and Saturday, where she could find both goods to buy and friends to talk to—Kim Ho and his wife Patsy Edwards.

Ama Posh packed several sandwiches, side dishes, and desserts for both of "*her boys*", giving them both her love, as she held tightly to their hands through a prayer she had learned as a child of the Cherokee Nation near Oologah Lake in Eastern Oklahoma, a little over a hundred miles from where she lived. With Nick's family back in Scotland for the summer months, Ama had hoped to spend a little time with her now-famously known detective son, whose name seemed to find its way into all of the local and regional papers.

A call from family friend Gabe Hanshaw of the Edinburgh Evening News kept Ama's mind jumping hoping Nick's name would remain domestic; it had not. Detective, turned private investigator, Nick Posh's name was usually linked with some extraordinary capture of someone less favorable in the eyes of a concerned mother. She knew he had been successful, but wasn't sure she wanted him to continue these quests; she wondered how it all came to be in the first place.

"*Nick, you'll promise me you'll keep to the road and not go off track too far when you're out there in the hard lands. I know you've got a good nose for finding your way; for tracking, but son, it's not safe these days with nearly everyone driving every which way, not keeping the laws in the front of their skulls when they're not being watched from every side the way they are in the city limits.*

"*You'll be careful to keep the speed limit too, mind you. I don't want to have to hear how you were scraped off the pavement and stuffed into a wooden box waiting to be shipped for burial.*" She teased.

Turning to Ralph Ferguson, Ama placed her hand over his before encasing it with her other hand as well. "*Ralph, you'll have to be my ears and eyes out there. He won't remember a thing I say to him if you don't. You remember how he was, how he still is.*" Ama's voice tapered off before she found herself releasing Ralph's hand so she could wipe away heavy tears that seemed to well up without warning.

"*Mama Ama, you know I'm your man!*" Ralph stated consoling the woman a bit before nodding to his silent friend who had turned his back to them both so they wouldn't see his own eyes begin to fill. "*He's not that hard to wrangle once you get the hang of it. Heck, he's got a few tells that I know, so when he gets to pushing his foot to the pedal, I'll start in on him, and make him think about it. I'll even poke him in the ribs twice if you want me to!*" he laughed.

"*We'll be OK, and believe it or not, my mother will be following every move we make. She's been watching over me since I was about thirteen I guess. She's one good angel that woman. She'll be in the desert before we are, and I'm more than sure she'll keep all the dangers as far away from either one of us.*

"*If she were alive today I'd bring her here to stay the summer with you. You'd like her, she was a firecracker too.*" Ralph said assuredly before a final kiss was given, and the two men packed the last few things they'd need for the trip and drove slowly out of the gravel driveway. Stealing a glance in the mirrors of the car, Nick gave his mother a slight nod and that smile he knew would keep her heart warmed for a while.

"*Your mom is something else.*" Ralph started. "*I can't remember really what my mother looked like; it's been too long since I held her close enough. You know how it is when you're that age, thinking you're all grown up; you don't want your mother wrapping herself around you and giving you kisses in front of everyone.*" He quietly admitted. Ralph Ferguson thought about her lovingly once again before he spoke; she had been taken too quickly from himself and his father and the rest of their family.

His mother, aged only thirty-seven, had succumbed to tuberculosis; her last few months were unbearably painful. Choosing to be institutionalized, his last true memory of her was the day she made him stand up straight before she was taken by ambulance to the sanitarium. *"Be brave son, you're the one who will keep this family together now. Your father needs you. You'll make us so proud of you; prouder than we already are."* She told him.

He was almost a teenager when she told him these things. Her letters and cards were delivered to their modest home nearly every day until they stopped coming, and a call to the general store manager was made informing Ralph Emerson Ferguson Senior of his wife's passing. She died three days after young Ralph turned thirteen years old.

Driving through the smaller towns of the Oklahoma City metropolitan area took a little longer than either of the men expected. More than once they discussed the fact that Oklahoma City seemed spread out almost like an octopus with eight long arms extending in all directions. To the north, there was Arcadia where Nick's parents had settled, and just to the west of it, still north of the big city was Edmond with the normal college; an institution to teach teachers to become teachers. To the east, cities called Midwest City, Del City, Spencer, and Forrest Park; all rural to some degree, but hoping to expand and populate, giving the Capital City a run for its money.

To the south was an area called Capitol Hill, though still part of Oklahoma City, it rallied to its own rules and seemingly looser regulations. Meridian Flats, as well as Mulligan Flats, were seedy and unsavory areas to which law enforcement hesitated to enter. The cities of Moore and Norman, Oklahoma were further south, but still close enough to almost be considered a part of the Metropolitan area.

Norman bordered Oklahoma and Cleveland counties, had its own police and fire forces of course, and another university; the big one. The University of Oklahoma had been established the same way Nick's parents had laid claim to their land near Arcadia. It had been a part of the Land Run of the Unassigned Lands, officially being "*claimed*" a couple of days sooner than anyone could rightfully expect following the official sounding of the guns on April 22, 1889, allowing folks who had been lined up along the unmarked and unquestioned borders to claim a full one hundred and sixty free acres of land all for their taking if they could stake it correctly and make it to the filing stations up in Guthrie, still in Indian Territory.

Those fine and brave souls who had claimed the original grounds for the university had done so by hook and crook according to those who had wanted to claim the name "*University of Oklahoma*" for themselves up near the city of Stillwater, Oklahoma; west of Tulsa, which was the far eastern border of the land run of the unassigned lands.

Nick thoroughly enjoyed recanting the story of how the University ended up in Norman, and how the folks proudly took the nickname or mascot of "*Sooner*" even though strictly speaking, to be called a "*Sooner*" was to be called a thief, after all, those who waited for the boom of the guns and cannons could never have made the fifty-mile trek in one day; and yet, somehow they did.

"*They called us 'Sooners' Ralph. I guess that's supposed to be a kick in the pants, but you know what, we took it. We accepted it, and we live by it. We show up before anyone, we take care of business, it's what we do.*" Nick joked, trying not to show too much of the pride that he had for not only the upstanding football team that boasted wins each year but for the fact that nearly every medical doctor and nearly every legal attorney in his state and several others, had come right through the halls and doors of the great University of Oklahoma.

"*I will say this now, and I mean it...*" said Posh, "*I wouldn't want any of those lawyers or even the good doctors we produce out of Norman to stick his hand down my horse's mouth or to do something medical for one of my dogs. Those boys, and yeah, maybe a few women up in Stillwater at the Ag and Military school do a damn good job. It's the best place for being trained to work with animals that's one-hundred percent true.*

"*I'm hearing every week how they take on new assignments and find cures for things I didn't even know a cow could get. They're tops, they are, but you know, they can't touch us on the field....it's a fact.*" Nick laughed, before turning into what could be the last gasoline station before reaching the Texas panhandle's border.

Gas stations along the newly formed Route 66 motorway had become something akin to the office water coolers in that everyone had to stop by them from time to time, and when they did, they found themselves staying just a bit longer than perhaps they had initially felt was necessary to have their tanks filled and their windshields cleaned. Managers, pullers, and servicemen alike at these places were just as apt to talk to a stranger as they would anyone who lived locally.

Some of the gossip exchanged was solid of course, but there were times when some of the tales that were shared seemed somewhat too colorful and even outright outlandish. Bob Pettigrew, owner of the Hi-Fix station just outside of Elk City in a township called Erick, had found himself a whale of a tale to spin to just about anyone who would listen.

"*It was like this...*" he'd begin, making sure he had the full attention of his captive audience. At times he'd hold the nozzle of the gas pump just far enough out of the reach of his customers, sort of eye-balling them to be sure they were willing to let him talk as long as he did his job in a timely manner.

He took even more time wiping down their windshields and rubbing any excess mud or clay dirt deposits from the two windshield wipers as he talked. "*I guess it was about two weeks ago now, but Jimmy Durante came through this place. He did! I'm not lying to you. I wasn't the one to fill up his tank, mind you, but I was there and could see him from the window.*

"*I didn't know who ol' Paddy was talkin' to at first, but when the guy turned his head toward the winder there, I saw it... I mean, I saw him! I saw the nose first, of course, you can't miss it, but it was him alright. He was in here driving a new model and I can't tell you if it was a Ford or not, but I think it was. It had a few stickers on it, sort of advertising where he was going or coming from.*

"*I didn't mind much, and I didn't pay no attention to them at all. I was thrilled pink that he came through. We get a few you know...stars and all. This new road will probably bring more of them....oh yeah, lots more of them for sure. It goes all the way to Hollywood and up back the other way to Chicago I think."* Bragged the gasoline attendant.

"I'm just waiting for Laurel and Hardy to come speeding through town. That would be something, really something," he said as he finished his duties with the Buick and made one last pass to make sure all the wheels were filled with the appropriate amount of air, to their capacity, before setting his charges free to take on the open road before them.

Climbing into the driver's seat of the sleek blue car, Nick cranked the engine pressing heavily on the gas pedal to send the engine into a roar. The sheer power of the thing sent shivering vibrations through the frame as both men prepared to embark on their united journey. Nick joked about how his father would have either walked to Las Vegas when he was younger, or he'd have to find a horse to get him there; though riding a horse through the desert could prove deadly for more than one reason.

With a quick check of his timepiece, Nick gauged the timing and the planning he'd mapped out in his head for what would be the next few hours of his life before pulling back onto the road leading to their destination out West. As they drove alone in what could have been mutually agreed silence, Ralph pulled out a thick folded newspaper dated that day, to read not only to himself but purposely to his good friend to keep the minutes rolling and their heads buzzing with interesting tidbits that seemed to interest one or another reporter who took the time to write and print them for the public to enjoy.

Ralph laughed to himself when he found something amusing in print, and said, *"Did you know that people are buying up property on this road just to put in soda pop stores and coffee houses? This paper says, some will make a killing, but others bet they'll die out waiting on the traffic to make ends meet. Maybe if they put out something interesting in the front of these stores for people to talk about it'll catch on. I know Stella would make me pull over to the side of the road to see a giant ball of yarn or something hooky like that. She'd pull out that Brownie camera of hers and make me take a picture."*

The wind whipped up a hot dusty breeze cascading through their hair as it rustled the flaps of the paper Ralph clutched with both of his hands. Boxes of supplies sat behind their seats filled with everything possible including case files, pencils, paper, ammunition, and extra firearms. Ama had packed enough sandwiches to last until they had safely arrived at their first solid destination where more food supplies could be bought.

"Your mom must have packed about a half-hundred of those good potted meat sandwiches, and I see some peanut butter and jelly in there as well, do you want one? Are you hungry yet?" Ralph asked.

Laughing lightly, Nick glanced over to his right at Ralph as he rummaged through the assortment of bags and boxes, containers stacked neatly as if organized by the best accountant on the planet. *"I think she put them in here using some sort of unique engineering feat of some kind of magic, she's probably labeled them alphabetically or something."* Ralph teased.

"That's my mom" Nick proudly added, *"...she always did that, raised me a bit too tidy for any good too."* He said. *"She always believed in being ready, always*

believed in being prepared for everything and anything." Reaching forward Nick adjusted the mirror on the side of the car mentioning it would be great to have a mirror in the center of the windshield so he could see who or what was coming up behind him.

"Maybe they'll get around to making that a real thing in the future now that more folks are driving on these paved roads." He stated, *"...and I want the credit for the suggestion. That's all I'm sayin' about that."*

Mesa

FOUR

Rubbing his hands in the dust under the front right tire of his Buick, Nick checked for inconsistencies that perhaps only he was aware could be found. Ralph Ferguson had been in Nick's life long enough to know that from time to time the Native blood in his best friend came to the surface of his soul in ways that could explain some of the more interesting details about life and in some of the most unusually peculiar ways.

"What's ya looking for there in the dirt partner?" asked his Chicagoan friend. *"Is that some new-fangled, or maybe knowing you, it's some really old-fangled way of telling the future."* He laughed. *"Are we gonna make it to Clovis tonight or are there meteors falling from the skies that are sending their radiation rays down upon us...is the dirt going to tell us it's going to rain? I'm not sure what to think when I see you doing things like that, pal. I gotta tell you, sometimes...sometimes you worry me."*

To his surprise and possibly his chagrin, Ferguson had to deal with a quite simplified answer, one he hadn't expected. *"It's fine...not like the soil we have back in Oklahoma. This may be a clay but it's not the tough and rugged thick stuff I'm used to kicking. This is a lot more like sand; it's not even sediment, but more like topsoil. It must have blown in from the west or maybe the southwest. It covers everything from the tops of the trees to the ground here. Look how it's piled up along the side of that wall on the barn just past the station."* He said.

Jude Stringfellow

"The constant blowing of the wind keeps things fairly clear of it, but it's here alright, and it just keeps moving along with the next gust."

With that, Posh pointed just to the south of where they were standing. Before getting into the driver's seat to pull out of the shoulder and back onto the newly paved highway, Ralph noticed perhaps for the first time that the sandy tannish red silt Posh had gathered up into his hand was now snaking its way across the street, leaving in its wake a slight and airy dusting of some of the finest sand particles he'd ever noticed outside of the beaches of Lake Michigan.

"Topsoil? Do you think it's blowing in from the west or the southwest; OK, I'll give you that. What do you make of it? I mean, is it something we need to consider as being a possible driving hazard? Seems to me that it could be the makings of or the tail end of a dust storm.

"If it is one, we don't wanna be caught out on the empty motorway with no one to help us get unstuck," Ferguson said. *"I think you may be right. I hadn't seen it before you pointed it out. We may need to think before we commit to the next several hundred miles, what do you think Posh?"*

The Texas Panhandle stretched out in front of them, a vast expanse of rolling hills and golden plains that seemed to go on forever. The skies, an azure richness punctuated with white dotted clouds drifting lazing across the broad unbroken horizon. The panhandle itself was less than two hundred miles wide; but with nothing in view from either direction, it seemed a lot bigger. There would be at least one major city and gas station right about in the middle of it; Amarillo, Texas.

Mesa

"We've got a little light left in the skies for now, Ralph, and that storm has probably passed or come into this area already. If I had to guess, and guessing is all it would be, I'd say we'll make it to Amarillo by supper time and we can ask around to see if traveling to Tucumcari will be the better bet, or if we need to wait it out." Nick advised.

"Tucumcari? I thought you said something about staying in Clovis, is that out of the way? I sort of had my heart set on the new hotel I read about on the train on the way down here." Ralph stated with some of that northern hopefulness he seemed to carry around in his veins whenever he traveled. If the man wasn't getting his news from a paper, he was not too shy about striking up a conversation with literally anyone with a set of ears on the side of their head.

"I don't get to see the world much like you have, Nick. I get a rush out of having a ring-a-ding-ding time in the better hotels when I can. A hot bath, a good meal, even listening to the live jazz bands they have; some of them anyway. I love me some wailing of the licorice stick! Clarinets and saxophones…that's my party." He added, smiling his way through the eye-rolling he knew was coming his way.

"Licorice stick? You call the clarinet a 'licorice stick'?" Nick laughed. *"What will be next, maybe the trombone is a lip-stick!"* he laughed, purposely giving his good friend the eye-balling he deserved for the use of the gangland slang he'd picked up while policing the Stateville prison in Chicago, where Ralph Ferguson had been recently promoted to Sergeant.

Jude Stringfellow

"Yeah...yeah, I'll start calling it the ol' lip-stick from now on, and when I get back to the tombs and do my rounds I'll throw it out there and see if one of the dons I keep tabs on can give me a good nod for being such a pip!" Ralph laughed. *"I'm in you know, they respect me and that's saying something. I don't call the gangsters names or cut them down in front of their rivals like some of the cops do. It's paid off some to have them know who I am and know they can't get something past me, but at the end of the day, they're men you know --- they want to talk and they want to be heard. I listen."*

Listening was one of Ferguson's strong suits. He'd been around too long to have a heavy tongue or loose lips. Surviving the war was in and of itself a feat, but the war was over fifteen years ago, he was a very young man then, he'd need to keep sharp, keep his mind, and mind his own if wanted to survive the real battles he faced every day.

Ralph Ferguson, like Nick, had been older when he married and started a family. He wasn't some young punk fresh out of the university working the family business with all the expectations that come with it. At just under forty years old, he was about to become a father for the first time; there was more than one reason to keep his head on straight, to listen, and to be aware of literally everything that surrounded him.

The road was hot from the summer sun beating onto it most of the day and into the evening hours. By supper time they had reached their next gasoline station, and hopefully, they'd hear a bit more of the gossip that was more or less local to the panhandle. It was a unique place in that the station took in visitors from every direction.

Some came from the West of course, others from the East, but other folks coming up from the heart of Texas

Mesa

or those going up into Colorado would also stop at the larger stations to fill up, wash up, eat something, and talk a bit to the workers and other strangers just because they could, and they had something in common, they were moving, going places.

Dennis Rockford ran the Rockford Bar Ranch just to the east of Amarillo. His cattle weren't eating much in the way of good grass out that far, but what the man lacked in greenery on the over fifty-thousand acres he owned, he more than made up with in oil deposits. Rockford could wheel and deal his way in and out of any conversation being had. Anyone would recognize the man.

Standing well over six feet four inches and weighing in somewhere around three hundred pounds, Dennis Rockford could hold his own. No man with a brain would ever think of going up against the barrel-chested brute, but most of them wouldn't need or want to. Rockford's voice boomed when it exited his robust lungs; it rang strong and clear with every drawn-out syllable he offered.

Most of what the oil man talked about and shared dealt with money; some had it, some didn't, but he talked about it. If it wasn't his or other people's money on his mind he talked about politics and recent decisions being made in the counties around his place that would affect his and other people's money. Politics played a part in every man's decision; that was Rockford's statement when he spoke. There wasn't a question asked or answered that hadn't at some point, hinged on something related to someone else's point of view; someone in an office – telling folks how to live their lives on the prairie.

Jude Stringfellow

When the two men pulled the car into Dennis Rockford's favorite gas station they met the man as he was holding court with a few of the locals and three or four outsiders who had found his company simply too charming to leave. "*You boys on your way to Tucumcari?*" He wanted to know. "*If you are, you can make it there by dark now that the sun don't go down before ten o'clock!*" Dennis added. "*Then again, with the winds kickin' up like they are, you may only get halfway there and find you need a tow to get you out of some ditch alongside the road. Maybe it's best you sit a while and have a hearty meal with us; we don't mind sharing if you don't*" He bolstered to the strangers.

"*I'll bet you haven't had a good steak since you came in from the other side of hell; come on over here, both of ya, and sit a spell with us. I'll get Barb to throw another two T-bones on the grill. We're having potatoes with sour cream, butter, and cheese and a fist full of that rhubarb I've been trying to get rid of.*"

Rockford's invitation was more of a strong suggestion, one Nick and Ralph thought to be too generous to pass up. While their dinner was being prepared just outside the station on the make-shift grill the man carried with him for just such gatherings, and usually on a Friday or Saturday evening, Dennis began questioning the lawmen about their mission. He wanted to know everything, claiming he'd already been told they were coming out through Route 66 from Oklahoma, and that one or the other of them had been recruited from the bigger metropolitan complex of Chicago.

"*Which one of you is the Yankee if you don't mind me teasing you about being one?*" he asked before taking a stronger look at the two men. "*Oh wait…no, don't tell me,*

Mesa

I'll tell you." He said. *"The darker one...you there, you're Native. You're driving the car and you're coming from Oklahoma. You're not so hard to peg.*

"You're the private eye and the other one, the...the...well, the red-headed white boy there, you're the Yank." Rockford gaffed; and as he did the audience he commanded gaffed right along with him. Rockford made it impossible for Nick and Ralph not to enjoy the roasting. It somehow solidified the fact that he was a friendly sort, not one to shy away from making new acquaintances.

"Aw, yes, you are one hundred percent on that one friend." Ralph started. *"I'd be the northern one. I can't claim anything remotely resembling pigment. I've got a few freckles here on my arms and more of my legs that if I ran them all together I may have a spot of color; that's about the end of that."* He smiled, rubbing his left forearm with his right palm.

With introductions out of the way, a good dinner in their bellies, and the needed introductions they needed from law-abiding friends such as Rockford, Nick knew his objective was shared to some degree, possibly by Chief Moore who had been building up a collection of lawmen he called "*The Link*". Men in blue across the country helping one another when and how they could. Telegrams and phone conversations made it that much easier than sending coded messages in newspapers the way they did before wires were installed.

What Nick needed to know was how far widespread the knowledge of his assignment had gone. He wanted to be sure that none of the people he was going to possibly

Jude Stringfellow

bring in for murdering the two women he was avenging would be all the wiser to his position or his mission.

"Your secret is safe with me, and by me, I mean anyone who hopes to breathe any of the air I own from here to where you can't possibly see from here. Anyone who knows me knows I support the men in uniform and I don't care if it's a police uniform, a mailman's uniform, or a soldier's. Anyone willing to put their life and limb on the line to bring me what I need, to protect me, or to help my family in some way has my pledge.

"If I support them then they best support them if they want to gas up here or buy and sell anything over the next twenty-five miles. It's all mine. I don't charge a toll for anyone to pass through it; I let the Route 66 folks cut through my land to build that motorway but that don't mean they can tell me how to run this part of the country." Rockford stated plainly. *"No sir, if I know you and I like you, you'll be liked. It's just that simple."*

Something else that seemed to put Posh at ease when it came to the larger-than-life man Dennis Rockford, he had little choice in putting his trust; the man mentioned having met with and having interviewed one of Nick's heroes, a man by the name of Chris Madsen. Hearing Rockford talk about Madsen so casually, as if they were still acquainted made the cultivating of friendship all the more pertinent considering the circles the two men ran in were so very different. *"Madsen is a friend of mine as well,"* Nick admitted.

Telling Rockford more about the times he had spent time with the aging lawman in his home state of Oklahoma. *"Are you telling me we might run into the old guardsman out West? Will he be joining us on the posse, or has he kept his word and hung up his spurs, so to*

49

speak?" asked Ferguson, knowing the two men could go on for hours comparing notes about the world-renowned Dutchman who once took the southwest by storm alongside his two best and most trusted friends, Bill Tilghman and Heck Thomas.

Posh felt less intimidated by the man's statements and in fact, he felt an instant bond with Rockford, asking him questions about the police forces between Amarillo and Las Vegas. He wanted details and offered the same in return.

"I'll be upfront with you if you'll be upfront with me. I'll let you know where we're going because you just never know if we'll need an anchor back this way to hang on to. We may find ourselves in a pickle we can't swim out of once we make it to Lake Mead.

"Things are sure to be delicate, to say the least; the minds and hearts of the people we'll be in contact with can only be trusted to the slightest degree. Most of the people we'll do business with, if and when we find the business to be what we would partake in that is; will be men of less than stellar reputations.

"If I had to put labels to them, I'd tell you straight that they're gangsters, mobsters, casino owners, and the like; one of them is a lower-level individual who may or may not run with or for the bosses, but he's not unsophisticated. He's been around the block a time or two; he's likely been incarcerated for at least one serious crime. Posh waited a few seconds before continuing; holding Rockford's full attention.

"I'll need men I can trust to get word back to you if I need you. I'll leave myself, and I'm sure Ralph will agree, he'll leave himself open to you when or if you need

us. We're both for hire when we can get the time to work outside of our regular assignments. Being a private detective I can move about more freely; Ralph is pretty much stationed in Chicago, but that in and of itself is a gold mine if you need intel." Nick implemented.

"We're international too; as a matter of fact. I've worked a number of cases for the Crown and under contractual arrangements during the war and after for both sides of the Big Pond. You'll only need to ask, and we'll help you to any extent you need us to." Nick stated as Ralph gave a silent nod, not wanting to appear rude by speaking with his mouth full.

"This...this steak, it's probably the best-damned steak I've ever had. I'd ask if it was homegrown, but you already said you own fifty-thousand acres and I can only imagine that part of that is cattle country." Ralph asked with the statement.

"You're not wrong. You said you worked some for the Crown; these are Black Angus beef steaks, they come right out of the lowlands and borderlands of Scotland and upper parts of England.

"I bought my first load of them about the time our boys...well, you boys were coming back from over there; right about twelve years back. I've had several head of them born since, and they do make the best meals...they are what they are; heaven on a plate", the man stated plainly.

Mesa

FIVE

Route 66 got its start sometime in 1926 when the Bureau of Public Roads created the nation's first real Federal motorway system, the initial plans for the roadway wasn't a typical linear highway tracking from east to west. It was more or less a diagonal one that assisted rural communities with a means to haul and transport their goods to the larger cities to distribute them; thus making the motorway one of the most popular routes in the world for free trade.

Making one's way from Los Angeles to Chicago would be a breeze when all of the roadways from Point A to Point B were covered or paved. Several patches of the route remained cut out but more or less packed dirt streets; maybe wider, perhaps more traveled, but hazardous for motor vehicles when dust and mud infiltrated their churning hot engines.

Ralph, as he usually did, had picked up a paper or two in Amarillo, and began reading the headlines and some of the more interesting bits of news to Nick as the Buick took them further and deeper into the last remnants of civilization. *"Says here in the Amarillo paper, that the route has better weather than the ones up north; the Lincoln Highway and the other one, the...the...oh nuts, I just read the name of it."* He paused, *"...the Dixie. It's called the Dixie Highway, that's the other one. They have better pavement but they go through some of the more mountainous areas making it difficult to maneuver those big trucks in the winter months.*

Jude Stringfellow

"This route, they say, will put an end to that, and it's already seen a huge increase in the number of truckers making their way up from just about everywhere out this way. Maybe that's why the clowns decided to leave Vegas and come to the big bright lighted streets of Chicago to screw around with our dons. They did it because they can!" He finished, looking over the paper, folding it to make it easier to hold.

Thick semi-arid air seemed to hoover from both inside the car as well as outside as they passed through what could only be described as tan-colored air, only slightly brightened by the sun that seemed to take enormous pleasure at beating its heat directly into the glass windshield and through their bodies.

"We gotta get some water soon if you see a place, Nick. We're down to about a jug or maybe a little more. There's that thing in the back but I think you said you have to save it for the car. If we don't get to a place soon I may have to drink it to die faster than I am now." Ralph complained but with a joking tone to his voice.

"I hear you, friend. I have the note I took from when I was talking to Rockford. He gave me a few places to stop along this route; and said it was just east of Tucumcari by about fifteen or twenty miles. I think he called it Odell or something like that." Nick's eyes scoured the empty road before him only seeing brush-type dried vegetation, loose arid air assaulting him as his tongue caught a taste of the gritty flat earthy particles silently making their way to rest inside his mouth and nose each time he took in a breath. *"You know it's bad when you see the catfish stand up and walk right out of the dry riverbed looking for new quarters. That's bad."* Ralph joked.

Mesa

"Odell's? The gas station? There's another one called that in Illinois, and come to think of it, it is on Route 66. Maybe the ol' boy has a string of them leading people from one to the other from all the way back to Chicago and then out to Los Angeles." Ralph thought for a moment and laid the paper down.

Turning to his friend he asked, "*Posh, this is a dumb question, but I've never heard you say the words. How do you pronounce Los Angeles? Is it like I do, Los and then An-ja-less or do you say it the weird way, the way some of the cops up my way say it? It's sort of a...Los Angle-ees thing that I can't for the life of me understand why someone would do it that way.*" He asked.

Nick looked over at the man, who to his surprise, was genuinely asking the question. It wasn't something he was rousting about or even half-heartedly wondering. Posh laughed a little, choking back a dust-soaked drop of sweat that had fallen from the top of his lip.

"*You're worried about the way I say a word and not about this damned wind-worn heat that seems to have a vendetta against anyone stupid enough to drive through it?*" he laughed. "*I guess if I had to think about it, I never think about those things. I just say it as I say it, but let me think...Los An-ja-less...yeah, Los An-ja-less...that's how I say it. Are we blood brothers now, now that we say the same word the same way?*"

Nick's poke at Ferguson was received with a good and sturdy nod, a cough for good measure, and a swipe of his brow. Ferguson's decision to remove his shirt made less sense to the Native American who had been in and around such extreme weather. "*You're looking to tan yourself up a bit, that sun coming at you through the glass will scorch you rather than toast you. You might want to rethink your last decision. It's apt to start a fire in my car and then I'd have to scrape what's left of you off my front seat."*

A landscape of loose sand, harsh wind, and hot air lined the horizon giving them reason to hate the next few hours. Towering red rock formations, barren of any life stood on either side of them as dead or dying cacti stood their guard. A flash flood would bring them back from their tombs no doubt, but this was not their lot on that miserable day. Dead grass, if there was grass to be seen, laid in thick dry patches here and there. Baked earth crumbled under the stress and weight of the wheels of the car.

If they listened they could hear the screeching of a lone eagle making its way from one bluff to the other in search of food. "*I'm hoping that's just an eagle, and not some lone buzzard thinking he's gonna have his dinner before we reach Tucumcari,*" Ralph stated, picking up his paper and reading from the more interesting bits again.

It was something Monty had said on the last call the men had engaged in that made Ralph repeat what he had heard. "*The Chief said Gabe Hanshaw is running another story on one of our fellow Americans; a man by the name of Albert Fish. He's not even human, Posh! He can't be.*

"*He is suspected of killing children, he's a serial killer. It would be bad enough to tell you the unspeakable things he's been accused of and what perverts like him do alone with children, but this man.... he has likely murdered dozens of them, and according to the New York papers, he's written to one family to tell them what he's done with their daughter.*"

Mesa

Ralph paused, "*Posh, the papers say he's eaten the flesh of at least one of his victims. A little girl about eight years old. Her name was Grace.*" Ralph thought more on the matter. "*Stella says if the baby is a little girl, we'll call her Grace. I'm not so sure I want to even think about that after hearing what Monty said about Fish.*" Ralph sighed.

"*He's been caught, he's escaped, and just about a month ago a sweet little girl in Far Rockaway, New York was found dead and the cops there put Fish at the site; he was seen. He wasn't apprehended – they said he had an alibi, but you can pay for those. She had the same name as Monty's sweet wife Robin. This man,*" Ralph Ferguson managed to say, shaking his head in disbelief, "*He's not human...I know I've said that twice now, but it's true.*"

Ralph unfolded the morning paper and held it between his hands shielding his face from the wind before reading various headlines. "*Oh, says here John Cunningham of Otago, New Zealand died. He was seventy-nine years old. He was born a Scotsman. I wonder if the boys knew him – he was well respected by all.*" Ralph took pleasure in trying to make Posh snort, an involuntary and obnoxious result of being caught off guard; Ferguson was one of the very few who knew how to bring about the sound.

Ralph picked up a second paper, "*Chicago, Illinois this time....seems a man called Raymond Pullen Jr. had his last meal on Friday last. He was electrocuted for killing a man several years ago who from what I can tell, didn't have an autopsy until recently...meaning, they dug up his body to do it.*"

Turning to Posh again, Ralph mentioned that he didn't know until recently himself, that because there were so many dead people in the city and just outside the city limits of Chicago, the medical examiners didn't always do an autopsy. It wasn't something they were mandated to do on a body just because a body died. If a person killed themselves they rarely performed an autopsy; especially when a note was left behind to do their job for them.

"I guess I just assumed everyone got one, but you know what, when a person dies by suicide or if they think it was a heart attack or some sort of a natural cause, they don't perform an autopsy in Chicago without an expressed request by the family. I bet this Ray Pullen guy thought making it look like natural causes was all he'd need. Says here, he was the caregiver of the man for almost seven years. He couldn't wait I guess for the guy to kick off, so he laced his tea with something that worked like a heart attack on a body."

Ralph continued to read, *"...goes on to say Jr. was twenty-nine years old, married and they just had a baby, it was their second. He's got a wife, a family, and a home, and he goes off and murders a man to get a small inheritance! Damn...you'd think he could wait for the man to kick unless maybe the old man had told him he was cutting him out of the will for some reason."* Ralph said thoughtfully.

Ralph recounted more strange details about something he and his fellow officers at Stateville prison had been told regarding the processes that take place after an execution; the one-sided conversation turned into a bit of a monologue after a while with Ralph detailing such facts that a medical examiner has to remove a person's organs if or when he or she will be cremated; he didn't know why, but knew they did.

Mesa

"Did you know if a person has any metal in their body from fixing a bone, the doctors have to take that out too?" he asked. Ralph seemed to be uncovering information by the buckets. His endless spewing of facts both entertained and concerned his friend, who had by this time decided to tune out some of the words unless Posh believed they had some merit to them. Ralph could be a handful most of the time.

"There was a rumor going around, and between you and me and these cactus Posh, I'm not so sure it ain't true. There was a rumor spread through Chicago anyway, that the medical examiners would put the inmates into a stupor before actually allowing them to die so they could harvest their organs. I know there was a pretty good side complaint about using the electric chair because there was hope among the medical people to use kidneys and livers. Maybe someday they can put someone else's heart into a man who needs one.

"That would be amazing...unless," Ralph thought cautiously, *"...unless maybe it's a ruined heart with sin and corruption. You put that into a good man or some mother of three or four kids, and God only knows what could happen."* Ralph thought out loud.

"Docs told me that if a body comes in mummified, which of course it wouldn't at the prison, but you know, in their regular line of work it could – if it comes in mummified they check to see if it has a brain, or any of its organs. Mummies don't have decomp like the bodies that naturally shrivel up and dry out; that's another process. It's been going on since Egyptian days." Ralph added, before stating the obvious,

"...I mean, I guess we still have Egyptians today too, right? So, these days are also...Egyptian days when you think about it; that is if you're in Egypt." He stopped and laughed. Nick's quick response in the form of a nasal short snorting was all the reward his friend needed; Ralph Ferguson smiled.

"Murderers don't much like autopsies, do they?" asked Posh. *"A man decides to kill and he does it. He has his reasons no doubt; reasons that maybe he alone can understand. This guy Pullen, take him for example. He may have only been a teenage boy, eighteen or nineteen when he became the caregiver. Didn't you just say he had been the man's caregiver for seven years and that he had died years back?"* asked Nick.

"He's twenty-nine now, but say ten years ago, he'd have been a very young man and excited to have a good-paying job like he had. He probably lived in the house and had his own place to stay, maybe he felt trapped after an amount of time.

"Maybe he fell in love but couldn't bring the gal home to his place to be alone with her and maybe they couldn't go to her place either if she had family. Maybe, and I'm just spit-ballin', but maybe after he got married the old boy told him he'd be cut out of the will for moving out and only coming back to the house a few times a day to check on the man. Maybe it was hard on everyone, but still, murder can't be the answer.

"You'd think there'd be some reasoning and maybe some discussion going on between them as to what was right and equitable." Nick questioned, *"But still money is money and some people will do anything to get it."* Ralph set the paper down again, smiled enigmatically, and made a severe gesture of rubbing his hands together over and

Mesa

over again to show his mocked agreement with Posh's money statement.

"*Holy Moly!*" exclaimed Fergy in one of his more animated moments. *"...let me read this to you; you're not gonna believe it. I don't think you heard about it or we would have already talked it over; this is a good one. Says here in the Chicago Tribune I picked up, that a week ago a group of men dressed as circus clowns were openly roaming the streets of Elgin, that's just outside of Chicago.*

"They were performing, doing their thing on the street for free, and people came out to see them. They were promoting or said they were promoting a small circus that was in town for a few days and when they were accepted by the locals as being just good-hearted men wanting to entertain the citizens for whatever they could get for tips, that no one in the bank...no one in the bank stopped them or even questioned them when they came in through the doors in their get-up! Can you believe that?" asked Ralph.

"The paper goes on to say they wore painted faces, and one had a red nose that looked like a rubber ball had been sliced open to fit over his nose but allowing him to breathe. There were three of them. They all walked in, smiling, laughing and then they went to three corners of the place and drew guns!" Ralph exclaimed.

"Nick, they drew weapons in the bank and forced everyone on the ground before going through their wallets and their purses. One of them told the clerk at the window to unload her drawer and she did. They got away with just over forty-thousand dollars!" He said. *"Geez Louise! Can you imagine the nerve of these guys? Clowns! What was I just saying about clowns before I read the*

article? They dressed as clowns to rob a bank Posh....and no one thought anything about it when they walked through the door like that because they'd seen them all for hours out on the streets entertaining!" He stopped before exclaiming, *"That's crazy!"*

After thinking about it for another dry-aired moment, Posh nodded to his friend to indicate that he could see the beginning of what looked to be some form of city limits; it could only be the outskirts of Tucumcari, New Mexico. *"If I had to guess, I'd say they wore the disguise to blend in. That statement sort of bothers me now that I've said it, but yeah, they were outstanding at first, then accepted, then trusted...and that allowed them freedom, access, even being welcomed into the bank.*

"It's a whole new world out there Ferg. Where men once rode into town on horseback and raised their handkerchiefs over their faces so they wouldn't be seen, these guys put on grease paint, rubber noses, maybe hats or big ruffles about their neck, who knows? They were right in plain sight for at least a few hours or more; it's more than planned, it's calculated."

Rolling into the city of Tucumcari meant they'd rest a good half day and most of the night before rising early in the morning to beat the heat trying to make their way through to the next stop. Another day another paper for Ralph Ferguson, the man seemed to relish news from every corner of the world. He and Posh both found it fascinating that civilized societies had reached a point where a man in Tucumcari, New Mexico could pick up a daily newspaper from Dallas, Chicago, or even New York dated the same day.

Knowing they may not be able to make their usual weekly calls overseas to their good friends in Scotland.

Mesa

Posh decided to try and put through a call before the two of them packed up the Buick to forge through yet another heavy-aired day facing torrid heat, body odors that neither man could control, and possible dehydration or numbness from it all.

"We may not be able to call the others every week like we do if we get in too deep out that way. I'll see if the operators here can put us through to Eoghan and Monty at this hour. I know they work around the clock in Oklahoma City, but there aren't as many....Oh, hello, operator, yes, can you put me through to an international operator, please? I need to make a call to Edinburgh, Scotland. The number is....OK yeah, I'll wait."

When the call was placed, Posh drew a long and hard sigh which wasn't ignored or overlooked on the other side of the line. *"Good early mornin' to youse Detective Posh! I'm sorry youse feelin' so bad an' so lonely so youse have tae make the big sigh when ya hear me talkin' on the other side of it. I'm happy youse no forgot me; tae be honest. It's been some time since I've heard youse voice. Are youse alive or is this your ghost callin' me?"* asked Eoghan MacRae, the first voice anyone heard when they called the Edinburgh Chambers Street precinct.

"You're right Eoghan, I did miss you. I couldn't go another day without hearing your rough and edgy Scottish voice, man. You're the beat of my heart, and the wind in my sail, what can I say?" teased Posh. *"...and it's 10:35 p.m. here in Tucumcari, New Mexico."*

"Well then, since youse finally admittin' it, I can tell my bonnie wife so we can get that divorce an I can be with youse soon enough. It only takes a little over two years youse ken tae make something like that happen

here. You'll wait for me, yes? I'm sure ya will. I'm sure ya will."

Eoghan's laughter could be heard throughout the front lobby of the marble-tiled police station. *"I bet that's Posh!"* stated Police Chief Nicholas Montgomery, making his way to the extension phone at the front desk with a fist full of his morning mug, so he could join the conversation. *"It's been at least two weeks Posh, what have you and that Yankee scoundrel been up to? We've been dealing with a snag here from the MK case we seem to be dragged into, thanks to you."* Monty stated.

Posh put in a good word for himself as well as for his good friend, the Yankee scoundrel, who had finally become part of the *"family"* where the Scots were concerned. Had it not been for Ferguson's quick reactions in the Scottish border town of Kelso just about a year before, Posh would have been shipped back to Oklahoma in a box; all who were involved in the Brian Cashion case were pleased to call Ralph Ferguson their friend.

Mesa

SIX

Clowns. When he thought about it, and he did think about it, Posh couldn't have thought of a more ingenious way to fool an entire band of people at one time. They go in, make people happy, make them laugh, involve them in crazy stunts and play, and then a few minutes later they join them in their daily routines.

"You go to the stores with them, maybe pretend to harass or tease them somewhat; you pretend to be a police officer in the streets, but all the while you know you're gaining the trust of everyone around you. No one suspects a clown of doing anything but play; it's all for a show, it's the perfect means of disguise. It was brilliant; absolutely brilliant.

"You're not going after the clowns though, are you Posh?" asked Monty. *"You're going after men or a man who killed the niece of one of your statesmen. You told me he was a known bully, who maybe faked his own death before stealing the identity of another man and making his way out to the casinos in Las Vegas. Is this the guy? He's doing side work as a bank-robbing clown?"* Monty wanted to know.

"No, I'm going after the man who took the lives of probably two women in Oklahoma, the one you mentioned; the former governor's niece, and her best friend. Both girls were college friends and had plans to....wait, they did have plans to invest in the newly formed circus circuit that got its start out west. You made me think Monty...you made me think." Posh admitted.

"That's usually something Eoghan has up his sleeve before I can breathe, he's up there in my head pulling out thoughts in my brain. What is it with you Scotsmen? Do you have a bit of that pagan witchery in you or something? You're able to make a man recall what his brain knew already but hadn't released?" Nick laughed before continuing.

"You're right. Maybe this particular clown isn't involved in their disappearance or murders, but he's clearly involved with that world and he's from out that way. It could be connected in the long run. I don't know about you, but clowns aren't the nice and jovial creatures we once thought they were. The older I get the more I realize that most of what I thought was typical ain't all that typical, and then that becomes the norm.

"I remember a time when you could call a spade a spade, but now with all the get-ups and costumes, makeup, and whatever they choose to use to distinguish themselves and to create individual characters for themselves, it's hard to tell what or who a man is supposed to be under all that colored grease paint" Posh added. *"They have personalities under that stuff – they can put on a face and become a new man. Good, bad, sad, happy, even blank-faced like those guys wearing black and white who move but don't say anything."* He said. *"They make their money that way."*

"We'll know soon enough. We're in a town called Tucumcari, New Mexico. We have another day or two before we hit Las Vegas. We'll stop just outside of it in a town called Lake Mead. That's where we think the man holes up; where he may be living as a hired hand and now I'm thinking maybe he did more than work for the circus set he may be part of their means of operation. He's good

Mesa

with horses, according to his criminal bio, and they have stables for dude-ranching up and around this part of the world. It's a way to make money outside of the casinos," Nick explained.

"Guests come out to the lake and rent a horse to ride for an hour or so before settling into their rooms for a good shower and a fine dinner. The whole thing is a good money-maker for those who have money. The average folk couldn't afford the prices or want to take the long drive out; both places have slot machines, tables, and a few under-the-table tables if you know what I mean." He implicated and openly suggested that the sale of cocaine was a heavy part of the lure for those willing to leave the safety of the glittering streets of Las Vegas.

"Most of the 'guests' if you can call them that, have ties to the underworld. They either make the powder, process the powder, or they prep and pack it for wholesalers to come out and get their load before using the newly almost paved motorway Fergy and I are using to get to them ourselves." Posh stated.

"The big road is an amazing feat to be sure. I think we talked about it, but just over two Scotlands can fit in the state of Oklahoma. New Mexico is even bigger. You could fit four or five Scotlands inside of it. We're headed west from New Mexico into Arizona and then up to Nevada. This country....Monty, it's big. This country is like nothing else on this planet. You can have all four seasons across the damn thing at the same time in the dead of summer." He added.

Eoghan's fascination with the United States had been completely taking over his thoughts since he and Posh became acquainted. Asking questions, reading articles, papers, and anything he could to better understand the differences, Eoghan MacRae began speaking and when he did, he did so in a calm and serious tone.

"Posh, I want tae come tae America. I want tae see it for myself. You've been here, it's my turn. Let's see if we can make that happen. I dinnae have tae see it all. I dinnae even ken if that would be possible. I cannae even imagine what it would be like tae drive a car all the way across the United States.

"It would take weeks tae do that, I'm sure. When I get in my car an' drive tae the south border of my country just before I cross into England, I realize I've driven several hours but tae drive for days....for weeks tae get tae the end of it...that boggles my mind." MacRae said.

Ralph waited patiently in the room for his turn at ribbing two of his closest newest friends. He had been listening to their conversation as best he could through the receiver as Posh held it outward; a musty smell from the room's carpet or perhaps the linen had preoccupied his mind beforehand. Posh had his way of communicating with the men back in Edinburgh, a way Ralph admired and wanted to emulate. He wanted to ask a few questions to keep his distinct standing with the lads overseas as being a part of their "*club*". "*Let me talk to the boys Posh, I have a few things I want to ask too."* He said.

Before handing the phone's heavy handset to his friend, Posh covered the mouthpiece to say something privately to his friend about having been told recently about the passing of Chief Montgomery's wife Robin. Her illness had been sudden but intense in its manifestation. The doctors said it was cancer, spreading or metastasizing faster than they had ever seen. The news of her passing had been delivered only briefly and in a manner understood by Posh to be off-limits for the time being. He knew Ralph was aware of her passing, but he also knew Ralph hadn't known Nicholas Montgomery long enough to know he was very much the grieving sort.

"I've been asked by Eoghan not to mention the passing of Robin, it's been hard for Monty enough with the MK case revving up and the changes being made around the station with incoming personnel he has to train. I sent a telegram for both of us last week, and mentioned how sorry you were for his loss." Posh handed the phone to Ralph with a nod of understanding.

"Monty! Eoghan! It's me, Ralph...you know, the police officer who does his job, and keeps his nose clean where others in the room I'm currently in may not be so professional." He laughed. When the men heard his voice they instantly returned the good humor with laughter and their keen way of tormenting their good friend Nick Posh, who seemingly couldn't do anything right if his life depended on it.

For the next few moments, the room was filled with friendship, comradery, and a sense of belonging. Every man knew that they had support from everyone involved. When Posh took the receiver back he added the name of Dennis Rockford to their growing list of men who could be trusted. Though Rockford wasn't a police officer, a detective, or had anything really to do with law enforcement, his presence alone was commanding enough that anyone thinking of breaking the law anywhere near the man would take the time to think twice.

"Eoghan, I'll make you a promise now. If I can talk Rockford into funding it, and let him know that he'll not

Jude Stringfellow

only meet you but let you play that guitar of yours at his hometown church on a couple of Sundays or so. I'll ask him if he'll bring you out sometime in the fall so we can see your ugly mug again and maybe take you on a train up to Chicago to hook up with Ralph so he can show you what the inside of a maximum-security prison looks like before locking you in for a night so you can get the full experience.

"What do you think, buddy?" asked Posh before sending his friends off for the rest of their work day some eight hours ahead of whatever time it was in New Mexico. Daylight savings had started a few weeks back but the state of New Mexico never turned their clocks back to begin with, so trying to keep up with that sort of thing could be a challenge for anyone who wanted to be aware of the differences.

Two uncomfortable crows sounded the early morning alarm the next morning before the roosters had a chance to see the cracking of the eastern sky. Sometime just before five o'clock in the morning, Posh and Ferguson found themselves without a cup of coffee to open their eyes, but with enough water and food supplies to see them through until they reached their next stop. Why coffee hadn't been on the list of things to buy in town had eluded the pair. "*I just thought the hotel would have it; who thinks otherwise?*" Ralph asked. "*I guess I'm a little spoiled from what I know about hotels up my way. Maybe here in the southern parts of the States, a man has to beg for his morning juice.*"

Along the line somewhere, calls had been made and arrangements as well, to see to it that the two men were given fresh sandwiches, fruit, jerky, and a strong bottle of Kentucky bourbon as well as three or four large

Mesa

two-quart green glass jugs filled with fresh spring water to aid them on their mission. It had to be Rockford, but the man behind the counter at the hotel said he didn't have a name to go along with the gifted supplies; he was just told who to give them to. He also mentioned that the best coffee in town was in fact, out of town; it would be opening soon. He told Ralph the name of the café that was about a mile and a half up the road and on the right.

"Remind me to send a telegram to Rockford when the sun comes up Ralph. I can probably find a Western Union in the next big city if I put my mind to it." Posh's gratitude was visible. He hadn't allowed anyone other than Ferguson to creep so deeply into his life as a true friend so quickly. Thinking back as to how he felt about Eoghan and even Montgomery, they had been held at arm's length for a while waiting for the pieces to fall into place for each of them. Rockford on the other hand, had somehow pushed his way through the layers and folds of the man's soul quickly and had penetrated his core with genuine true friendship almost instantly.

"Hey Nick," began his friend, *"How's that dog of yours that you gave up to MacRae, you haven't talked about him in a while. Keeper, right? His name was Keeper. You said Eoghan's girls are all over him and won't ever think about giving him back to you. Do you suppose your boy will want him now that he's in Scotland for the summer? Do you think Brenna and Maylene will surrender the pooch to their 'cousin'?"* he asked.

"Not a chance. That dog is so far ingrained in those girls' lives he'd have to be pulled from their cold dead fingers before they'd give him up. If one were to almost let go the other of them would come sew it up!

Jude Stringfellow

Keeper is being kept! We'll say that. He's been the best dog for them and even stopped a bad guy from delivering a box to the door I'm told....a bad guy in the eyes of the dog anyway, the poor mailman probably doesn't see it that way." Posh laughed.

The miles stretched out aimlessly and barren from Tucumcari to Newkirk before endlessly stretching further into the abyss of desert loneliness through the cities of Cuervo and Bolton before finally opening up to the very welcomed oasis of Santa Rosa. Miles upon dusty dim isolated miles leading the men to the first Euro-American settlement of that open hard land. First called "*Little Black Water*" by the natives the name of the city was changed about the time locomotives made their appearance and began crisscrossing the country. Saint Rose or in Spanish, Santa Rosa was named after or for a small chapel built to honor the grandmothers of the founder of the city; Don Celso Baca.

When the Civil War broke out among the states Baca organized a group of men who soldiered for the Union; he was commissioned as their commander. He served in at least one battle, the battle of Val Verde, and through other smaller skirmishes before being decorated for his service to his country. The quaint little township was nestled among the rolling hills dotted with cattle and sprawling ranches; not unlike those owned by ranchers in Texas – more men like Rockford no doubt; and ranchers had a way of communicating just the same as cops or for that matter, criminals.

Santa Rosa offered a good hotel, hot meals, a much-needed shower, and rest before the men met up with men who were stationed purposely through a chain of secreted telegrams and coded messages; all seeming to

Mesa

know exactly who the men were and what their assignments had been even though neither man had made a point of letting on exactly who they were.

Back in Scotland, when Nick had found himself in need of performing an undercover operation, he had little trouble inducting MacRae to assist. On one occasion, the two men had dressed as homeless vagabonds roaming the mean cobbled streets of Edinburgh making their way into a temporary sanctuary to catch a murderess red-handed. When that job was finished they both took a few days off to recover from the stress of nearly being killed by the pint-sized pistol-packing pixie. Eventually, the woman was sentenced to hanging for her crimes, but the liberal-hearted citizens of the city petitioned for her sentence to be reconsidered; a sentence of life without the possibility of ever being paroled was handed down to Fiona Faye Hayes.

Only a few had been privileged to their operation, and as far as he knew, no one had been brought in on this one, except maybe...yes, Rockford, had been told, and it was Rockford who had assisted the men with supplies. It was Rockford who had telegraphed the Santa Rosa Western Union to leave yet another encrypted message leading Posh directly to a meet-up with men of like-mindedness who would take a slice of pride in being able to assist their interstate comrade by giving every ounce of support they could to the unnamed private detective and his equally anonymous law enforcement friend.

"Ferg, it looks like Rockford has us going from one point to the next to meet up with men who may very well be our greatest asset. If nothing else, we have a chain of people to fall back on for advice or help if we need it. I

think I'll dig through the stash in the back seat to see if I can find the pencils and pads of paper I know are there somewhere.

"I'll want to keep a record of these names and where I can find them if I need them again. You can't be too careful and you can't have too many connections." He stated. Ferguson nodded as he stuffed a bit of sandwich into his mouth making some sort of comment about the dirt of the skies lending a bit of southwest flavor to the potted meat.

"You'll want to keep good records of them just in case one of them isn't as helpful or as honest as the others. When you get a group together, there's usually a Judas in the middle of them. Sometimes the mole isn't as clean-cut as the one we found in Kelso; they may not be upstanding and maybe they'll let their guard down, but it's been my experience that you can't be all wide-eyed about it when you seem to get the best help out of nowhere.

"Someone may be riding along to play the game for a while before he pulls a gun on you in the hallway of a secluded hotel in the middle of a perfectly good investigation....speaking from experience you may remember," Ralph added, then stuffing the last bit of the sandwich into his mouth.

Before settling into their rooms for the day both men noticed a small-framed Hispanic maid entering each room with her wheeled cart. Before she had entered the room a few doors down from theirs, her cart was full of fresh white terry-cloth towels stacked one on top of the other, and of course, there seemed to be cleaning supplies on the lower tray of her cart. When she exited the unattended room she seemed to have even more towels than before she had to begin with, they seemed thicker;

thick enough to catch the attention of both Posh and Ferguson.

Their silence held taunt between them, as their eyes met and both men understood that there may very well be a mole of some sort working right up under their noses; hiding in plain sight. When the woman exited the room her eyes caught those of the private investigator lurking just outside his door. He hadn't been there before; she would have noticed.

"*Excuse me...*" Posh stated, catching up to the small-statured woman holding tightly to her wobbling metal cart. "*I think I'd like a few extra towels, please.*" His words tapered off while he helped himself to the thicker towels closest to the cart's top tray. "*I'll just take these three if you don't mind...*" he added while turning himself from the maid, using his back to block her from trying to stop him. "*No...no sir, not those towels, please. I can...I can bring you fresh towels to your room...I...*" her words caught in the back of her throat.

Staring into his eyes she had been caught and she wasn't able to move. Nick Posh stood facing the woman, holding the heavy-laden clean towels in his left hand while reaching for his gun with his right. "*What is your name*" he quietly asked her, "*What is your name, and who sent you to that room to pick up these particular towels?*" his eyes were fixed upon hers; he wouldn't release her, not before he knew everything she knew.

Her dark eyes flashed before welling up with tears. Immediately she felt a hot troublesome rush of blood flowing into her face and behind her ears. "*I'm sorry sir...I'm so sorry. I'm not...I don't. My name is Maria,*

Jude Stringfellow

Maria Gonsallis. I have been at the Santa Rosa Motel and Bistro for a while, maybe a year now.

"I have never had anyone ask me to do this before, I promise. I didn't know what to do. He paid me. The man...he paid me to go into the room and remove the towels just like you see them. I wasn't to look...I wasn't to pull the top of the towels to see. I was told if I did he would know. He's waiting for me to bring them to his room on the other side of the lamppost...please, I know he must have seen you. Please, let me take these towels and bring you more." She begged, not realizing Nick's gun had been drawn and was now pointing at her waist.

"I don't think I can let you do that Maria. I believe you when you say you haven't ever done this; maybe I believe you that is, but I can't let you have them, not now." He said, allowing her to pull her cart away to see his true position. Maria's stare was fixed; her mind raced as her heart began to fail her. Shaken, the woman withdrew within herself and began to shutter.

"Do you know who the man was who asked you to bring these towels to his room? Which room did he want you to bring them to?" Posh quietly asked. As he asked, Ferguson took a few paces back from where they had come, he made himself seen in and around the front desk and lobby, making eye contact with anyone who may have been looking out of the glass front encasement to monitor the maid's actions.

"You're not expecting any fresh linen today are you, sir?" Asked Ralph raising his eyebrows to imply intimidation. Reaching out he caught the wrist of a man who couldn't keep his eyes off the happenings in the parking lot. *"You're not thinking of running now, are you? We've just met. I've not even introduced myself. You don't*

know me...but I think I may know you." He said, before giving a nod to the front desk manager, taking his key, and walking the man toward his shared space with Posh; Room 110, a mere few steps from the room Maria was instructed to take the towels to. The two rooms shared a common wall.

"I bet if we put a glass up against this wall I could hear whatever it is that your partner is saying right now. Do you wanna bet I can?" asked Ferguson to his silent rugged captive who hadn't opened his mouth or closed his eyes once. Ralph turned to his good friend and partner to say, *"Looks like Rockford ain't the only one who knew where we'd be staying tonight, Posh. What sort of man goes up against a wrangler like Rockford and lives to tell about it?"* he asked.

At first glance, anyone might mistake Nick for a statue – his face impassive; his posture rigid. But beneath that hardened exterior lay one sharp intelligence, a keen intuitiveness that made him one of the most formidable detectives on either side of the Pecos. Before he could answer Ralph's rhetorical question, the Chicago cop fired off another round of questions; Nick remained stoic, calm, and collected as Ferguson beat the man verbally into place.

There was no doubt in his mind whatsoever, that the bravado of Ralph Ferguson was anything less than stellar – he had it in spades. He knew better than to ever underestimate the sheer willingness and cagey courage of his Irish counterpart; biding his time until the right moment to ask his questions of the red-handed, and no-doubt paid thug caught between two rocks and two very hard places.

SEVEN

The only thing the man hated worse than elevator silence was elevator conversations. If he couldn't ride his way up to the top of the building where he could then exit to the roof to have a smoke alone, by himself, and without any disturbance, at least he wanted to not have to speak to someone else who happened to push a button that would stop him from making his destination as quickly as humanly possible; he knew he should have taken the stairs.

"*Good day, Chief Moore.*" Stated a stranger who just happened to be waiting on the Chief at that exact moment. "*I believe you're about to take your morning constitution on top of the roof for your ten o'clock smoke, am I correct?*" the man asked. "*Before you ask, you don't know me. I'm one of those people who pop into a man's life now and again to drop information about this or that, to bring light into an otherwise dark and dangerous moment. You might say I'm the voice of reason...yes, good reason.*" He continued.

"*Your wife, she doesn't know about your smoking habit does she? Organist at the First Presbyterian Church there on Western, she's also the head of the Ladies Auxiliary Club, and she's the first woman to beat out a man in taking over the Vice President's position at Standard Oil, am I right? Is that your wife - Ulla Mansfield Moore?*" When he spoke he did so with an air of confidence not usually offered by a stranger.

Mesa

With a soft clang, the old iron cage door swung open, revealing a dimly lit hallway on the fourth floor; two floors short of the roof entrance. The solitary figure stepped out onto the cracked linoleum floor, adjusting his hat as he squinted against the harshness of the morning sun bursting through the open windows. He was dressed impeccably; Moore noticed. There was an air about the man; something cagey or on the edge. He seemed to know his way around the building, he knew which floors to be on and which would lead to trouble.

Chief Moore held his tongue as well as the instinct to finish the man. He began to think he was being targeted for a reason; he didn't answer. The stranger took his leave quickly, without so much as an inkling of explanation as to his reason for the unusual interruption. Moore quickly punched the floor selection buttons – stopping the car one floor up. When the elevator car stopped on the fifth floor, Moore forgot about his morning smoke; he exited the car and walked directly to the office of the Police Commissioner, Mike Ballinger. Having taken a mental note of the man's description, his clothes, and his voice, Chief Moore entered the lobby of Ballinger's office and promptly closed the door behind him.

"Mike....Mike, there was a man in the elevator with me. He got off on four; it'll go to the top before he can come back down. I've pushed the button to force it to return to this floor. Get a couple of men to guard it. Don't let him leave. You and me, we'll take the stairs to the top to see if we can catch him that way. He's not one of us. He knew my name, my wife's name. He knew her habits, her job, everything. Something is going on; he's trying to scare something out of me. I didn't budge. Let's go."

Jude Stringfellow

The Chief's movements and the way he handled himself led the younger less experienced Commissioner to follow his every direction. As the older more seasoned civil servant, Chief Moore exuded an air of authority few could or would argue with; he commanded respect simply by reputation. Even the younger, less experienced officers and men around the city looked up to him with reverence. His movements were fluid yet deliberate; each step was calculated to maximize efficiency in his everyday life and his work.

"I've said it before Moore, you should have my job. You know more about what's going on than I'll ever know. You have the steel for it too. What did he say, the man, what did he say to make you stiff up like you did?" asked Mike Ballinger, a man in his mid-forties who had moved quickly and steadily through the ranks over the past several years, starting as a routine beat cop making his way through the office of being a detective and then taking a political turn to sit where he was sitting; as top dog of the force.

It was Ballinger's job to determine who worked where, what assignments they took; who could be counted on, and who could improve with more training. When the two men reached the top of the stairs and quickly opened the door leading to the roof they found no one. Both men surveyed the scene carefully, their eyes darting back and forth between the surrounding buildings of the downtown metroplex. The mid-morning jolt had been stronger than any third cup of coffee for the Chief of Police. He wanted answers, and he wanted them immediately.

The two guards positioned on the sixth floor and fifth floor, as well as the first, also found no one as the elevator doors opened, revealing an empty car. If he hadn't been found on the roof, and he hadn't taken the car back down from the fourth, there was only one other route to take; and that was unthinkable. He had to have either jumped two stories from the six-story police building to the roof of City Hall, or he had to have somehow made it across the rooftop and down the fire escape before Chief Moore and the Inspector had time to climb just one set of stairs to the roof. Either feat would have been amazing to see.

"*I don't know what he wanted.*" Stated Moore. "*He said he suspected I was taking my 'morning constitution' whatever that means. He knew I smoked a cigarette each morning around this time, and he knew my wife didn't know about it. He said she was the organist at our church, which she is, and he knew she had recently won the slot of Vice President over at Standard. He knew her name.*" Chief stated.

"*Describe him to me. Do you think you could do that, or maybe to the sketch artist we have on payroll? Could you tell her what he looked like; maybe in detail? Did you see his face at all?*" The questions were pouring out of Ballinger as he tried hard to recall his days as a detective long enough to form an idea of who this stranger could be. He came out of nowhere and he had retreated into it the same way he had materialized in the first place.

When they were back on the second floor and able to talk freely, Ballinger pulled a small folded paper from his pocket, telling the Chief he had found it on the stairwell. He hadn't had time to look at it before, but he could make out a crude diagram made by the lead of a sharpened pencil. There were buildings represented by crude square forms; a straight line was drawn between two of them with another line joining the two – like a cross or a *"T"*.

"He had to have taken the hard way out, but to do it he'd need to have known he'd have a place to land without hurting himself in the process. Maybe he's an athlete or something, maybe he's a tightrope walker!" Ballinger stated, *"If he is, he may very well be connected to whatever Posh is stirring up in Vegas with that circus crowd."*

How could a man like that come into the building, make it to the elevator, and know Chief Moore would enter the hallway and the elevator at exactly that moment? Had he been waiting several minutes in the elevator? Since the police station didn't have an elevator car escort on payroll anyone who rode the caged car would know they had to hoist the doors open and close them by themselves. This man knew how to do that. He either had experience with that elevator in the past, or he had experience in other elevators like it.

This one, this car was a little different than most, the closing bar had been installed as if the operator was a left-handed person. It was always a bit awkward for anyone who hadn't been in the thing before they were. That issue, that unique situation wasn't a problem for the dapper fellow who placed himself into Chief Moore's life that morning. That fact alone was enough to convince the Commissioner that the person they were hunting had to be in and out of buildings of all shapes, sizes, heights, and purposes. He had to know his way around to be as smooth as he was.

After describing the man to Anita Cranston who had been recently promoted to Director of the Oklahoma

Mesa

City Arts Counsel, Chief Moore's impromptu recollection of the man who had met and accompanied him in the police station elevator had suddenly come to life on paper. Through the keen and subtle strokes of lead being manipulated by the artist, an image began to emerge. Tall but not over six foot one or two inches, the man was of medium to thick build. He had short cropped hair, with only a touch of grey, setting his age likely in his mid to late forties.

Without facial hair, the Chief assumed the man's habits, saying he could recall a slight menthol scent that could have come from the man's freshly shaved face. Since the scent was still strong enough to be noticed, it was believed he either lived close enough to the police station to hold the scent or perhaps he had met up with one or the other barbers in the neighboring streets surrounding the downtown precinct.

Only two barbershops were within walking distance of the police house; the Commissioner took a man with him to question the owner of one while Chief Moore attempted to draw information from the second. They'd get their answer if they had to break down doors to do it – when the Chief of Police came knocking in Oklahoma City; no one was going to say no to the man.

The stranger's facial expression had been a happier one. He had been smiling, showing a dimple on his left side close to his lips. He had green or hazel eyes that had a heavier deeper setting while his teeth seemed pristine; almost as if he were a model or advertisement for a dentist wanting their patrons to remember to brush their teeth at least twice a day. A man like that, a man with such handsomeness would be remembered the Chief thought. If he were athletic enough to scale the six floors of fire escape ladders in mere minutes, he would be strong enough to run in or out of the downtown area when he needed to.

The clothes the man wore were loose; a bit uptown for the Chief's liking, if he had to be honest about it. Once Ian Moore clocked out for the day and drove the eight miles toward the eastern city of Spencer, Oklahoma, he liked nothing else but to lay himself down on the couch for a quick nap wearing his gym pants and maybe an old tee shirt. Dressing up for a day's work meant the standard blue uniform of a cop; not those wild plaid pants, a crisp linen buttoned shirt with leather suspenders; not if he had any say in the matter. The man's shoes had been expensive as well. Moore knew he couldn't afford those shoes if saved his paychecks for a month of Sundays.

Having only looked up at the man while he was entering the elevator car, the rest of the time the good Chief kept his cool by staring at the man's laced brown brogues with patent two-tone styling, something a dandy would wear, maybe a pimp or a mobster. Now that he thought about it, he had probably just encountered one of the up-and-coming hoodlums in the city who wanted to make a name for himself on the streets. What better way to make a name for himself than with the cops? It was the fastest way to put anyone's name at the top of their list.

A telegram was sent ahead to Posh and Ferguson to address the encounter. Whether it made sense or not, Detective Sean MacArthur wanted the Chief to think about putting a bug in Posh's ear about the matter just in case he needed to keep it in his head for where he was going and for what he was doing.

No other major cases seemed to warrant the use of a leg-breaker to make a polite and cordial visit to the Chief

Mesa

or anyone else in the police precinct; just the one case, the governor's niece's murder. *"Let Posh know what's happening here Chief; it could make a difference to him out there if the two things are somehow connected."* Sean MacArthur suggested firmly.

When they arrived in Albuquerque, Posh checked in with the Western Union clerk first thing; even before settling up the rooms for himself and Ralph at the Guidestone Hotel on Main Street. With its ornate wooden countertops and antique brass fixtures, the telegraph office oozed with character and Western charm, transporting Posh back to the same almost exact styled offices of the Western Union office in Edinburgh; where his good friend Wayne Stringfellow rules the roost.

Ralph walked ahead of Posh as he stepped up to the counter to ask the attendant if they had any messages to receive. At first, there was no answer; it took Ralph a few seconds to realize the clerk was in the middle of sending a telegram – it would be a few minutes before he could make himself known. The clerk, a darker-skinned man of foreign descent; greeted Ralph kindly enough, his weathered face breaking into a friendly grin as he handed Ralph two folded pieces of paper. One telegram was from Chief Moore, the other was from Dennis Rockford.

"Posh, you've got a message from Oklahoma City, you need to read it. I'll pay the tip; you need to call Chief Moore as soon as you can." Ralph stated.

Paying the tip to the clerk was something he'd learned from being a northern man. Folks in the South didn't seem to cotton too much to giving money to folks for doing their job, but Ferguson found that painting the palm with one or two coins for doing next to nothing, could bring about a world of unknown information and oftentimes when the information was needed the most. He began talking it up with a second clerk, a young woman in her early twenties who spoke better English than her Peruvian partner; her Americanized name was Elaine.

"You know, that ugly mug over there has a beautiful wife with your name! She's from overseas too; Scotland." He told her. *"She's a real looker. I think moms must have it in their heads to name the really pretty ones Elaine; wouldn't you agree with me, pal?"* Ralph asked the man standing only feet from the blushing young girl who couldn't be more embarrassed but flattered at the same time.

"Oh, she's OK I guess, for a kid sister. You can't go around telling people you think your sister is a looker, that sort of thing can get a man in deep water 'round these parts anyway." The male clerk said before they all had a good laugh at Nick's expense. *"Look at him, does he look like he deserves a gorgeous wife with such an amazing name?"* teased Ralph.

Before they closed their doors on the Buick, Ralph had intel he needed to share with Nick, and Nick had word to go by the office of the Greater Arts and Supply House just about a mile down the road. *"We'll head up to the Arts House now and see if the woman there who spoke with our police sketch artist could do justice to what she heard as a description over the phone, Ralph.*

"This man, an unknown gangster probably, made his way into the police station and somehow threatened the Chief without so much as lifting a finger or raising his voice. Chief said he made his way either across the roofs for a getaway or high-tailed it down the fire escape six stories in no time. He's given a full detailed description of

Mesa

the man to Anita Cranston and she's called a woman she went to university with to do the same drawing for us. We'll take it with us to show around if he's coming out this way to stop us or if he has connections out this way.

"When you think about it Ralph, we have connections and they have connections too. You're probably right about needing to be careful reading between the two lines. There has to be some blurring from time to time. A man can't be all good and he's just as likely not to be all bad either. I hate to say it, but we're living in darker times. When men can dress as clowns to blend in rather than stand out, and other men can boldly walk into a police station to threaten a top cop…we only thought the war was dangerous."

Nick turned to Ralph to ask him what it was that he wanted to tell him before he went off about the sketch artist, and their need to find out everything they could about the evasive stranger in police headquarters. "*Nothing much I guess*," said Ralph with only a bit of sarcasm in his voice, "*Except Elaine told me that the last telegram her brother Emilio sent was to Aldo Restani in Lake Mead, saying two messages had been received at that office addressed to Detective Nick Posh and he was expected to retrieve those messages within the hour.*"

Jude Stringfellow

EIGHT

Ralph questioned Nick about his wife Elaine and their nearly nine-year-old son being back in Scotland for the summer. He wondered if Nick thought it would be difficult to convince them to return to Oklahoma once their vacation was up. Both Elaine and Alistair were born and raised in the United Kingdom, it was truly what they knew and they loved it with their core being. Nick, nodding thoughtfully, shifted the car into first; the mechanical lever resisted somewhat, perhaps some of that sand had managed to maneuver its way into the gear shaft. With a firm hand and careful coordination, the gears meshed together seamlessly, sending a jolt through the car's newly constructed frame.

"*I imagine so...to be honest with you, Ralph,*" Nick admitted. "*Elaine's family has been there for generations, and she loves being able to educate and inspire Alistair to dream of one day being a very important man in his own country. It's where she and Alistair both grew up, it's where I fell in love, it's where I thought I would live the rest of my life if I had to be honest with you pal.*"

He said, his voice trailing off into silence before thinking of a few more words to strengthen his resolve about the matter. "*But then again, maybe the newness of America, the rough and tumbled life in Oklahoma, the Southwest, will be enough to inspire him to be something worthwhile here instead of there. Maybe he'll be the next Roosevelt or own a big ranch like our friend Dennis*

Mesa

Rockford; it's an open world here. It's a clean and open slate, anyone can be anything they want to be, but in the United Kingdom things aren't as easy to change," Nick postured.

"If a man is born into money he usually dies in it. He's expected to make more of it and leave it to his kids when he's gone. Here, a man can teach his son to hunt, fish, camp, fight, run a business, take over a business, or even make his own dreams. Americans are encouraged to be independent you know, maybe Alistair will see that for himself." Nick voiced with more hope than he even thought he could muster.

"Then again, perhaps the future here and there will change enough that we can't ever know what a boy his age can end up doing over time. He's at that age where he's so curious about everything. He's into learning math and science, how things are put together, how engines work, and how to build a staircase without using nails. The kid....Ralph," Nick stated frankly, *"...the kid has a great head on his shoulders. He learns fast and he keeps it inside himself, he thinks."*

Ralph nodded in agreement before mentioning something along the lines of what the family chooses to do together will make an enormous impact on the child as he grows up; Ralph more or less hoped the boy would choose to return on his own without being told to do so. Being nearly nine years old, Alistair was of course, too young to make permanent decisions on his own for himself, it was a good thing he had both an intelligent and strong-willed mother as well as his deeply thoughtful father who had never been able to surrender under any circumstances. For now, though, their focus remained firmly fixed on their current objective; which was to bring justice to those who sought refuge in the hills and cavernous hideaways of Nevada's neon oasis.

****

Elaine Posh drew her hand from the pocket of her tailored-made coral and peach-colored jacket before removing a soft linen glove to turn the door handle on their Tolbooth flat. The unit had been left in the care of a good friend and neighbor who had watched it while the family was overseas. Plans were being made to offer the flat for sale at some point soon. Inside the cozy abode, Elaine drew a heavy sigh of relief upon seeing that everything she and Nick had left behind appeared to be in place and order.

Walking slowly through the front room, running her delicate fingers across the back of the sofa, feeling its coarse material brought deep-seated memories back to the forefront of her mind. This was the first piece of furniture she had purchased immediately after Nick had left her when he returned to America to find the desperate and horrible man who had murdered his father in cold blood.

Somehow, touching the couch, knowing it was safe kept her mind centered on what and where she was standing; what those years of being alone had been to her. She had managed to work full-time, raise a child alone, and depend on herself for more than eight years. It was another time completely. As she walked across the hardwood floors of the two-bedroom flat, she glanced to the right and the left, making and taking a mental note of literally every small detail of each room.

The scent of lavender lingered in the air; perhaps a window had been left open in one of the rooms to avoid any stuffiness. She welcomed the intruder with everything in her being. Elaine couldn't help but feel grateful for this brief respite from what had become her reality. Since leaving for the United States and taking a job at the airport, where everyone called the flying cages *"airplanes"* now, she had not once been inside an aeroplane as an employee, as an attendant; Scotland was the place for that sort of work.

The United States, at least in the part where she lived now, expected women to remain outside of the cockpit, in a more acceptable position; that of a flight stewardess. This was her chance to reconnect with her past while she knew she would be creating new memories with her husband, her son, Ama, and all of her newly acquainted friends. Where Scotland was more open for a woman to make more choices perhaps in most industries, Oklahoma had pushed her to know she could be everything she had hoped to be as a child.

She could be a wife, a mother, have a career, volunteer, and make a difference, and if she wanted to, she could own her own business easily without needing to work her way through the ranks as she had in her first chosen career path. She may not be a pilot, but she could be vitally important to those in her inner circle; a circle that had grown extensively over the past year of her life.

Among such tranquility, she couldn't shake off the nagging sense of unease brought about by all of the recent events that had transpired in her life, and the lives of her family. With Nick's reputation and ability to fight crime the way he did, she all but knew she would have to be even more protective of their privacy, and of the privacy of their son. Every passing day was a gift in one way and a tightening of exterior ropes around their lives at the same time.

She couldn't afford or chance anything happening to her Alistair. With every passing day his language, his actions, everything had reminded her of the man she could never say no to; the man she had been smitten by – her son's devoted and mysteriously wonderful father Nick Posh. When Alistair entered the front door of their flat to find his mother seated at the small dining table he rushed to hold her.

"Mum, this is the best place ever, you know that right? You know I love it here, but there's something different about it now. I don't know what it is, it's not coming to me right away, but there's not as much of me here in my head. I don't feel that his place is really home anymore. It's like if someone said where do you live, I would stand up taller and say 'The Great State of Oklahoma!', just like Dad does. I like saying it." Alistair admitted.

"Maybe, it's because no one else here can say it." Advised his mother. *"It could be that you know both sides and you can see good in both and maybe something less than good in both, but you're hoping for a new future and a new start."* She said.

"...well, to be honest with you son, I'm thinking the same thing myself. I'm hoping we can say we were born in the United Kingdom, but we live in the United States. At least we know we can go to ether and be welcomed." She said.

Hearing her son's words, Elaine felt a pang of sorrow, a bit of sadness mixed with understanding. Of course, Alistair couldn't feel the things she had felt, having only been a lad, and having been born into a family rather than like herself, being adopted into one. There would be new and fond memories being made as well as being remembered. After all, they weren't just visiting Scotland; they were living among strangers in a foreign land now, and yet, the people she was beginning to know and beginning to accept and even love, weren't strangers after all.

She couldn't count on both hands the people she knew well while living in the bustling capital city of Edinburgh, but in Oklahoma, she was privileged to know every single neighbor for blocks and blocks, as well as most of the people who attended the same church as they attended. It was true, Scotland was their first home, and it would always hold a dear and cherished spot in their hearts, but Oklahoma was going to be the best part of the rest of their lives; they both knew it to be true.

"One day after the last day here, you'll find yourself smothered with friends at school and hoping to invite them all over for sandwiches and cookies. I know you, Alistair Ean Posh!" said his mother, squeezing the young boy with everything she had.

"We'll be here for a while, but when we return, returning to our true home of Oklahoma City, we'll reclaim the peace of mind, that piece, and the peace of Heaven right here on earth. In the meantime, let's resolve to cherish every single moment we're here." His mother told him. *"We'll start by having dinner at Bandy's restaurant tonight, and we'll load up on some good old-fashioned haggis tatties and neeps before bedding down tonight, and waking up to meet your two best cousins at the Red Door Café for breakfast. You know your uncle Eoghan has been waiting to see you, I'm told...although,*

Jude Stringfellow

I've been sworn not to reveal too much, that he has a surprise waiting for you tomorrow." Her words teased, as he lifted his small eyebrows into one of the most hilarious facial expressions his mother had ever seen; his tiny teeth flashing boldly.

As they settled into their seats at Bandy's, Elaine couldn't help but marvel at the rich flavors and the irresistible and grand smells assaulting her nostrils. It was as if she had been away from Scotland forever. The Scottish cuisine was one of the things both of them had missed more than anything else.

The tangy rich taste of the haggis melded perfectly with the thick and hearty potatoes and tenderly crushed mashed turnips; the meal transported her back to those exciting days when she had first met Nick, and when she had coaxed him into eating the meal for the first time in his life. Her memories returned as she retold the favorite story to their son.

"*Your father wasn't much for blood pudding either in those days. He only tried it because he lost a bet to me, you know.*" Elaine bragged as her son nodded silently asking her to continue.

"*He thought he could climb the old Adler tree out back of the boarding house where he and I stayed and he bet me I couldn't get as high into it as he could.*" She said with a wink. "*I took that bet, and I put everything I had into it. I'll show you the tree since I know it's still standing. I'll bet everything I own that you can climb higher than either of us did, and you'd have half as much trouble doing it too, I imagine.*

"*I had the weight of the world on me that day for some reason or the other, I don't recall now why or how I came to think that everything was crashing in on me, but there he was, your dad, making light of my terrible troubles telling me that if I could beat him to the highest rank, he'd eat his hat! Well, you know what I told him, don't you?"* she asked. Leaning in this chair his boyish face covered in goosebumps just waiting for the answer.

"I told your father that if I won he had to eat a whole plate of haggis, which would include both blood pudding and a large heaping of beans to boot!" she told her son. *"To boot! You said 'to boot' Mum!"* Alistair laughed, *"You must really be an American to say that!"* he added with another chuckle under his breath.

When all was said and done, and their meal completed, the two of them whisked away into the evening to race home, just the way they always did, only this time Elaine had to keep up to try and beat her boy to the front door. This was certainly something that hadn't happened in the past. Time was changing everything for her, as she knew it one day would.

Looking around the old established neighborhood filled with voices and muted laughter and conversations between so many tourists and residents of the area, Elaine realized that perhaps they hadn't strayed too far from all the things she had cherished about her homeland, she had simply remembered to pack them up with all of her belongings and carted them off to her new home; to her new life – proving positively that home truly lies within who we are rather than where we happen to be.

Jude Stringfellow

NINE

Elaine questioned within herself what she could have seen in Nick Posh in the first place. Was it the fact that he didn't look like every other man in the United Kingdom? He was different, he had a darker complexion and was so damned confident. He somehow stood taller than others his same height; his skin bore testament to his ancestry, a timeless ageless people of another world. His dark eyes pierced through anyone who saw them. Holding their stare and making them blink first; that was Nicolas Posh. Nick stood out in any crowd, that had to be it.

His unique blend of not only being an American, a foreigner among allies, he was born of a Native American woman who had engrained in him the beauty and strengths of her people. It gave Nick a distinct difference setting him apart from others, and highlighting his striking features; those incredible dark eyes and the way his thick jet-black tresses were straight, not a curl to be found.

It wasn't just his appearance, she knew that. She knew she could never be so shallow as to fall for a man simply because he was rugged and handsome. There was more; so much more to this man Nick Posh. It was the way his lip curled when he smiled; it too seemed to control her effortlessly; accentuating an incredibly handsome face marked by character and experience – she hated him for being able to stop her in her tracks, but would never change a thing about him.

An aura of quiet strength emanated from him, it hinted at a life marked with sorrow and resilience. He was

Mesa

a military man, a noble soul. Despite his outward differences, the man carried with him a sense of morality like no man she had known before. She recognized a greater purpose in him, an intelligence in his demeanor, and a kindness from his soul that seemingly poured from him when he spoke.

Nick Posh would never consider himself before thinking of others, even from the very first meeting with the man she felt that he had already committed himself to her in some way. This was the reason she followed him to Oklahoma when he returned. This was the reason she fell in love and could never consider being with any other man when he returned without her.

When Elaine and Alistair woke the next morning they readied themselves for what both knew would be an emotional and welcoming reunion with their closest friends Eoghan and Alice Ann MacRae along with Eoghan's young daughters Brenna and Maylene. Even though everyone knew that the families weren't related by blood, and that calling themselves cousins could be argued by those who kept protocol in check; the children's admiration for each other matched the love and deeply held adoration shared between every MacRae and every Posh; which of course, included the Broonsford set as well.

As they stepped into the cozy confines of the restaurant Elaine couldn't help but give a smile as her eyes fixed immediately upon the faces of those whom she loved and missed. The tantalizing scents flooding the air around them seemed to overwhelm them from the second they walked through the door. Freshly ground hot coffee, sizzling bacon, and fried potatoes with garlic and onion

Jude Stringfellow

flavoring surrounded them, filling the air with a greater welcome than they could have ever imagined.

A mingling harmonious sound of chattering voices mixed with the clinking and clanging of culinary cutlery only added to the feelings of being exactly where they both wanted to be. The only thing that could make the moment more enjoyable would be if Nick could have been with them. Greeting Eoghan with a smile, Elaine took his hands and shook her head slowly at how much she had missed his charm and his smile; always one for a quick and jesting banter, Eoghan teased both of them immediately questioning them if the Oklahoma sun had something to do with their new tanned faces; knowing the answer would be yes.

"*Elaine! Alistair! Good morning, welcome back!*" exclaimed Eoghan's ever-expanding pregnant wife Alice Ann, reaching past her husband to take Elaine into her arms for a hug. Holding her friend meant so much to Elaine; over the past few months in the States, she had few friends close enough to share her truer emotions with.

The two women took their seats beside each other and began their mutual exchanges immediately. Pulling out a chair for young Alistair, Brenna took it upon herself to play the dutiful and polite cousin that she was. Maylene, Eoghan's younger daughter had other plans for her "*twin cousin*"; she hadn't told anyone before they arrived at the café that she had pocketed a small toad she had found in the garden outside their Stockbridge home. She knew just where she would bring it, and just who she would give it to.

Retrieving the small creature and handing it to Alistair under the table sparked laughter and fright simultaneously, sending the entire table into an unexpected rowdy raucous of shrieks and chortling before civility demanded they all return to their more socially accepted conduct.

"*Is this the surprise you were talking about Mum?*" asked Alistair with a bit of inquisitiveness in his voice. When the table returned to themselves, Elaine, with an unconventional move amidst the chaos and laughter reached across the table to retrieve the small beast and placed it squarely in the center of her son's plate.

"*Yes, this is your surprise,*" she stated. "*Maylene has given you a friend to cuddle up with so you won't need your favorite pillow. This is it! This is your surprise, there's nothing more for you*", she lied, all the while knowing her son would never believe her. Meanwhile, Eoghan tried to remain somewhat vigilant, trying to maintain order while his two daughters scurried from seat to seat, each trying to push the other out of the way to be closer to Ali, whom they missed tremendously over the past few months.

"*I've got something for youse, Alistair.*" Eoghan teased, as he reached beneath the table to reveal an early birthday gift for the boy that would not only be accepted with extreme excitement but one the talented singer and songwriter had battled within himself to know for certain that being willing and able to gift it would be something he could live with. When a man gives another something that means as much as this gift meant; it was truly personal.

From under the side of the table, he withdrew one of his older and more worn acoustic guitars; the one he had purchased himself when he was all of thirteen years of age. It was the perfect surprise – bar none. Alistair's eyes grew wide with astonishment; he couldn't believe what he was being told. The moment he saw it his excitement took over; no toad could hold a candle to a boy's first guitar! Taking the instrument in both of his hands, the boy danced freely and openly in the presence of everyone in the small eatery. An eruption of spontaneous applause cascaded from one table to the next as guests realized what had just taken place.

Within their smiles, her son's screams, and both of their expressions, Elaine knew the bond between her own family and theirs was immeasurable. She knew they would always remain close-knit and playfully banter with one another in such competitiveness no matter the distance that separated them all from being in the same place at the same time.

Their bond reminded Elaine of her relationship with her husband. He wasn't with them now, but she knew he was. It was as if he were seated next to them; his long and deep drawl telling bits and tales of what has transpired over these past several months. He would tell them all about the heat in Oklahoma, the sunrises and glorious sunsets of the western skies; the way the clouds illuminated the brightest of blue skies day after day from very early in the day until often well into the later hours of an extended evening. He would tell Eoghan about the murders he solved, or the cases he was involved in.

Nick wasn't one to bring attention to himself, and he would never think of bringing up such macabre matters with Alice Ann or the girls, but because Eoghan was an investigator himself, their friendship had become so much deeper, that it had formed an increasingly strong nexus of trust and comradery. Nick understood Eoghan's sensitivities and how he would rather see something for himself so that he might grow to understand it. Details given over the phone often created wicked images in the mind of the Scotsman; his anxiety levels could pique and even become triggered. Seeing the gore, rather than hearing about it, somehow made things less intimidating.

"*I wish Nick was here to join us.*" Elaine mused wistfully as she sipped strong black tea. She imagined how delighted he would be to see his good friends and to meet up with Eoghan's lively brood again. Perhaps soon, maybe closer to the holidays, they could plan a trip to come back again and they would all be back together again.

"*Where's Donny, Nick's grandfather?*" Elaine asked. "*I want to see how he and Norma are getting along. She's bound to be the light of his life now. I haven't seen them since we landed a few days ago.*" She added, hoping to hear a bit of family gossip she could retell to her husband when he called next.

"*I'm sorry we couldn't have met up earlier this week, but Alistair and I wanted to take in a few days of the city and sites ourselves; you were working, and my family was visiting Perth and Kinross. It was good to breathe and good to rest before meeting up. My emotions have been all over the place just thinking about coming home, or coming back to Scotland.*" Elaine said, "*I hadn't seen my parents in two years. We needed to catch up.*"

Whether it was sharing laughter around a crowded dining room table at their favorite haunt, or simply being in the same room, any room, Elaine felt at home again. Seeing Alistair play so freely and openly with the girls

Jude Stringfellow

made her heart skip two beats. These lost but familiar settings meant that she could always be comfortable with these people in her life; she could and would always know she belonged.

With a faraway look in his eyes, Eoghan began telling the tales he had been waiting so long to convey about Donny "*Pop*" Posh and his new bride Norma Jean Gleason. Norma had gone by the name of Meredith Kuhlman for many years, as she purposely hid her true identity to separate herself from her Louisiana-based plantation-working, slave-owning vicious family.

After a lifetime in lower-class entertainment as well as a self-imposed lifestyle as an elite escort, Norma Jean after decades of decadent living had turned her life over to God and had confessed to many less-than-aboveboard activities which led to Nick recovering the body of her former lover buried within the walls of the shared apartment house she and several others occupied. "It wasn't my fault," she told him, "…he died of food poisoning but not like you think." She went on to confess. *"I just hid him so I wouldn't have to admit how he died exactly."*

Whisking Norma both out of the country and into the arms of his grandfather Donny seemed to work out for everyone involved, even the dutiful men and women of the Oklahoma City Police who couldn't find reason enough to try and place the long arm of the law onto such a sympathetic figure as the sweetest of characters. Fifty years of keeping and hiding such a personal secret was punishment enough they imagined. Norma, or Merideth Kuhlman was many things, but she could never be considered a murderer. The ruling of the case was officially an accident, though the mishandling or disposal of the body was questionable.

Mesa

"I'd love tae tell ya more Elaine, but all I can tell youse is that the last time I saw them Donny was wearing that cowboy hat that Nick had sent tae him tae wear. He called it a ten-gallon hat, seems tae me the fit was perfect for the old man. It makes him look younger an' certainly put a bit of a skip in his step." Eoghan teased.

"Tae see Norma for the first an' last time, you'd think she was already part of the family. The woman hugged me like she was my own gran, taking the breath right out of me she did." He laughed. *"According tae Alice Ann, the two of them made quite the pair – Donny sporting a smile like nothing she had seen before, an' Norma wearing bright red lipstick an' a sweet simple flowered dress, the two of them almost skipped off together saying they were going tae file immediately for a marriage license. They'd only just met for goodness sake!".* Eoghan laughed.

At their age though, every day is a gift. Despite their advanced ages, they seemed determined to accept and welcome one another into a bright and brilliant new chapter of their lives, inspiring awe and amusement for all who knew them. Elaine listened with her heart as well as her ears, imagining the vibrant love and energy that must radiate from the two spirited souls; she could only imagine that the feistiness and the overt confidence she found in her husband was a product of the hearty lives lived by both his Scottish ancestors and the brave courageous spirits on his mother's side.

After their hearty enormous breakfast, Elaine and Alistair joined the MacRaes for a stroll up Arthur's Seat, a lonesome volcanic iconic hillside east of the city's capital within Holyrood Park. Its impressive peak reached more

Jude Stringfellow

than eight hundred feet high into the overcast grey majestic skies over Edinburgh. The hill itself with its tough primarily volcanic rock formation dates back millions of years creating a unique draw that lures everyone within its path to walk it, climb it, be a part of it, and make memories of their own.

The children, taking their leave from the adults, chased one another to the top of the mound, taking different hard-packed paths to see who could make it to the peak first. Laughing and jutting among the winding landscape, dodging rocks and large mounds of grass-covered sod, their voices could be heard calling to one another as each pretended to have already reached their destination; each knowing the truth.

Once reaching the top, the three sat waiting on their parents, talking about the visions before them, how small everything looked from that height; how everything and everyone seemed to move about like ants on the ground. Watching the happenings of their city, they pretended to control the actions of the unsuspecting patrons below them. Making up stories and bluffing their way through childish small talk making up stories each "*ant*" had to share with the others in their company.

Mesa

TEN

As arid dust clouds settled, billing behind them, Nick drove easily, not wanting to invite the desert vista's loose remnants into his car's engine. He had already pampered it somewhat over the past several hundred miles since leaving Oklahoma. Things were only going to get worse the deeper into the vast and barren endless mural they trekked.

The scorching sun beat down upon their weathered faces like thousands of tiny mirrors, reflecting off the hardened clay beneath them; a patchy area of the route that hadn't found pavement or much in the way of any maintenance at all. The road was hard, the air quite thick, and their minds began to understand more of what they had agreed to take on for themselves. Each man realized collectively and independently, that this was a mission they had purposely started and it would need to be completed with favorable results as soon as possible.

Not a sound around them could be heard, nothing but the roar of the engine and Ralph's obsessive way of passing the time by reading out loud every headline of every paper he could get his hands on. When the headlines and interesting stories were read, he started in on the less interesting stories; often using his imagination to boost the actual events placed in publication.

"Nothing like using a little bit of creative license to spruce up these boring articles." Ralph joked. *"If you don't mind, I'll lie myself through this one and tell you that...that...here it is, Ella Mae Braden has finally*

returned home after a quick marriage and an even quicker divorce. Ella, aged seventeen, left her home in Matterson Ville, Arizona to find love in the arms of a one-eyed pirate of a man calling himself Arthur Robert Padillo."

Ralph added, "*Padillo, a middle-aged man from the hillbilly hills of West Virginia found true love in Ella Mae from the moment he first laid his eye on her at the carousel where he worked as a carnie for the Burlington Roadside Carnaval Corporation. With his bright orange mop of hair and boasting a near-toothless smile, the uncouth man caught the unlikely attention of the beauty queen debutante from Matterson Ville by juggling his way to her heart. Padillo, along with a host of other...other...clowns.*"

With the last word pouring easily from his mouth, Ralph quickly recanted his thoughts of adding spice to the matter, explaining to Posh that Padillo, considered himself to be a roadside entertainer; one who had made his way along with a small band of others on a less known circus circuit presently cutting through smaller less populated areas of the Southwest.

"*Posh! Listen to this*," Ralph encouraged as he read the paper's small tucked-away article word for word, "*Padillo, along with several other painted-faced men and women have been promoting their circus and side-show gig as part of a grass-roots means of bringing back the simple and often characteristically known acts of juggling, dart throwing, knife-throwing and target shooting that never ceases to amaze audiences wherever they go.*

Mesa

"Arthur Padillo, one of the long-standing members of the group, seemingly married the young Miss Braden after only knowing her a few hours. Their divorce came only hours after their union; the pair having admitted to the county registrar's office that they had made a mistake." He finished.

"Padillo. The name is too close to Patullo. Patullo is the name of one of the men on my list. I'm chasing this son of a bitch, Posh. He's one of the men known to have been up in Chicago, him a few others – more ethnic men they're telling me, not necessarily born here." Ralph mentioned. *"Patullo was stupid enough to sign into the Brixton Street Hotel using his real name, not Padillo. He even pulled out his driver's license when he was asked to show identification, it says."* Ralph mentioned that from time to time, according to police records, Patullo, a professional man, got a business degree or something so he could hide in plain sight. *"What's he doing working as a carnie? He's got a real degree from an accredited college."*

"I only know that because when he sent me out here to find the killers of the three businessmen on Michigan Avenue, Captain Pershing mentioned to my CO that Patullo had a mop of orange hair like a real clown. That could be it Posh. That could be his undoing. We can maybe find this Ella Mae Braden when we get up that way, and ask her what else she knows about him. If he's as dumb as I think he is, he did a lot of pillow talking, maybe trying to impress the dame; what'd you think?" asked Ralph, hoping to spark a long enough conversation to while away at least part of their time on the open road.

Jude Stringfellow

"We'll pull off to the side of the road soon and make camp, Ralph. We're not gonna make it to a hotel anytime soon. Besides, we need to finish off the sandwiches in the boxes Mom packed for us. We don't want them to go to waste, and if nothing else we can use them as fire starters." Nick laughed, *"...but if you ever tell my mom I said that, I'll ring your neck, pull off your arm, and stick it so far down your throat you can tickle your stomach. Do you understand?"* Nick jeered. *"Your secret is my secret. Your loves my love, your hates my hates. What are brothers for?"* Ralph quipped.

Nothing could be more desolate than the skies and ground before them. Not a soul stirred in any direction except maybe the occasional roadrunner chasing after some phantom prey which seemingly ran faster than the birds. Their stomachs called out for help, grumbling and turning to the point each man could hear his gut as well as his friend's. It had been hours since they had stopped for food and to fill up the car.

Settling down around what would become a crackling campfire once they found enough kindling among the prickly tall cacti lining the strip of smooth clay road, the men set up their camp using the heavy woolen blankets from their military days to cover the barbed and bothersome turf. *"Who knew these things would be welcomed?"* asked Ralph.

"Back in the day, we hated laying on them. The way they itched and knotted up every time we tried to make a nest out of them so they wouldn't poke us all night. I think your mom had another ingenious thought there buddy. She's always thinking; that gal. Your dad knew a good thing when he saw it. He probably had to fight off a

Mesa

few dozen men for her hand, but it would have been worth it!" Ralph laughed.

"Laying these things down and then placing a tablecloth over them makes a whole lot more sense than using a larger flat folded sheet. Where in the world does she get that kind of intelligence?" he asked. Giving his friend the side-eye he knew he would receive for even asking such a question, Posh silently thanked his mom knowing that without her he'd be one lost soul indeed.

Without stones or rocks to be found around them to make a small pit, Posh began thinking of things he could use to form such a basin for their evening campfire. Pulling out the short but sturdy shovel he kept inside his oversized duffle bag, the man began to dig out a small hole, using the sides of the same to fortify the boundaries of the fire. Ralph looked on as his friend demonstrated his survival skills; skills the cop from Chicago hadn't thought about in years; not since the war.

Choosing a flint stone and his pocket knife over the hardened peanut butter and jelly sandwich so he could start a small fire, Posh searched for abandoned driftwood or a thick tumbleweed that he could break down into kindling. *"If we don't find it now we won't have a fire to keep us warm tonight."* He said. *"Ralph, maybe grab some of the old papers you bought if you've read them, that is."*

"The open desert isn't the best place to sleep of course; it gets cold at night, but without any light, we won't be able to even see the road. I don't want to drift off into the abyss out there and not be able to get back onto the road before the car gets choked." As the two men walked through the massive empty wasteland gathering

what they could to burn, a lone flatbed truck honked; a man in the driver's seat waved at the pair before driving past them and into the dusk. Ralph challenged his best friend asking him what he considered to be his best tips or techniques for surviving; surviving anything, not just the harsh conditions of the desert.

"Well, if I'm honest, I would have to say that doing this, doing what we're doing now, and gathering sticks and rubble to burn and of course, being able to make fire out of nothing. That's gotta be one of the best things a man can do for himself. He's gotta learn how to do it, how to keep it, maintain it, and not let it get out of hand.

"Besides that, I don't know, maybe another is having a Plan B if you don't have a flint stone and a knife to strike it. It would be tough, but you can get a spindle reed or a couple of sticks to rub together; it takes longer, but is just as effective." Posh instructed. Looking over at his friend, Nick realized that his upbringing in the South could very well have been more than just a geographical difference between himself and his friend from Illinois.

Ralph, as Nick was aware, hadn't been brought up with much of a father after he turned thirteen and lost his mother. Ralph had been abandoned by his older siblings to forge on his own after her passing; doing what he could to sustain life for his younger brothers who managed to find shelter with other family members from time to time.

Though he had a loose tie-in with those family members himself, at his age, he was expected to work and be productive. He had managed to survive in the concrete jungle of a hardened crime-ridden city whereas Posh had pushed through his formative years mostly in a rural or semi-rural existence with both his devoted and dedicated family-oriented father and his overly protective mother who seemingly had angels guiding her from the day she was born.

"What about you Ralph? What's your best or most used skill when it comes to surviving?" Nick asked. After thinking about it for a minute, before setting down his load of kindling, Ralph quietly murmured more than spoke. *"I've been surviving every day of my life I guess, in one way or another."* He said. *"It's either physically making things happen like when we pushed through enemy lines using the training we got, or in my case looking on to see what you or the others were doing. I didn't seem to grasp all the details myself when they told us, I'm more of a hands-on kind of guy.*

"I have to do it to understand it." He paused before continuing with, *"...when it comes to surviving, for me anyway, it's mostly mental. I'm pretty good with the action side of things, but it's the day-to-day and the mundane in-between moments, hours, days, weeks, and even months, that can add up and creep into my head. I have to push through those times a lot harder than when I'm pushing with my body in some way."* He admitted.

"Yeah, it's mental for me. I get all wrapped up sometimes and think I'm no good, or I think I haven't got what it takes. I guess it sort of gets to me when I realize that I've not been the man I want to be, but somehow Stella doesn't think that way about me. She thinks I'm the proverbial knight shining in my armor, riding in on some dumb white horse to save the day." He said, staring out into the dusk and waning skies on the horizon.

Jude Stringfellow

"If I had to think about it, I'd say my best technique for surviving is just praying through the moment asking God to show me the way to do whatever it is I'm supposed to be doing because I don't know most of the time what that could even be." Ralph's voice shifted into lower reserved tones; his thoughts surrounding him like a thick blanket of darkness needing to be breached.

Turning to face Nick, Ralph Ferguson surrendered himself with all abandonment, opening his arms to invite his best friend to embrace him. *"Don't take this the wrong way Pal, but I need a hug right about now, and well, you're the only one out here in this God-forsaken patch of land we've decided to cross. Get over here and make me feel better, will ya?"*

The best friends clasped hands, pulling themselves together shoulder to shoulder, each wrapping his strong arms around the other. The two men stood silently bound together in a union that only brothers could understand. There was an undeniable bond between them, forged through shared experiences and life, through hardships they had faced together in the past, as well as the current times.

"You've kept me alive a few times, friend," Ralph said under his breath, his words sticking in his throat. The two men clung to each other for what seemed like a lifetime, Nick remembering the night Ralph stepped in just in time to save his own life when Officer Brian Cashion had attempted to fulfill a macabre assignment to assassinate the private detective; if Posh had one breath left in him, he would never waiver if it meant giving it to Ralph Ferguson. *"You don't have to worry about being alone in your head buddy,"* Nick stated.

Mesa

"I'm there too. I'm always in that head of yours doing the talking, thinking, telling you what to do, when to do it, how to do it, why you should do it. Just think about me kicking your ass if you ever get to the point where you can't take it anymore. I'm right there. Your secret...it's my secret. Your hates are my hates. Your loves are my loves. You are my best friend, Ralph, I thank God every day for you. We're gonna do this thing, and more things, and let me tell ya, we're going to not only survive, we're gonna thrive." Nick postured, as he released his good friend holding his shoulders and looking him straight in the eyes.

"We have a long night to go, but we'll get up as soon as the sun hits us so we can see clearly and the road doesn't swallow us. I think Albuquerque is just about fifteen miles in front of us. We've got enough gas to make it, and we've got plenty of stoney-hard tack peanut butter and encrusted jelly sandwiches to make it through." He laughed, *"...you know you may have something there with the fire-starting thing and these sandwiches."* Nick added. *"I bet if we toasted them over the open flame they'd taste a lot better than they would right now."*

Jude Stringfellow

ELEVEN

Their entrance into Albuquerque proved uneventful enough with Ralph carrying on as he read through the papers he had picked up the day before in Tucumcari. Although the Chicago Tribune copy he held was admittedly two days old by the time he bought it, the paper was thicker and had more interesting articles about events that could be more pertinent to him as a resident of the northern mega-metropolis.

"Says here, if you want me to read it to you, that Colonial Randolph Pittnegreft of just outside Chicagoland's southern borders was giving his last speech from his hospital bed before succumbing to his ailments and other age-related factors. The man was ninety-six-year-old Posh; he fought in the Civil War on the side of the Confederates before marrying his long-time sweetheart after the war and moving up North where he found work on a farm before owning his own.

"He raised chickens and turkeys for a poultry circuit I guess. Here he is discussing the same things we were talking about last night by the campfire. He's going on about how he survived hiding from the Union army in a cave up around somewhere in Missouri by Table Rock Lake. He said....he said... 'Lastly, a man has to stay calm no matter what is happening around him. He has to put on an air of confidence to not show his hand to anyone. Stay calm' he said." Ralph put on his best old man's voice to repeat the words of the recently departed.

Mesa

"The colonial then added, that 'conserving your energy while breathing can help too.' He said if you breathe through your nose and out your mouth you'll live longer. Well, I guess he'd know! Ninety-six years is a lot longer than I ever expect to be drawing breath." Ralph admitted to the air around him.

Situated in the heart of the greater Southwestern United States, Albuquerque, New Mexico is somewhat sandwiched between the majestic imposing Rocky Mountains and the ever-present vastness of the Mojave Desert. Boasting such interesting blends of Native cultures as well as those brought in by the white settlers of years gone by.

The city is dotted with clay adobe homes and offices, buildings made to withstand wind, heat, sudden rainfall, and every other natural disaster poured upon it. Vibrant colors invaded the territory that is the city of Albuquerque. Nowhere had been so diverse and rich hosting the Mexican cultures alongside many Native tribes all selling their vivid lively wares from every doorstep on every street.

Heavy silver and turquoise-laden jewelry, finely crafted blankets, and clothing all handmade with precision and care lay open in the ongoing makeshift market rather than being houses collectively under one roof. Each building and each store had its unique blend of wares and valuables to sell. Art such as paintings, pencil lead, and charcoal drawings stood proudly on natural canvases ready for framing. In the air, the spices of heavy peppers roasting over an open flame mixed easily melding together the sweet scents of pinon smoke; drawing every visitor from the harsh outside into the folds of this most welcoming of cities.

Despite what could be considered depressed times for the nation at large, the city of Albuquerque seemed bolstered, bustling, and even fueled by endless possibilities being offered up by its citizenry; the citizenry of a rugged openly honest frontier town. When they had pulled up outside the Moorish-inspired *Hotel Andaluz*, the two men knew they were being treated to something very special; something right out of a fairytale.

Dennis Rockford, their good friend from the Texas panhandle had called ahead asking that two rooms be held open for his new friends; the bill, of course, was sent to Rockford's estate and ranching operation. Inside, the guests were treated to the most luxurious accommodations featuring ornate furniture made of the finest of hardwoods, adorned with thick plush lavishly colored fabric materials probably imported from exotic countries. Each pillow, each cushion, a unique blend of color, texture, and design.

A grand piano stood stoically in the middle of one of two grand ballrooms, readily inviting the next master to sit to entertain those willing to gather around to hear them. Above them hung dozens of tinkling crystal chandeliers casting their warm intricate angles of light upon marbled tiles of greys and various hues of greens and natural shades of golden tones, while the handsomely dressed waitstaff stood at attention and greeted anyone who walked through the ornate glass and wooden front doors, and dozens of vases of fresh flowers voluntarily gave off their fragrance.

"This is the...this has got to be the most wonderful hotel I've ever seen in my life," Ralph stated. *"I can't imagine having the money it took to build it, let alone to*

Mesa

run it. A room here must cost at least forty dollars a night. How in the...how did...well, OK, I know how...cattle, that's how. That Rockford, he has it all, doesn't he? If you ask me, the whole thing is a bit quixotic – impractical as hell," stated the cop under his breath, not willing to draw attention to the fact that he was so easily distracted.

"It's not that big of a deal Ferg. Didn't we have a bang of a time back in Kelso? That's gotta stick in your head as being one of the most memorable stays in a hotel, doesn't it?" Nick teased, knowing that the moment he mentioned Kelso, his good friend would fold in on himself laughing from having saved his best friend's life in the time it took a hummingbird to shake its wings. *"Kelso?*

"You bring up Kelso in a place like this?" Laughed Ralph. *"Kelso can keep Kelso. I'll take the Andaluz friend. I'll flippin' live here if they let me. I'll call for Stella to come down. I can only imagine there's an on-site hospital inside this place somewhere. She won't have to have the baby in a stale old room like she's planning to do up there. I don't mind if my kid is born in New Mexico as long as he can say he was born in a place this regal. He can say he was born to greater things."*

Posh laughed slightly as he took the opportunity to rib his friend again about somehow being able to look into his wife's belly to determine what the sex of his unborn child would be. Boy or girl, Ferguson didn't care either way, but until proven otherwise to him, the baby was an heir to keep the Ferguson name living for at least one more generation.

Looking about the lobby before climbing the wide elegantly framed staircase leading to their second-floor rooms, Nick accepted a single red rose handed to him by a beautiful young maiden who seemingly expected a few coins for the flower; her eyes glancing over him as if she were capable of accepting more than the price of a token rose. Ralph couldn't help himself from laughing a bit too loudly at the silent yet devastatingly obvious innuendo of their first encounter with the locals at this most magnificent establishment.

"Do you think she has a whole bouquet of those things Nick?" he asked, *"Do you think you could buy them one at a time to see if she'll pluck something other than the flowers in her hands?"*

Even though the two men knew their limits as devoted married men, it was clear to them both that the young woman was a professional in her way, using the flowers she sold to detect any would-be interest for future evening enterprises, perhaps a postprandial industry of sorts involving massages before being treated to more amorous benefits; the type provided by one with enough time and expertise to deliver the very best in the hospitalities of that sort.

"You'll notice Ferg, that she waited until I was on the staircase to offer the rose to me, friend. I guess maybe she could tell from the start that you had less to share in the way of exotic lovemaking; you don't have to worry, I'll not mention it to Eoghan or Monty when we call them up here in a few minutes. I don't want you to pine over such sorrows to our good friends.

"It's just that I have this charisma going you know, it's in me, it's the Native thing, it has to be. Otherwise, she would have been interested in your pale skinny ass; but she wasn't." the man gaffed before he caught himself choking on the spit that had made its way to the back of his throat. *"Yeah, that's attractive right*

there, Posh." Ralph returned the jag to his good friend and comrade. *"That's exactly what that girl is looking for; that old man cough of yours. I bet you're at least half a dozen years older than her father!"* his words caused Nick to involuntarily snort again, which only strengthened the moment for Ralph. He continued jolting his best friend as they made their way into their separate rooms.

While they stood outside their respective doors Ralph shook his head again at the simple yet complex beauty of each floor of the exalted hotel. *"These floors! Look at them. Downstairs it's all marble and old stone while up here on the guest floors it's the thickest most luxuriously decorated carpet I've ever stepped on. Just thinking about it drives my mind into bankruptcy Posh."* Ferguson remained fascinated by the sovereignty of it all, while his good friend kept a cooler head about their surroundings.

"Meet me in about an hour and we'll place a call to Eoghan and Monty. I want to call Elaine first. Don't forget to keep the receipt for the calls, we don't need Rockford paying for our outbound comms with family and friends. I'll let him pay for the one we put out to the station, that one will fall under business expenses, and if there's anything we can glean from it and send by telegram to Rockford and his group, we'll be able to keep our costs lowered and bring this whole operation under budget."

TWELVE

Entering the spacious suite, Nick was immediately struck by the grandeur of the place. Towering ceilings adorned with intricate crown molding at least a foot wide gave way to floor-to-ceiling windows covered in ornately decorated treatments of matching upholstered materials that framed a breathtaking view of the city's main street with its bustling community down below. Rich wood paneling accented three of the walls creating an atmosphere of opulence and grand elegance.

A king-sized bed dominated the center of the room flanked by matching velvet accent sitting chairs and finely crafted nightstands, each with hand-carved twirls and inlaid delicate craftsmanship. Small brightly lit lamps stood guard over each nightstand, inviting their visitor to sit and relax between them, perhaps to read or meditate over the day's monumental events. Nick had rarely allowed himself to be so spoiled; it was a treat he could have gotten used to.

Nick placed the call directly to his former home in Edinburgh, having sent a telegraph to Elaine the moment they entered the city limits and found the Western Union station; it was a priority for him to send his wife a notice asking her to be available for his call at a certain time, a time he calculated perfectly in his mind and was eager to put into motion. The sound of his wife's voice filled him with warmth and a deeply felt compulsion to want to be anywhere he could be as long as he was holding her tightly in his arms.

Mesa

There was something about her, something organic that rose inside of him every time he thought of her, every time he tried to stop thinking of her, it was there; always with him. Before hanging up, they discussed their son, and his excitement to be back in Scotland, and to be nestled into the stone mansion with his cousins rather than staying close at home with his mother.

"The second they saw each other it was on, Nick!" she told him. *"Maylene brought Alistair a toad to breakfast! She took it from her pocket, not telling anyone in her family that she had picked it up outside in their family garden, and she presented it to him from under the table as we sat down to eat."* She explained.

"Brenna has grown so tall in just the time we've been away. I'm not kidding you, Nick, Eoghan is going to have to beat the boys off with a stick when she gets a little bit older. Maylene has some of the same qualities as her older sister in that she's pretty and somewhat natural-looking, but Brenna, she's stunning at her tender age now, I can only imagine how she'll look and present herself when her grandmother decides to adorn her in costume and makeup for the stage. She will be a show-stopper; one of the ones to keep an eye on, that's for sure." Elaine bragged.

"Perhaps when I lay down the cloak and dagger I can retire there with you and if Alistair has a mind to come back to Scotland he can take care of us in our older golden years." Nick teased. Hanging up the phone the man felt empty the second the two of them were no longer connected. He hadn't planned on being so very much in love that it would take a herd of wild horses and now a pack of would-be clowns to drag him so far out into the

Jude Stringfellow

wasteland of a forsaken Southwestern desert city, separating from the one he could no longer live without; the two he could no longer live without.

When he and Ralph sat beside each other in Nick's room, the two placed their later-than-usual international call to the Chambers Street station of the Edinburgh Police. There, at an hour when most citizens were enjoying their final meal of the day, Eoghan MacRae and Chief Nicholas Montgomery enjoyed holding separate lines in which to communicate with their American friends and counterparts.

"It's just after eight in the evening here, Posh." Stated Monty. *"I take it you fellas are looking at just around the noon hour or so, if I do my math and time zonings correctly enough. Is Ralph with you or is that bastard going to make us wait again while he whiles away the hour taking his own sweet time to join us?"* laughed the Chief.

"I'm the one who placed the call, you old coot!" bantered Ralph, before the three of them were giving and taking as much as the other. This back and forth, as lively as it could be, gave Nick time enough to refresh himself in the bathroom before joining the conversation a few minutes later.

Entering the main room Nick overheard his good friend giving it to his overseas colleagues saying *"Aye...aye...you've got that right, matey, here I am just another Scots on my way to becoming a damned American!"* Ralph trying to impress the others using what was supposed to pass as a thick Scottish brogue.

"You betcha you goat-headed bloke, ye're right aboot that one, ye are. This place makes yer pockets feel mighty light to be sure. I was just telling Posh I bet this

place gets at least forty bucks a night from each room; I wouldn't doubt it if they charged more." He added and ended before handing the phone's receiver to his friend, laughing and clearing his throat.

"Hey fellas, it's me, Nick. I'm having to beat the man off me now while I take the phone away from him. He can't stop goo-goo eyeballing this place. Every time I see him his jaw is dragging the floor over the last thing he saw." He said. *"He's not wrong, I'll give him that, this is one of the finest hotels I've been privileged to see, and I guess if you think about it, the palace itself isn't necessarily as gaudy or colorful. It's more reserved in an elegant manner of speaking where this thing is in your face and drop-dead stunning.*

"Oh, and speaking of stunning, Eoghan MacRae, my wife tells me that your young one Brenna is just about ready to break a few unsuspecting hearts with her good looks and charm. I don't have much to offer in the way of advice for that one, but I'll be there to stop anyone you can't handle on your friend. You can count on ol' Uncles Nick and Ralph to do the trick, and we'll leave quietly afterward so no one suspects a thing."

Eoghan's gratitude was expressed openly enough, and within a few minutes the four men were able to break their banter long enough to engage in more serious business, the business of keeping the law, finding and apprehending criminals, and investigating crimes that could lead to them to do both on either side of the Atlantic.

"Monty's over here listening intently at youse an' having a hell of a time trying tae keep up with us. I think he's thinking again about retirement but I've already told him he cannae do it. We cannae have a good force here

without him. Hanshaw said he's got the man's obituary written but not his retirement article, so I guess he'll have tae die instead. He'll be here when you age out an' decide tae leave the crime-fighting tae me, I suppose." MacRae bantered.

Monty listened alright, regaling at the details of the stories being sent across the many thousands of miles that separate the men. *"I just can't believe the changes I've seen in all these years I suppose, that's what gets to me sometimes."* The Chief admitted. Over several decades he had witnessed more brazen acts of criminal mischief as well as a lack of genuine care and consideration on the part of those sworn to uphold the law; in his experience, it was becoming harder to get a man to do his job when called upon to do so.

"When I was a boy I had a horse, that's how we got from place to place. There was the train, sure, but it was for transporting goods not people. We walked or rode a bike if the family could afford one. Nowadays we drive big engines encased in fancy boxes on wheels, we hop on a train or inside an aeroplane if we have to be too far away.

"There were newspapers of course, but you couldn't get the daily news twice a day like it is, and now I can find out what's going on in Chicago, Los Angeles, Milan, Hong Kong, or next door to me in the same day that the events happen.

"Wireless communication, electricity, and running water; all these conveniences and new technologies, and we're not the only ones to take advantage of them, the crooks and the lowlife criminals take full advantage of them too. We're no closer to ending

this thing than the day Cain killed his brother Abel. Where there is good there is evil, I suppose."

Ralph listened while Nick held the receiver out far enough for him to hear. When Monty spoke, unlike the times when MacRae was on the horn talking, you didn't have to have the headset close to your head to hear what he had to say. Sometimes it was even recommended or necessary to hold the phone receiver out further than closer to one's head to be able to maintain one's sanity when the Chief got too riled up. Throughout their conversation, each man expressed his gratitude for the others and offered insight and his full assistance in any way needed.

Posh spoke for a while explaining their assignments. He was going after one Titus "Ty" Rushby, supposedly out of Birmingham, Alabama, but he admitted that the name may be fake or even stolen from someone who may have lived and died years back. Rushby was called Burke, Dillon, and sometimes used the name Adam Greer. He couldn't be pinned down easily. If it wasn't for a port-stain birthmark on the side of his neck, he could pass for anyone of average size, height, and weight.

"This Rushby, there's a rumor going around that he's dead himself, the guy calling himself Titus Rushby anyway, the one I'm chasing down. Could be true, could be just that, a rumor that he's started to give the cops the slip. He's a roustabout, a traveler. Chief Moore in Oklahoma City had a profile built up on the man giving his description the best it could be given, but one piece of information is more helpful; says he lives in a mobile traveling trailer; the type you pull behind a car or a truck on a hitch.

"*He lands sometimes in the city where he can shower and shave but other times he holes up near a beach or lakefront where he can dip in the water to clean up. He's a loner but finds a woman from time to time to travel with. When he's done with her he lets her go, he's not been accused of mistreating the ones he keeps for company but he is being accused of killing the former governor's niece and maybe, even probably, her best friend when they were lured into his investment scheme.*" Posh stated.

"*Both women were said to have a bit of money wanting to invest it with his bosses. The man is part of a small circus circuit making its way on the west coast now, before heading inward a bit and traveling from north to south as the weather permits. They've been bought out it seems, most of the circuses have been, and there's some corporation witchery going back and forth between the old hats who inherited the shows and the ones who want to get involved because it seems like a good way to launder money from site to site, from city to city.*" Posh explained.

"*The more I think about it, the more I say it out loud like this, the more it all makes perfect sense. Ralph is chasing men down from Chicago to Vegas too, and they may have connections with this Rushby in they too are involved in the entertainment industry, one of their mainstays being the smaller circuses. I don't know how it works over that way boys, but here the whole show, the circus corporation if you will, was purchased lock, stock, and barrel by one John Ringling of Ringling Brothers fame. He's not bad, the Ringlings are good in fact – but the same can't be said for those on the inside; those who make the clocks tick.*

Mesa

"It was sewn up as a corporation about two years ago when Ringling became the owner and president of the American Circus Corporation. They even have a college here, more than one, where people go to become clowns, trapeze artists, flame throwers, sword swallowers, and the like." Nick stated.

"Seems to me, if I remember correctly, there was a string of circus or entertainment murders that took place right at the same time Ringling signed the dotted line on that acquisition." He thought cautiously, and added, *"Do you think there's a connection? I don't believe in coincidences. Ralph's been reading about it in the papers he can find from back then and some newer editions. He's telling me that Ringling isn't going after the smaller circuses because they don't advertise.*

"He incorporates what he can into one bigger company – the biggest most outlandish show on earth," Posh explained that to the same extent that the Ringling organization did things correctly, there were any number of other smaller, much smaller troupes who weren't above doing things quite differently. Nick postured, *"Money drives these smaller units; money drives everything about them. If they think they can take it and take a powder, leaving the folks behind to wonder what hit them – they'll do that, and just move on as if nothing has happened. They're banking on the fact that the days of the posse on horseback have long since died away."*

"These smaller sets show up and let the town folk know they're in town for a few days. They set up in the back areas of the city, maybe a mile or two from the outskirts and they camp really, all of them in the same spot under the same big tent. They keep their animals

close to water, and one article Ferg read to me said they walk the wild tigers, lions, and bears, even the great ape one of the circus group has; they take walks with the wild animals in the open. Which doesn't sound safe at all if you ask me. I don't want to be anywhere near a place with a loose ape, I can tell you that." Posh exclaimed. *"Eoghan, ask Alistair about the Lowland Gorillas in our zoo back in Oklahoma City. He tried to convince me they were from Edinburgh, you know, the Lowlands. I have to give the boy credit for trying."*

When he had the phone again, Ralph explained that while the two of them were driving through Moriarty, New Mexico they had the pleasure of meeting with a group of lawmen who like them, were keeping their eyes out for some of these gypsy-type circus vendors if only to keep them in check while passing through their small towns. There were half-dozen of the shows milling about the Southwest; some going north toward Oregon and Washington, while others headed out toward the Great Plains.

Most banks and places holding money wouldn't have the extensive securities expected to be found in larger towns. Honest men and women were counted upon to keep the peace and to keep themselves free of any robbery activities. A smaller off-duty police officer in Moriarty told Ralph that because of his smaller stature, he was offered a position with a group of entertainers going under the name of The Bollen Group, the same group Rushby is associated with. In exchange for him keeping his eye out for anything suspicious they would pay him a handsome forty-five dollars a week; seeing how the work was seven days a week and not five.

Mesa

"They told him he'd need to dress up and make up his face all painted up a clown so he fit in, so he didn't distract people who came out to see the show. Ralph explained. It was reverse psychology, he told them; he had read about it in the papers and he remembered their good friend Dr. Francis Moynihan mentioning it last year when he met him while he was on tour up in Chicago.

Reverse psychology is a fascinating concept in and of itself. The tenants of it held Ralph's mind captive the moment Moynihan began to explain it. Ralph closed his eyes to try and recall all that the famed psychologist had told him about the theory.

"You use someone's behavior or thoughts against them to achieve your agenda. You tell the people that you're one of them, you act like it and gain their trust, and as they trust you they give you everything you want from them. They do it willingly sometimes" Ralph stated. *"I mean, it wasn't willingly when they robbed the banks, but you get my point. The towns folk were flimflammed into believin' that the clowns they thought were harmless were their friends but they weren't."*

"By dressing in the costume and wearing grease paint the man wouldn't be recognized and he could go about the town during the day meeting people and telling them the show was going to be on for a few days. If he didn't have the makeup on they'd know exactly who he was. They knew him. He was with them every day, but by pretending he was someone new, and not being known, they would believe him.

" He could bring candy to the kids, shake hands with the men, tip his hat to the ladies, they told him." Ralph explained, *"Then, like it was just another everyday*

conversation, they told him he could walk straight into the bank the day after the show, still wearing the costume so folks would love and admire him, and he could pull a gun, asking them to get on the ground while other men behind him came through the doors and robbed the place.

"They told him that like it was another everyday thing; he's a cop! Maybe he didn't look like a cop to them. Can you believe it? They told him of course, that he'd get a split from whatever they took. Him being the lookout and all, his position was important to them."

Shaking his head in disbelief, Eoghan let out a low whistle. *"That takes a pair, doesn't it?"* he muttered, *"I mean, I ken people have tae make a livin' but this is something else. This is incredulous. It's downright brazen."*

He paused for a moment considering the implications of it all. *"And tae think, these guys probably thought the man would jump at the chance tae leave a lower-paying job that had a bit of monotony tae take up the life of a rambling roustabout on the verge of taking the wind by the sails and sailing away like modern-day pirates."* MacRae couldn't put it all together to make sense.

With a few more minutes to spare, Monty and Eoghan filled their ears with tales from their side of the world; mentioning the MK killing Posh had been involved with a few months back, that it had a bit more unraveling to do, but there was certainly a connection between the initials MK and the numbers behind them; they just didn't know yet, what it could be. They would discuss it further, and in time. For now, it was good that they were able to keep in touch as the next two or three weeks may prove to

Mesa

have fewer opportunities to find hardwired phones or even telegrams.

"I'll call you when I can Eoghan, but do me this, keep an eye on my family while I'm working, make sure they know I love them. I hear Alistair is a fixture at your place now. He's grown accustomed to my mom's biscuits and gravy, he likes grits too, but I don't know if you can find them there.

"I did tell him you had mom's recipe for the biscuits though, so you're welcome for that, and good luck trying to get him to help you clean up the mess afterward. He's a good boy, I'm telling you, but tidiness is not his stronghold."

THIRTEEN

The afternoon sun beat heavy on the residents of the growing metropolis of Albuquerque, sending most merchants as well as their clientele indoors, to find protection from the searing heat of the afternoon. Posh, turning to Ralph, suggested they turn in for a couple of hours' nap before heading out to meet with the three lawmen Rockford had set up for them to meet and go over their plans to ferret out the men they were to apprehend.

"I've got another idea, Nick," Ralph said, *"We've got a little time to kill, let's head out into the streets and take in the sites of the city; the art, the food, the people. Let's see if we can understand a little more about what it would take to acclimate to these conditions.*

If the men I'm looking for are from this area, and if the man you're looking for has been out here any real length of time, they'll have learned to suffer through and even adapt to the heat and the way things crop up out of nowhere to try and stop a man from doing what he needs to do."

As they strolled along the main streets of downtown Albuquerque, Ralph and Nick marveled at the sheer beauty of literally every storefront or open space along the bustling streets. The blend of the Old West and its charm mingled perfectly with modern urbanity, creating a timepiece like no other. They felt the comforts of electric fans alongside the rustic facades of the stone and clay buildings opposing one another from across the busy streets.

Mesa

Cars and trucks scurried by some at a more leisurely pace, allowing the men to cross the street without needing to do so at the corner of an intersection. *"That's something we can't do in Chicago."* Ralph commented, *"You'd be hit by a bus or a car if you tried that there. We'll dip into this restaurant and grab something to eat if you don't mind partner, I'm about to cave into myself from starvation."* He laughed.

Despite the overwhelming heat and the dusty air surrounding them, there was an undeniable energy about the place; it simply pulsed through the air giving it a sense of rejuvenation; a possibility and opportunity that resounded deeply in both men. They stopped for lunch at a small Mexican restaurant and an eatery that seemed to transport them straight over the border into the old country of Mexico itself.

There they indulged in spicy beef and chicken enchiladas, refried beans with Spanish rice, soft fluffy hot stove-top roasted tortillas with thick creamy queso cheese, and fresh Pico served generously to every guest. Ralph ordered a side of ghost peppers, something Nick couldn't believe he would do; something Nick wasn't inclined to share.

"I don't know Ralph; you think you know a man. You spend years with him, you save his life, he saves your life, you share the most intimate of secrets with him, and then you find out he eats fire. You find out he's a walking time bomb about to explode when you least expect it." Nick teased.

"You eat more than one or two of those things and I'm not taking you across the sands to Gallup; you'll need

to find another way to get there. I don't need to clean off the seats of my car from whatever comes out of either side of you." He laughed.

They enjoyed their meal, washing it down with ice-cold beer from the tap, stopping just short of overeating and putting themselves into a misery no man deserves to go through. As they ate, they exchanged ideas and thoughts regarding the meeting they'd soon have with the undercover officers Rockford told them to keep an eye out for.

Believing one of the men was there in the restaurant with them, Nick gave a quick direct nod to the man indicating he knew he was being watched. If the man was one of Rockford's confidential acquaintances, he would return the gesture; which he did.

Recognizing the subtle signal, Nick returned the same discreetly, feeling a renewed surge of anticipation coursing through him. It seemed their contact had followed them from the Andaluz through the streets, and into Rosita's Palace, where he had subsequently ordered his meal while keeping an eye on his query.

As the man approached their table, Nick stood to welcome him. Offering his hand and quietly introducing himself, as well as his companion, Posh informed the man of their connection with Dennis Rockford, telling him that though it was only a brief encounter, he felt that Rockford was a man of great integrity; one he would respect and show his gratitude to. To that, the man gave a simple nod towards Ralph before settling into the chair next to Nick.

"Dennis sends his regards to you both," he said, *"...he's looking forward to hearing what you may have to say or think about these indiscreet robberies taking place in our smaller rural areas by these clowns, these literal*

clowns that dress up and gain the trust of the folks before going out and robbing them blind.

"*He wanted me to go over a situation you boys might be interested in; that is, you might be interested Posh, seeing how Dennis mentioned you were going after a fella named Titus Rushby.*" The man's casual understanding of the matter took Nick somewhat by surprise. Had Rockford telegraphed him to let him in on the more intricate details of his situation? He could only think this had to be the case.

Nick raised an eyebrow, his expression rather plain as he processed the words coming from the stranger's mouth about his mission. It was strange how readily spoken the man was – too ready. "*I'm sorry, you said your name I suppose, but I didn't catch it. Can you tell me again and tell me how you know Dennis exactly?*" Nick questioned.

"*The name's Jeff Dickerson; Jerry Jeff to some out that way I suppose. My dad went by Jeffrey so some of the older folk call me by my first and middle name to keep it all separate. Rockford and I go back about ten maybe twelve years or so. He and I met up in Amarillo just outside where he lives. I ran a cattle drive from outside Austin to Denver a few years back and every year we'd need to pass through part of his land to have good water for the herds.*

"*He didn't mind but needed to know because there was a patch of the land we weren't allowed to go through. At first, he didn't tell any of us what it was, but over time we've weaseled it out of him. I'll let him tell you the gory details, but in a nutshell, what it is…it's a body garden, to be honest with you.*

Jude Stringfellow

"Sixty acres of his vast and endless ranch hold is a feeding ground for maggots, wildlife, weather, and other conditions that give insight to investigators like medical personnel and law enforcement so they can physically understand and prove how and why a dead body will decompose the way it does." He mentioned it almost as if it was a very common thing to discuss.

"When a body dies...say at midnight, and the weather outside is cooling off, but not cold, say it's around sixty-five degrees, well the body will start to show signs of rigor within an hour or so, but if its colder you know it takes longer for the muscles to tighten. On the contrary, if it's hotter, something like we have out here in the desert, that same dead body will shrink and start to eat away through the heat faster than if it had been placed in cold storage.

"Then, I suppose he decided to experiment with the elements and with certain conditions, so he added a pond to the area where he could dump a body, and built a saltwater pool underground so he could see what differences the chemicals had on the process." Dickerson again, spoke plainly, not flinching as he described the more intimate details of the most bizarre experiment ever to be revealed to either lawman.

"He's added animals to it both naturally, and he's brought them in purposely to see what damage can be done. He's used rats, raccoons, dogs, coyotes, whatever he can get his hands on. I came in a few years after he started the gardening or research and put my own two cents into the mix, giving him ideas of what one or the other condition could have in terms of aiding or halting decomp to the point of being a viable means of investigating murder and other forms of death; but

mostly murder. He tries not to interfere with nature, or what would naturally happen, but he has reasons to bring in certain animals and the like.

Dickerson took a long drink of his beer before continuing his story. *"He's an author, Dennis Rockford is. You didn't know that probably, he doesn't use his real name when he writes. He wanted to be as accurate as he could be when he wrote, so he got with the proper authorities with this body research thing and they put their John Hancock on the matter."*

With every passing moment, the details became clearer and more intricately gruesome to the point Posh stopped the man to ask if he knew the pen name used by Rockford to write his murder stories. *"I'm just wondering if I've heard of him."* He said. *"Heard of him? You've heard of him. He's one of the best-known authors in the United States. His books have sold well into the millions, and even if you live under a rock you've heard of Justin Zane."*

At the mention of the man's pseudonym, both Ralph and Nick sat in silent astonishment. Neither of them knew how to react or respond to the fact that they had been accepted by and into the life of one of the world's most prolific authors, not to mention now, because of his body garden type of research, one of the most interesting of human characters ever to walk the planet.

"You're telling me that the man...Rockford has bodies laying out there in the field somewhere, on that ranch just openly exposed to whatever hits them? He's dropping them into the water with and without sea salt, and he's allowing animals to feast on them to see how long it takes to turn a body into what, a skeleton?" asked Ralph, not necessarily seeing the bigger picture. *"Ralph,*

it's not that alone." Stated Posh, thinking through his next line of explanation. Leaning back in his chair, Posh started.

"If I have it right in my head - if I can wrap my brain around it, by doing this sort of work, experiment or if you want to call it research, he's helping the medical industry as well as law enforcement to put two and two together when they have questions about how a body reacts under controlled circumstances and conditions." He said, asking Dickerson if he was on the right track.

Listening attentively, Ralph leaned against a halfwall of the restaurant, his chair now placed soundly on the floor. His expression grew increasingly stoic, even grim. *"So this fella's using people, dead bodies, to push research and get answers to things we only thought we were able to figure out through what we thought happened to a body if it's exposed to rain, snow, heat, animals, and whatever. He's writing about what he finds I guess but is anyone...wait a minute."*

Ralph stopped himself suddenly, thinking instantly about how a man like Rockford, who wasn't in the medical field, and who wasn't in law enforcement could even be given custody of the number of dead bodies he would need to create and recreate his experiments.

"Who are these people? Where does Rockford get bodies to bury, or throw into ponds?" he asked. *"He not only buries them with and without wooden or concrete coffins, he hangs some of them from various things such as trees, and meat hooks, he's even got one laid out in an open or shallow grave with a load of lye poured over it to see how long it takes to dissolve,"* Dickerson answered. *"But you asked me where he gets the bodies."* He said, *"...well, that's where the medical personnel and the law enforcement had to come together.*

Mesa

"See, he gets a body from any place he can when it isn't claimed. He picks it up himself or sometimes they bring it out to him. He even pays for them so the county isn't out anything for bringing the body to him. He doesn't keep the fact a secret around town, but he's not publishing the facts about it either because he don't necessarily want someone coming across that part of the ranch messing up the process by adding something or taking something away." Dickerson mentioned.

Turning to face their newfound associate, Ralph squinted against the forcefully strong light now coming through an open window on the western side of the eatery. *"Well now, that ain't surprising really, guess money talks. He's not being paid to do the research, but that sort of knowledge would sure bring a genuinely more accurate description to his writing now wouldn't it?*

"He's sitting pretty that's for sure, and hell, he deserves it if he can stomach going out that way now and again to check on how those bodies are faring. But tell me something Dickerson, what do you expect us to do for you now that we're grouped and working with and beside one another? Do you have anything for us now, something we can hang our hats on regarding our cases? Do we need to fill you in as we go along, or tell you what we found?" asked Ferguson.

Jeff Dickerson paused a moment before answering. Straightening himself in his chair he reached slowly into his hip pocket to pull out a folded somewhat crumpled piece of paper with names, numbers, and notes written by two hands. *"These gentlemen, are the names and last known whereabouts of a few men who are operating outside of the good side of the law. These abbreviations and symbols beside their names reveal information about what we already know about them, and these numbers to the side tell us their last known addresses."*

Dickerson then waited for some of the gravity of the situation to set before continuing. *"What we're hoping to get from you boys is cooperation in turn for the same. We have intel on your men, we can give that to you, and you can take these notes or write up a new one I suppose, and you'll have intel on some of our cases.*

"We'll keep a sharp eye out for yours and you keep the same for us. We talk, we communicate through typical means but also through a little of the necessary covert actions as well – I'll fill you in on how we do that if you're interested." He said.

Posh nodded twice, giving a quick glance toward his friend indicating that the answer was as good as done where he was concerned, but he could never speak for his partner. *"I'll do what you need done, Dickerson."* Nick added, *"I think banding together is good for the long haul, but I gotta be honest with you too; too many cooks in the kitchen can ruin a good stew if you know what I mean.*

"How many others know about what we're supposed to know?" asked Posh, expecting the answer to be greater than what he was thinking. When their new friend indicated the number of men involved in the cases at hand was only a few, those numbers including the rancher, the number was six. Six men, but it was bound to be more as they could be trusted; Chief Moore was one whom the team was willing to include. Dennis Rockford, Jerry Jeff Dickerson, now Posh and Ferguson, and only two more made up the current number. *"These other two men, are they law enforcement here in Albuquerque or spread out over towards Las Vegas?"* asked Ralph.

Mesa

"Vegas. The short answer is Vegas." Dickerson claimed. Nodding thoughtfully, Nick considered the man's proposal internally while waiting for Ferguson's response. There was certainly something good about being able to pool their collective knowledge and resources together with each man having and sharing different thinking processes and skills, but there was something to be said about holding information closer to one's chest and not compromising their independent assignments.

After a moment of stilled silence, Ferguson spoke again, *"Alright then, let's do it."* He said, *"You said you had information that Posh may be particularly interested in, but you didn't say yet what that is. Can you tell us now?"* he asked.

Dickerson turned his chair inward slightly putting his back against the sun now beating through the place like a furnace to add quietly that most of the talk regarding Titus Rushby was that he was dead. It was known and relatively accepted that his name wasn't always Rushby, that he had taken the name from a man he either knew or had killed back in Alabama. Ken Burke is the best they could come up with for the fugitive, but even that name was suspect to them.

Rushby had traveled about the Midwest for a while. He had been in Oklahoma City posing as one of the roustabouts for The Bollen Group sometime last year, but he had not been a party to it directly, or a member of it in any way. The thought that he could be responsible for the murder of Asta Pate, the niece of the former governor of Oklahoma, and that of her true and best friend Dorothy Eischer was something to consider.

Jude Stringfellow

"Your Rushby would have been in Oklahoma about the same time The Bollen Group was promoting themselves, sometime after Ringling bought out the circuses in '29, maybe he was there around Christmas of that year and through the next as well. He would have coaxed the ladies into taking a trip with him out this way too, as the winter months are much easier to travel the roads if you don't go up into the mountains near Flagstaff, Arizona, or closer to the canyons.

"We get a good amount of snow in the mountains, but not so much on the ground that you couldn't drive out and enjoy the day most of the time. Along the way he would have had them believing that they were investing in The Bollen Group, all the while planning to take whatever cash they had and putting it in his pocket. He would have waited to kill them out this way so that their bodies couldn't or wouldn't be found." Dickerson added.

"There's enough desert out this way and enough caves to hide one in that it might be years before anyone discovered them. By that time the animals and the elements would have carried them off completely." He said, *"...but that's where Rockford comes in again, and this is the part where you might be interested Posh."* He said.

"Rushby being found dead was big news to the circus folk. They had heard about him and put up with his shenanigans enough to hate him themselves, but word is that not one of them put an end to him. He was good for business in other ways. He promoted the circus without them having to pay for advertising. He knew it, they knew it. He wasn't on the payroll, but they compensated him fairly; at least the owner did.

Mesa

"Several folks took a liking to Rushby; he was a likable guy. He stepped over the boundaries at times, but never so far that they couldn't reel him back in, you know." Dickerson's demeanor changed when he faced Nick to give him the next bit of information. It was something he felt he could say with some level of confidence now that more information had been revealed, and their rumors or speculations were beginning to gel into actual fact.

"A body was delivered to Doc Hambrick up at Lake Mead after the first of the year. She was in her mid or early twenties and had been raped as well as strangled. Because she had no other marks or punctures on her body other than the ligature about her neck, and she was unclaimed. Two days later another body, that of a woman was found half-dressed and mangled by animals.

"The first was carted off to Rockford's place and that's the body I was telling you about that was hung up by its neck to see how the elements would continue to affect it. The second, the one that couldn't be put together again, was buried by the county in a common unmarked grave for paupers. We now think that woman was Dorothy Eischer. We asked the sheriff's secretary to keep a lid on Asta Pate's body simply because we were almost certain we knew we'd finally be able to place her after we found out about you and your mission. Dickerson stated quietly.

"See, Asta died of strangulation, and she was found only days after being left out in the winter elements. It never got below freezing, but not all that hot either, and the body remained about as good as one can

expect. Rockford was notified and told he could drive out and take her back to the ranch if he wanted to. We now think, because of her height, weight, and description, that she's most likely the governor's niece.

"Not one of us knew the women, but after getting word that you were coming out to find her killer a few of us put our heads together, met with Rockford, and made sure he met up with you back in Amarillo on your way out. He wanted to tell you that night, but we had to be sure the two of you were on the right side of it all; now we know you are. He could have let you drive on that night, but he needed time to telegraph and phone me to let me know what you told him."

As Dickerson openly shared his findings without expecting anything in return, the other two men listened intently without making a sound. "*Rockford didn't want to tell you what he had out there; he didn't want you to think that was all you needed to do. He knew, like we knew, that Rushby had been found the same day this dead woman was found, but until we found out about you and your assignment, we didn't know there were two women and we didn't know Rushby was even Rushby.*

"All we had on him at the time, was that he was found dead from being lit up inside his trailer home with nothing on but his socks. Whoever did us a favor by taking him out knew enough to know he gets really stupid when he gets sexually excited. He must have agreed to let the woman tie him up before she left the trailer after she poured a gallon of gasoline over the man's body and lit him up." Dickerson snickered.

Nick Posh furrowed his brow in concentration, rubbing his chin with his left thumb. Ferguson watched as his long-time friend gave one of their covert signals indicating that he believed the man sitting with them was telling the truth. When Ralph slowly rubbed his right ear before interlocking his fingers and placing his hands on the table, Posh understood that they had silently agreed to take the position of helping Rockford and anyone associated with him.

"*This woman, the one who torched the trailer, would you by chance know anything about her? Could she have been a part of the killing of either Asta Pate or Dorothy Eischer? Could she have known them, or been privileged to whatever it was that Rushby was doing to convince them that they were truly investing in The Bollen Group?*" Posh asked Dickerson, as the men paid their bill and walked through the doors of Rosita's Palace.

FOURTEEN

Maudine Cooke wasn't the sort of woman who gave up easily or took no for an answer. She didn't seek the freedom of being vindicated, but she knew she would be in the end. She owned her place, drove herself in her car, made her money when and how she wanted to, and did it without the heavy eyes of the law poking its nose into her business.

Finding the woman took time, when she wanted to be seen she showed herself to the world in an unmistakable fashion. When she stepped out into the tranquil streets of Lake Mead that morning, the morning after she had less than quietly, murdered the man she knew as Ty Rushby, Maudine couldn't help but feel that she was being watched.

She couldn't shake the feeling that hundreds of eyes were staring directly at her, through her, and these eyes were telling her in no uncertain terms to break away as fast as she could but not to make a scene in doing so. Moving too quickly would draw unwanted attention to herself; something she had never been accustomed to doing.

She still had two days to go under the registration she made at the Conner House bed and breakfast. Leaving too soon after arriving, and without reason would make anyone think she had something more pressing to attend to, something more urgent than her needed and well-deserved rest. Having booked the place was easily done, all she needed was a driver's license; she borrowed one.

Mesa

As far as anyone knew Maudine Cooke, the auburn-haired beauty with big green eyes was named Cathleen Walters of Colorado; she was said to be a recently widowed woman out of Aspen seeking a place to grieve the loss of her millionaire ski resort owner of a husband whose tragic accident only a week before had landed his beautiful and well put together young widow on the doorsteps of the elite and secluded boarding house; one of Nevada's best-kept secrets for those hiding in plain sight. The place was an automatic iron-clad alibi for anyone who needed one for any reason.

There was no Cathleen Walters, just as there was no millionaire ski resort owner, but to use her own driver's license to prove her identity didn't make sense to someone whose sole mission for the weekend was to murder her two-timing, casino-loving, hard-drinking supposed real estate managing boyfriend who not only had promised her the moon, but he had assured her the gift would be wrapped up nicely in a package remarkably resembling a five thousand acre tract of useless land somewhere up in the Sierra mountain range with a sweet little cabin to spruce up, and endless countless free roaming land for every last wild horse that had captured her imagination and her soul as a young girl living among the animals for the past two decades.

Ty Rushby promised her the land, but he hadn't delivered it, and when she had found him and realized that the first and second installments of her investment had been falsely propagated by Rushby, she realized the land, the cabin, literally everything out of that man's mouth was a lie from Hell. Well, if it was Hell he wanted, it was Hell he was going to get. No one makes a promise to a woman like Maudine and reneges on it; not if they're smart enough to want to breathe again.

It wouldn't be that hard to lure him back to the trailer, she knew that, but getting him away from the two women he'd been seen with about town, now that may take some finagling. Maudine waited them all out. She played her cards cooly and carefully, using her womanly charms to say all the right things she needed to say before he willingly invited her back to the beachside campsite a few days later, where he kept his rig hidden among the croft of pine.

Stepping up into the trailer she couldn't help but notice a spot of blood on the tiled floor just inside the doorway. *"What did you do love, cut yourself shaving again?"* she teased, rubbing his prickly face, taking it in both of her small delicate hands and lightly squeezing both cheeks to prepare him for what she knew would be his last arousal on earth. She teased him with worded foreplay, undressing herself almost immediately upon entering the trailer.

Following her into his home, a grotesque smile stretched across his face. Rushby's tongue tickled and lined his lips; he hadn't expected to skip dinner and go straight to dessert, but if she wanted something sweet, he was certainly willing to give her anything she wanted.

"That ain't my blood Maudine. I need to clean that up before anyone else sees it, and you don't need to go around tellin' anyone you saw it either, you understand?" he coarsely told her rather than asking. Smirking to herself, where he couldn't see her face, the woman cooed over her shoulder, *"Baby, I don't care who you kill in this place. I don't care who or what you do here; you have time for me, I have time for you. That's what matters.*

Mesa

That's all that matters now." Her words caught his attention and put him in the mood she needed him to be in for the next few moments of his miserable life. Glancing past the man, she couldn't help but take in the serenity of the isolated campsite he had chosen to set up in; it was perfectly secluded. No one would hear a thing.

By the time she had convinced the man to allow her any wanton freedoms she wanted to take with him, he had all but fully submitted to her dominant manners in the back half of the trailer where the bed was permanently fixed. The cozy trailer had a perfectly quaint interior filled with warm comfortable furnishings. To the left, a small kitchenette which offered everything needed for simple meals; he had rigged it with a small cook stove, quite fancy for the times. She made mention of his genius more than once while she moved purposely slowly toward the back where she knew she would find a way to encourage him to join her.

At first, she pretended loosely to be the submissive one; she kept her cool, and whispered her words desperately, pleading into his ears how very much she wanted him to play the dominant male to her abject menial submissive female role. It was her game, and she knew it. In the end, it was an easy sell – sexual prowess has always been the downfall of most men; it had also been the weapon used by many women willing to wield the sword, in whatever direction they chose.

She calculated exactly how long it would take to plead with the man, begging him to take the lead, while all the while holding the very real and very proverbial reins herself, and using those reins to twist his wrists above him as she mounted his naked body in what she could only hope would be the last time anyone would recognize him as a man.

"One thing I love about these mobile trailers sweetheart, they have so many interestingly useful places to tie down whatever is in them so they don't bump around while being dragged behind the truck on the open road." She managed to keep his attention as she wormed her way across him, rubbing him with her taunt bare skin, allowing him to watch her finish undressing herself with one hand while holding him in place with the other.

"Oh...oh my...daddy's going to need to help me, I can't seem to unbutton my blouse any further. Can you lean up and use your big strong teeth, Daddy? Can you...can you just...there, yes, that's how I like it. Push against me, let me feel your rough, powerfully thick thighs."

Her words cascaded over his left ear; the man struggled some but was able to bend a little to give warrant to her command. While he was otherwise preoccupied, Maudine straightened herself long enough to breathe a heavy sigh, she took the few seconds of respite to purposely tighten the reins she held so forcibly. She managed further to secure them several inches above Rushby's head creating several tight hard knots, all in a row, one right after the other.

Lifting herself from the man, she redressed the lower half of her body and finished by rebuttoning the open gape of her fine white linen blouse. She gazed at him inquisitively, almost feeling sorry for the man, but not quite sorry enough to simply walk away.

"I don't know what you did with my money lover. You could have spent it, I don't know. I don't care. I don't

Mesa

give a damn if you have it here or if you spent it all on those two bimbos I saw you with these past few days when you came pulling up to the country club bragging about how much they had invested in the old circus routine you got goin' on for yourself." She continued.

"Honey, no one believes you. No one thinks you're taking our investments and making something out of them. I've given you over six thousand dollars. I wanted that land. You promised me if I could just come up with another four grand I'd be the sole owner of the great Sierra range of my dreams; wasn't that what you said?" she questioned the man, who by this time had somewhat figured out most of what was about to happen. If he ever actually knew his fate he never actually let her know.

Titus "*Ty*" Rushby or whatever his name was, was simply too preoccupied to mention the land deal at a time when he believed he would be enthusiastically making love to his feisty bobcat of a partner. He was too busy begging her not to do what he thought she might do. Seeing her exit and return to the trailer with a five-gallon can of gasoline gave the man reason to pause.

It gave the man reason to sincerely beg for his life, but all the begging couldn't have moved the woman in any direction that would favor him living. Her mind was set. She lit the match; and when she did, she simply left the trailer. As she did she wondered again about the large spot of blood on the tiled floor just inside the doorway.

FIFTEEN

Understanding the challenges ahead, Nick prepared himself mentally and physically for the task at hand. Reaching into his front pocket he retrieved a worn leather notebook and pencil, ready to jot down any pertinent details that might arise during their investigation. Rushby may very well be dead, but that wasn't the end of his assignment, and he knew it. With a determined glint in his eye he turned toward his company to say "*Let's hit the streets again and this time, we won't stop until we know what we need to know.*"

Every cell in his body told him he'd need to stay focused from that point forward. Too many people counted on him to bring in the murdered women's killer; bring him in even if he was already dead. Visions of wanted posters from times past spun around in Posh's head. He couldn't help but imagine the brutal face of the killer, his squinted eyes beating out hatred while a snarled lip curled in disrespect.

"*Dead or alive, Ferg...dead or alive, we've got to find the bastard and bring this case to a close. If he is dead, they're sure to have buried his body by now. I can't see them giving it to Rockford for the ranch; not if he was burned the way they said he was.*"

Ferguson strongly agreed; he'd sooner live out the remainder of the summer there than to turn back without the evidence they needed. "*If your man is dead, Oklahoma City may want you back. I hope they'll understand your need to stay on with my case; I hope they won't ask you to pack it in before these families get the closure they deserve.* Ralph mentioned.

"*We'll need to prove it was Rushby who took the girls. We'll need to prove they died there, and at his hand even if it means combing through every cave, every home, every backstreet or alley; we can't let him rest in peace.*" Ralph stated. "*All we have so far is a description of one, and a good maybe.*" Their determination was fueled by the knowledge that Rockford held an ace for sure, and he was willing to show his hand to stay in the game.

The new route took them further west through numerous smaller communities before reaching Gallup, New Mexico there they made their way to the local library, just as it was closing for the evening. With the help of a kind assistant, they managed to track down and locate another influential figure connected to Dickerson. The musty smell of old books filled the air as they navigated through aisles upon aisles of yellowing dusty tomes. Eventually, they stumbled across an obscure article from an old journal containing handwritten notes that had been purposely left for them to find.

"*You can't tell me these people didn't know we were coming, Posh,*" Ralph whispered, tipping his hat to the eagle-eyed librarian flanking his right side. Keeping her watchful eyes on the door to be sure the two men were uninterrupted. "*They may be pretty much in Vegas, but the others in our circle travel about and they know how to use a telegram service.*"

A few minutes later they found themselves piecing together enough details to track down more clues leading to the men being described as a trio of rugged lugubriously gloomy souls, two of whom were known to don costumes and paint. The other perhaps the driver or the lookout. These were quite possibly the same men making their way back from Chicago after a string of shameless murders after the circus corporation had been bought out and their free-for-all enterprise was exposed for what it was; taking investments without providing results. It usually ended in the murder of the money lender before all was said and done.

As a heavy-laden grey sky loomed over the desert landscape, the horizon made itself understood – the ambiance of it was not to be mistaken. The two made their way to the only hotel in sight. The Coffer House stood strong and imposing on the small nearly naked Main Street of Gallup, New Mexico where storefront windows displayed an array of goods ranging from fresh meats and vegetables at the corner grocer, to sparkling diamond jewelry, enticing passersby and visitors to stop and take in their offers; to stop and browse.

A thick dusty wind blew up around them, carrying with it the faint echoes of gunfire and the sound of distant laughing. "*It's gotta be a tavern or a casino or something Posh, I can't imagine the sheriff allowing such a fractounatious raucous in the city limits if it was just a regular store or something; do you wanna check it out before we head to the rooms?*" Ferguson asked, hoping to unwind a bit with a little excitement. He wasn't one to relax too early or without a reason to resign. If there was noise, there was action. If there was action, Ralph Ferguson wanted to be either in the middle of it, or on top of it; or the one causing it.

A broad slow smile broke out over the rough stubbled face of the detective, he hadn't necessarily wanted to end the day any earlier than he had to. "*Yeah, why not?*"

Mesa

he said, giving off a short chuckle under his breath, "*Let's check it out. God only knows if we'll hit pay dirt, but we sure can't know until we go. We gotta be in it to win it, right? Isn't that what they say in Vegas?*" he laughed.

As they approached the all but ramshackle lean-to posturing as a public gambling hall, they heard sounds of increasing revelry growing louder – a mix of rowdy voices, clinking glasses, and the occasional strains of some old western favorite ditty being sung by men who could barely stand let alone carry a tune. The place somewhat reminded Posh of a hole-in-the-wall establishment he had worked at as a bar back while growing up in rural Oklahoma. He had wanted to strike out on his own to see if he could do it; he was fourteen years old. The place was a dive, but in working for the rougher set of men who ran the joint, he learned how to duck when bottles began flying through the air aimlessly.

Choosing their seats at the bar, the two friends ordered whiskeys and began purposely scanning the room for anything, anyone, and any sign of who might fit their idea of being suspect. It didn't take long for them to spot three men huddled together, holding themselves separate from the rest of the bawdy crowd. While most of the others seemed engrossed in play at card tables, pitching dice, and spinning roulettes, those three seemed to be casing and gauging the room for any move they could make to pull off a quick and unnoticed operation.

Catching the eyes of one of them, Ferguson gave an involuntary nod only to regret his action instantly. Turning himself around to face the bar he gave a short curse for having possibly been made so quickly. "*Damn, I did it.*" He said. "*I let him know I was here and that I had him in my sight. If I can't stop being a cop when I need to stop, I could end up on the business side of a hot bullet someday*".

Sensing the tension in the room, Posh knew he didn't need to say a word; his quiet solitude was his best defense now - he only needed to listen. Now, that they knew they were being watched, and that those who were watching them knew their plans had come to a halt, everyone present realized that this was going to be a delicate operation indeed. The loser moves, and the winner sits still.

Nick remained immoveable, calm, and collected; his gaze fixed on the tables and the men milling around the room as if he were merely observing the games rather than planning an ambush. Meanwhile, Ferguson shifted his weight nervously in his seat; fingers drumming impatiently on the wooden surface. Lifting his glass he finished it, tapped it on the bar, and asked the keep for another round.

A waft of chaotic smoke blew in from the open fireplace; a crackling fire had been started providing its meager warmth against what locals knew could be a sudden drop in the desert air that seemed to creep through the cracks in the walls. The games continued for hours, each player losing before swearing he'd return to earn back his own; round and round the wheels turned, their little white balls popping as they determined the fortunes and misfortunes of those reckless enough to remain.

With a sinister grin spreading across his face, Posh suddenly reached for his sidearm; his pistol instantly leaped into action. Grabbing hold of one man's arm while simultaneously pushing his weapon against the side of the man's temple, Posh knew instantly he too, had been made. There was no time for words; their lives depended on both swift and decisive action. Begging for release, the man apologized quickly for any misunderstanding – removing himself as quickly as he had been caught.

The saloon suddenly erupted into chaos as the first shot rang out, sending patrons and lookers on diving for cover under tables and behind the stronghold of the large imposing bar in the back. A second man drew his weapon, aiming directly toward Posh, he pulled the trigger trying to shoot past Nick, aiming directly for the man who had shown too much attention. Bullets flew, piercing the thin wood panels lining the walls of the small bar, shattering bottles as they passed through the air.

Amidst the madness and the mayhem, Ferguson sprang into heated action, pulling from himself every bit of training he had all the way back to his boot camp days. Ducking low enough to fold himself at the waist, he lunged forward charging into the lower body of the second man, the two of them falling together, tumbling into the third and onto the ground in a wild grappling of fists and kicks.

The battle spilled out toward the back of the room and onto the dirt floor near where the bartender and owner of the joint kept his supplies. *"No, no, you don't you dirty bums!"* he shouted, *"You don't take it to my storeroom, you don't. I'll kill you all myself if you break another bottle, I swear it!"*

Taking the opportunity when it presented itself, Nick swung his right fist lower and landed a strong hard upper cut to the side jaw of his opponent, knocking him unconscious immediately. Standing solidly on his two feet, Posh turned forcefully toward the keep to say *"You have it! I believe you. I won't go near your stash."* He said. *"If you help me take this trash out I'll do what I can to stop the rest.*" He promised. The bartender complied.

Returning to the main room, Posh thrust out his hands to grab whatever piece of a man's shoulders that he could. Turning the man around, he put another strong and violent hook into the first man he had managed to subdue who had somehow regained his senses from the pistol whipping he'd received earlier. "*Stay down!*" Nick commanded, pinning the man to the floor with the heel of his boot.

"*I'll not tell you again, I'll put a boot up your ass if it's the last thing I do tonight*." The man struggled somewhat before submitted, cursing and then pleading for whatever mercy the dark detective would give.

"*No, I can't trust you*," Nick said, before landing a final blow to the side of the man's jaw, all but guaranteeing his silence for the rest of the night. Turning his attention back to his friend, he saw Fergy gaining control of one situation, but blindly about to step into another.

With a quick forward kick, Posh thrust his heel into the lower part of a would-be assailant, crumpling the man where he stood. With a final blow to the gut, Ralph finished off the man he'd been so apt to watch before all the hubbub. Panting heavily, Ralph shot off a smile stretching from one side of his face to the other; as he surveyed the damage done.

Several beaten bodies lay strewn about like discarded ragdolls, weapons, money, cards, and hats lay scattered among them. A hard fast silence fell over the once-rowdy saloon; the sound of it was deafening. When the air began to settle, and the noises rose to a tolerable roar, the two men left standing took a mental note and understanding of what had just happened and why it had.

Mesa

This couldn't be anything less than a setup; they were at the right place and at the right time, but the men who challenged them had underestimated their opponents to the point of complete disaster.

For a good long moment, neither man spoke, caught up in the rush of the adrenaline rushing through them, carrying them from one side of the bar to the next as they gathered and stacked the three men who they believed had been as transient to the establishment as they had been themselves. While the dust settled and the ringing in their ears began to fade away.

Posh and Ralph exchanged a few glances with each other and with the barkeep in the back. Their clothes were torn and dirty, a testament to the sheer roughness and brutality of the fight. The police were called, and with them, Jerry Jeff Dickerson came bounding through what was left of the front door. Outside, the cool night air began to force its way into the bar mixing with coal from the fireplace and the sticky smell of sweat from every man present. Looking over his newly acquainted friends, Jeff Dickerson shook his head as he holstered his gun. "*Put 'em away boys, I think it's under control now.*" He said, nodding toward the back to the nod of the man behind the bar who had placed the call a second or two after the first shot was heard.

"*Posh, you and Ferguson seem to know what it takes to keep the peace in our peaceful little town, I may have to deputize the both of you right here and keep you around a bit.*" He laughed, shaking each man's hand before pulling up each toppled man he found piled up on the side of the back wall. "*Take these three into custody,*" he told one of the officers, "*I'll see to it that our guests make it to their hotel safely enough.*"

"*Well now, that was quite a welcome party there, if I say so myself!*" Ralph spit out somewhat sarcastically. Chuckling softly, Nick replied "*I see you had a long drive to here from Albuquerque just to come out to meet us. Didn't you maybe want to stay here and wait for us to come to you instead?*" he asked. "*Or maybe you've got a twin brother that looks just like you; I swear we just keep running into you wherever we go – don't we?*"

Dickerson, smiling and keeping his cards closer to his chest gave a wink to both of the outsiders, allowing them to know he had been tailing them long before he showed up in Albuquerque at Rosita's Palace. "*How do you think I knew you there? I've been on your tail since Amarillo.*" He said. "*Where one goes we all go*". He told the boys. "*The only thing I can't figure for the life of me is why you decided to sleep out in the rough that night when you could have gone another mile or two and made it to Grand Cavern Lodge – like I did.*" He laughed.

Mesa

SIXTEEN

The miles rolled by beneath the sturdy Buick's wheels, and Nick and Ralph found solace even gratitude in each other's company. Nick knew he had made the best decision to bring Ferguson along for his mission; the fact that he had one of his own and was eager to share only made things better. At least, he told himself, he was fairly certain he wouldn't have gotten into any rough and tumbling fistfights if he hadn't brought the angry Irishman with him. There is something to be said about the mettle of a man whose red blood runs green.

As they had always done before, their conversations took a sharp turn down Memory Lane; both men reminiscing about family life current of course, but more pointedly, how their lives seemed so very different from one another's as they grew through their more formidable years. Nick couldn't help but feel a certain determination within himself when he sat beside a man whose sole purpose in life, like his, was to be true to the good Lord, his country, his family, and the truth that represented itself in the form of law.

Both men marveled at how far they had come since those challenging difficult days; Nick become a man under the tutelage of strong Native traditions, religious piety running along both sides of his parentage, and the strictest of Scottish family traditions being adhered to no matter where they called home. It was bred into the man.

Ralph, admittedly showing less of himself to God through any regular church attendance, worked harder on weekends than most young lads his age because most young lads his age didn't have to work as hard or as many hours to help the family bring food to the table. Had the horrors of a world war brought the two recruits together? If one or the other of them had not made such high marks in boot camp they wouldn't have been chosen, singled out to become dedicated hardcore trained United States Army soldiers, trained for the elite Special Forces.

Reliving their lives and times in the hard, dark, damp, impassive trenches together, but together alone, Ralph recounted the story of a seemingly impossible situation they had been thrown into under impossible circumstances. It involved crossing enemy lines deep within no-man's land under the cover of night and then needing to navigate through possible minefields, machine gun fire, and more while carrying with them vital intelligence to their Allied command post.

Nick remembered how their wounded Staff Sergeant had ordered the two men, who hadn't formed their life bond yet, to tear the orders in half, placing one half with Nick and the other with Ralph. "*This way,*" whispered their commanding officer, "*...you both have to live to save the others...you won't let the other man die. You can't...you can't.*" Those words would prove to be some of the last words ever spoken by Gerald Palmer, a man whose belief in his men stood strong through the end.

The memory brought forth a mix of pride and terror as they relived those hallowing moments again. Despite any odds stacked against the two, no matter what, they would prevail; they had no other option – and it would be so now; if need be. As weighted darkness

Mesa

descended upon the vast expanse of desert surrounding them, they pulled the car over to a nameless roadside diner where they filled themselves with a hearty good home style meal before pulling back out onto the road to drive as long as far as they could through the night; as long as the paved road held out, they could remain on course, on time, and point.

A thousand neon signs flickered in the early predawn hours of the morning as the two men pulled onto Fremont Street, smack dab in the middle of the mix, smack dab in the heart of Sin City; Las Vegas, Nevada. When he fully realized the ride had come to an end for now, Ralph Ferguson leaned as far back as he could in the passenger seat and let out a holler loud enough to make his best friend proud!

"*Quite the sight to behold,*" he shouted, allowing his lungs to fill with the crisp morning air beginning to lift as the sun poked its head just over the eastern horizon behind them casting its golden rays across the desert landscape. The city appeared almost ethereal in the morning light; all the hustle at that hour! Chicago woke up rather early, but these people never went to bed; there was a clear difference.

It was five-twenty in the morning, and the sound of a hot live Jazz quartet could be felt as well as being heard. Six men all wrapped in colorful street garb stood on the corner just under the electric lamppost pumping trombones and blasting trumpets, every note heard twice as they rifled their arms and blew out their cheeks. They played with a passion so real, so alive it radiated from every note they produced. Their loud and forceful music filled the air, weaving itself effortlessly around the movements of the very early crowds who were either getting off work to go home to sleep or just arriving to work to take their daily posts.

The party seemed to spill out into the streets from every door of every establishment running up and down the main street. Countless clubs, former speakeasies, all of it mingling with the raucous laughter of after-midnight revelers eager to forget their woes long enough to spend their last week's wages amid the raw bright burning lights. Oh, the endless possibilities in this place, thought Nick, with the hypnotic sounds of the quartet lulling them all into an irresistible groove.

Such a sight to behold indeed, like nothing either man had ever encountered; it could either make their job that much easier or that much harder depending on whether or not they could catch a few hours of sleep before finding one of Dickerson's envoys to fill him in on what they knew was already wired ahead. Confirmation would be necessary before too many details could be shared.

Before checking into their rooms Dickerson's man made himself known to Ralph quietly, handing him a note with instructions to meet just after ten o'clock in the Freemont Café directly to the south of their hotel. "*Isaiah Hartman. I'll bring my brother Amos when we meet; you could use a good attorney in your corner I'm sure.*" Spoke the man quietly, without being noticed. Slipping away, he neither turned to his left or right. He never looked back but was gone before Ralph could turn to share the encounter with Nick.

"*Our rooms are across the hall from one another,*" Posh stated. Looking past Ralph to catch the sight of the enigmatic stranger as the lobby door closed behind him, Nick questioned his friend with a silent glance, lifting his brow to inquire as to who the man was. *"Dickerson's man. His name is Hartman, I think he said Isaiah, but I'm sure he said he had a brother named Amos and he'd bring him with when we all meet up at ten o'clock just across the street for coffee and maybe an early lunch.* Ralph noted.

"I don't know what this one does, but he indicated his brother was a lawyer; said we could use one now and again, and I didn't disagree. I didn't tell him about Ramsey either, but I guess a man could use a few good lawyers in his quiver, right?" he asked, already knowing the answer.

After settling into their rooms and catching a very needed rest, Nick and Ralph met up with the Hartman brothers over steaming cups of hot coffee and a few leftover biscuits, a stack of bacon, and several scrambled eggs. They compared notes on their suspects, men they knew they were chasing, and men they were now being asked to keep an open and respectful eye on while the same was being promised by their new accomplices.

As they spoke, news of the impending arrival of The Bollen Group circus spread throughout the establishment like wildfire. Flyers littered the tables around them boasting the times and dates where the shows could be seen. People buzzed excitedly about the spectacle that was sure to unfold. Rumors abounded and were on the lips of every employee and guest of the café; the shows were to start that very next day just outside of town in an open area to the west of Lake Mead.

Incredible feats and stranger-than-life attractions were being pledged; anything and everything anyone could imagine would soon grace everyone under the Big Top. With admission being free for children under the age of ten and only fifty cents for anyone else, the place was sure to be packed. Free parking of course would be provided, and if you happened to buy a bag of hot roasted peanuts at the gate, you could share them with the loosely chained family of elephants waiting to greet you before you entered the *"Show of a Lifetime!"*

Despite their initial skepticism, curiosity got the better of the lawmen. With nothing else pressing on their agenda that morning other than planning their means of tracking down the very men who may quite likely be working the circus itself, they decided to check out the circus grounds firsthand, excited to find any clues to any answers and any explanations to any clues they might stumble across. Little did they know their very lives were about to collide with the obscure and cryptic world of the most mysterious parade of oddities, where beauty intertwines with horror, wonderment masked depravity, and truth hidden behind illusion.

"We'll need to duck into a second-hand store somewhere before we drive out there. We'll park the car about a half mile away so enough dust can cover us before we arrive." Ralph suggested. *"We can't go in there looking like cops or any sort of professional whatsoever. If we're going to make them believe us, we've gotta look the part.*

"We're roustabouts now. I can say I'm a mechanic – I know my way around that world, and you…" Ralph added, *"…you're a bouncer; you know, a muscle man. You can pull that off pretty good. You still got that shiner from the other night! You're a shoe-in!"* he laughed. Nick's lips slightly split, his teeth firmly set, holding back his tongue. *"Seems to me friend, you were the one winking at people and causing the entire thing to erupt in on us; if memory serves me right,"* Posh suggested under his breath.

Mesa

Finding the store they needed the men bought denim dungarees and overalls, some heavy work shoes, threadbare cotton shirts with missing buttons, and even an old straw hat. Posh said he wouldn't want to put anything other than his signature tan Fedora on top of his head, but wouldn't argue that Ralph made a mighty fine ruffian if he had to say so himself.

"We look the part, and I'm not worried about breaking in, but we'll need names and backstories to go with it. We'll go over the plans with the Hartmans just so they know what our strategies are; they'll likely want to join us in some way or another to keep us out of trouble if nothing else. They've put a lot of man-hours in on this operation as well. We may need that attorney before all of this is done." Nick chuckled.

"I'm sure they'll pay us in cash, so we won't need any real papers, but you're right. I need to call you something other than 'Posh', you're famous now. We can make it easy and just pick out names we both know. You can be Paul Tanner and I'll take Duke Cockburn. Remember them? They were both in our regiment with Staff Sergeant Palmer; they were his men too. They were our brothers for a good amount of time." Ralph reminded his friend.

"They'd do the same for us, and you know old Duke would love to stick something like this on us if he could." They both laughed, they needed the levity if they were going head first and headstrong into something as dangerous as what they knew they were about to do. Nothing could have stopped them; but then again, no one was trying to do that.

Jude Stringfellow

As luck would have it, as the men walked a little less than a quarter mile from where they had left the Buick, they caught the eye of the ringmaster himself; Gino Restani, who for professional reasons called himself by only one name; "*Rashnell*".

As was his typical way of doing things, Restani cased the local cities wherever the circus took them; he found local talent to recruit for various needed short-term employment. A few dollars here or there could do him and the men he hired some good. No one knew more than they knew, and if anyone asked, they were volunteers. Everyone loved a circus. It was the perfect form of employment for any on-the-lam criminal type who had bones to pick with the authorities. These small circuses and carnivals could blow in and out of an area in a week and get their next two weeks' worth of pay. The roustabouts kept to themselves, and they kept busy. There was always something to do around a show.

Introducing themselves as Duke and Pauly, respectively – the men pitched their skills to the impressed circus manager. Nick played up his physical attributes, and openly demonstrated how he could handle himself in sticky situations, while Ralph made it clear he was better at turning a wrench than being out in the middle of the show on the back of an elephant or in the cage with the lions.

After a few hearty laughs over what it must have been like to imagine such a scene, the two interlopers were hired to be what Restani called "*general help*", meaning they could be expected to do just about whatever was needed; but he mentioned to Duke that having a skilled grease monkey around may be an interesting thing. He implicated that Duke Cockburn may end up running away

Mesa

with the circus on a more permanent basis – if he wanted to, of course.

To their surprise, they were offered positions on the spot, with Restani pulling out a roll of cash, and peeling off two five-dollar bills; one for each of them. *"You'll see five dollars every morning like this, and then again at night if you do your job right, and we don't have to clean up any mess you make.*

"We all pull together you see; all of us. If one of us is having trouble making the time, we chip in. I'm not saying you have to get inside the cages to feed the beasts, nothing like that, but you may be asked to cut up the chickens or the beef we keep around for the cats. You could be asked to take down a trapeze line so no one outside of the tent gets hurt on it.

"You wouldn't believe how many outsiders think they can crawl up under the sides of the tents to see how things fit together," Restani mentioned in passing as if to send the men in the right direction toward the open field where everything needed to be assembled...everything.

As the sun began to center itself above them, signaling another hot and sweaty day of hard work ahead for them, Nick and Ralph joined forces with their newfound colleagues. Assisting in the erecting of massive strong tent poles and stretching bountiful colorful canvas panels, they quickly learned the intricate skills required to set up camp for a traveling circus.

The air rang with excitement mixed with nervous anticipation as everyone pulled their weight, doing their part to prepare for opening night. They'd have one day to practice and get their acts ironed out; to work through any troubles that may crop up from the chaotic measures

Jude Stringfellow

needed to push the process into reality. Everyone knew that every city and every show hinged on a lot of tiny quirks that either worked their way out for themselves, or they got worked out; it was what it was, the show – and it would go on!

Animal handlers, jugglers, clowns, and every unique artist and act slowly entered the Big Top to introduce themselves to the seemingly dozens of recruits. "*You'll all be one of us soon enough!*" spewed a smaller man with a mouth larger than most. "*I'm not in my paint right now, so you probably don't recognize me or even think I'm anyone to give a damn about really, but you'll see for yourselves soon enough!*" he promised.

"*This circus has a hook like no other circus in the corporation. We're not just the average run-of-the-mill or fly-by-night gig. We have more clowns than anyone! We have more clowns than any show or any circus on the planet.*" He said. "*It was Basket's idea. He goes by Basket; I don't know if any of us know his real name. Like I said, I'm not in my paint right now, so when I'm not wearing my face you can call me Joe; Joe Whitfield. But when I'm in the whites and my eyes are done up, and my mouth all painted as it will be, I only answer if you call me Jewel.*" The little man's strengths were in the way he carried himself, and how he spoke.

"*You'll be required to wear a lesser suit when the folks are around. We all use the same type of gear so we know whose with us and who may be rattling in to get a look at things so they can poke around for their owners. All of our costumes have two colored sides in the front, and then in the back, the colors are reversed. Two orange and two blue, or maybe two purples and two greens.*

Mesa

"We don't care what colors you use, but it's two in the front, and then two in the back. You'll need to go see Shirley out to the side by the jugglers; she'll hook you up and get your robes made. We use the same collars or ruffle she's made a lot of those, but you'll bring your own shoes and if you don't work with your hands you'll need to bring some sort of gloves. I guess if you do work with your hands you may want to bring a set too!" the man laughed.

Joe couldn't help but explain himself clearly, not wanting to have to repeat himself. Shirley Tipson was many things to the circus including their seamstress, main cook, and the one to roast the peanuts out front before each show. She would be busy that evening and all the next day putting together a dozen or so uniquely pieced clown outfits so as Joe put it, *"They all fit into place, and everyone knows who is with The Bollen Group...if he ain't in gear, he's not us."*

Of course, anyone who had their own act wasn't expected to don a clown costume, they fit in by who and what they were; the animal trainers wore elegant tightly fit costumes with dark rich colored capes fastened at their shoulders. Capes they could remove and use to sweep about and dazzle the crowds. The jugglers, trapeze performers, gypsies, and others chose costumes to best suit their crafts and personalities.

There were more clowns because anyone and everyone who wasn't an actual part of the circus looked as if he were a part of the circus. Of course, the actual clowns who performed were also easy to spot until they too blended into the spectacular façade of it all. The Bollen Group boasted more clowns than in any other show because even those who weren't in the show were dressed as clowns to fit in if they wanted to be paid; and of course, add the lure of being the show with the most clowns. It was their thing, and it worked.

The animals took their places with controlled guidance by their handlers. Human performers practiced their death-defying stunts beneath the watchful eyes of Restani and his two associates; the other two of the masterful three ringmen who ran the show all at the same time. From aerialists suspended high above the ground by their teeth to the sword-swallowers risking life and lung for the sake of family entertainment; there wasn't anything these cataclysmically daring individuals wouldn't do for a round of deserving applause.

Yet, even among the glitz and glorious glamour of it all, Nick couldn't seem to shake off the feeling that something sinister lurked beneath the surface; he knew it did. It was the reason he and Ralph had made their way halfway across the country so far. He could feel it through his bones. Amidst the orderly chaos of it all, Nick spotted a group of performers gathered near one of the tents' entrances; they were loading bullets into long-barreled pistols. The sight of it nearly stopped him in his tracks. Instantly, his right hand fell to his side where his larger loose pockets concealed his .38 revolver.

Ralph hadn't come right up to him and said it, but from across the expanse of the tent, he caught Nick's attention with a low whistle to alert him to try and keep him posted or informed if he thought he needed to be included. He knew his friend too well. When Duke approached Pauly he set his friend's mind at ease. *"They do a pistol act. They shoot ballons with blanks."* Ralph said, *"Relax, you're not in a freak sideshow; that's in the next few tents outside."* He laughed before adding. *"I think I've been assigned to that part of the shows; that's where the most cars and engines are anyway. They even have an electric icebox that's big enough to hold one thousand pounds of meat. I've never seen one before, but maybe when this is all over I'll check and see if Sears and Roebuck sell them; Stella could keep her pies in it for me, and I could keep that thing full of steaks after we get chummy with our rancher friend."*

As darkness fell on their first night of ragtag employment, the two men knew it was only a matter of time before they uncovered the truth about what was hidden between the folds of the canvas, and behind the curtains of those very curious and wickedly intriguing sideshows Duke had mentioned. Whatever it was that bothered Nick, or now Pauly, he knew instinctively that this was the strangest most unorthodox place he had ever stepped foot in; he felt like a fish out of water.

SEVENTEEN

Lights flickered to life; music pounded through the air being pumped through big wide speakers; a Victrola stationed at one end of the large tent, inviting any within its range to meander their way through the withered tall-grass fields to find their way in through the open broad flaps of the main tent where hosts of oddly smiling human caricatures greeted each of them.

Some of the clowns, those who performed for the circus, flitted about the gathering crowds choosing pantomime as their means of communication while still others boldly sauntered up to folks laughing, bowing, taking them by the hand to lead them to their seats. Such was the expectation of all who didn't have dedicated stationary jobs; Duke made himself available, running in all directions up to and through the legs of the giant man on stilts who from time to time made a scene of false aggravation; it was all for the show!

In the distance a lone barker called for those who hadn't paid their admission to do so, "*Don't be lured by these clowns ladies and gentlemen, they know nothing of commerce! They have no idea what it is or where it is they're taking you. Keep your eyes and ears peeled! That smile you see may just as well be a smirk*!" He laughed, giving off a purposely false sense of security to keep the people on their toes and the edge of their curiosity.

As evening closed in on everyone colored-filters covered lamps cast long and vibrant hues of shaded mystique off the canvas instantly attracting every eye. The

Mesa

main event would have to wait; for now, the audience, as they were being instructed to find their seats, were mesmerized and entertained by a small herd of pure white horses being led into the arena by two young and beautiful women, each more gloriously animated than they'd ever seen.

Lifting their hands in sync the two petite beauties began violently cracking their whips which seemed to punctuate the rhythmic thud of hooves pounding the dry hard earth beneath them. In the center of the arena stood another row of fine proud steeds, all so very magnificently black and sleek, all so magnificently still and strong. The contrast was dynamic; creating the perfect illusions even before the show truly began.

Before long a shill command cut through the din, sending all of the horses into a wild mix of black, then white, then black again. One by one the horses fell into rhythm into their places charging around the track at breakneck speeds. Keeping their distances between the next and then the next, each horse calculated their steps in a queue with one another in perfect timing; perfected rhythm.

Another round of merriment, another sweep of dust, and just as suddenly as they had begun the monumental live carousel had stopped. Now, taking their perch upon particularly well-trained beasts, the two taut and beautifully decorated sisters once more held their whips in sync with one another, while simultaneously ordering their animals to break from the herd, determined to showcase even more raw power and control.

Jude Stringfellow

Perched precariously atop each horse, the stunning ladies were dressed in skintight costumes that revealed far more flesh than most society norms. Their faces contorted into fixed smiling masks hiding sheer determination as they urged their mounts forward again; and again into a joining pattern racing past the cheering spectators and drawing in the attention of every eye instantly. No one could take their eyes off of what was happening; it didn't seem real.

This was no ordinary trick or act; this was a masterful display of raw power and elite control. Nick couldn't help himself; he'd nearly forgotten his cue to drop the ropes he was charged to allow his side of a large freefalling banner to let loose, cascading its way over the entrance of the big tent. Not only was this curtain a means of closing off much of the incoming light, it was another unadvertised rule of The Bollen Group; a way to separate themselves from other circuses.

"You're watching the greatest feats you'll ever see...sit back, relax, laugh, applaud...today may be the best day of your entire life" boasted the heavy canvased drape in boldly colored two-foot lettering.

Backstage of it all, Ralph observed what he could, taking in the rumble and tumble of all the interior activity through his ears; he felt as well as heard every second of the enterprise. Around him, men and women alike scrambled to apply various layers of clothing, makeup, and more. Some adjusted their sequined costumes until they were perfected fitted and snug. Among the entropy, he spotted a small group of unsavory characters lurking near one of the prop storage areas. Listening intently to them, trying to hear their conversation over the drumming noises coming from the Big Top, Ralph overheard one of the men calling to one of his cohorts and using the name "*Bams*".

This couldn't be a coincidence he told himself. Elliot "*Bams*" Russo was one of the names given to him by the mayor of Chicago as being the most likely of the three men he was chasing to be the shooter in the multiple homicides he was investigating. The other two names weren't Italian that much he knew; he was sure of it, but they were likely to be usual aliases for sure.

Listening to the men he could tell one of them was trying too hard to put on an uncomfortable accent to pass himself off as something he wasn't. Could he be from overseas? Ralph wondered; trying to drown out the music and loudspeakers was difficult at best; he could make out only a few words, but even those words were enough to give the man away as being anything but an Italian or even a Brit; he had to be from another part of the world and a recent immigrant as well.

Noting to himself that the men hadn't donned anything resembling his dual-colored outfit, he immediately took note of their covert ways. Recognizing the danger signals, Ralph followed his gut; stalking the men as they made their way from one tent through to the next. Their body language left no room for misunderstanding; these men were there to cause some sort of trouble for the troupe.

Ralph didn't know what, but he knew he needed to try and stop them. He knew he hadn't been detected, and thought hard about inching his way back to the main tent to try and signal Nick, but the chance of him doing so without being seen was next to impossible. Still, he told himself, that Joe Whitfield had mentioned the very reason

Jude Stringfellow

The Bollen Group roustabouts dressed in costumes was to fit in, to blend in, and not be a distraction for the audience. He could use this to his advantage if he thought about it; he had been a bit of a player himself as a kid; often impersonating his teachers and other figures of authority when wanting get the best of them in a rouse.

Perhaps he'd not need to be so discreet in his attempt to signal Posh. Perhaps an open act of harsh discordant and boisterous slap-stick could do the trick, and do it well enough to bring not only his good friend Pauly but a few other handlers with the good reputation of the group as well. It was certainly worth a shot! Makeup on, costume in place, gloves on the ready as well as his penchant for making a scene when he could, Duke Cockburn delivered his best!

Before he could be picked off by any wayward bullet on the off chance one or more of the men had been packing a gun, the clown mechanic threw himself into a frenzy of dance, tossing his arms and legs in every direction, his voice whooping and hollering as if to beat the band. Dancing in circles, jumping to the right and then to the left, the man threw himself onto the ground face first and somehow managed to bring half of his body upward while virtually swimming along the ground in a half-pushing half-flailing manner creating quite a pageantry of comedy indeed.

Realizing they'd been seen the men readied themselves for the inevitable to happen. Within seconds of his calling for them, several clown-clad men descended upon the smaller tents some armed with pistols, others with whatever makeshift weapons they could find; a stick, a hammer, one carried his switchblade in a long side pocket.

Mesa

Still, another grabbed a folding wooden chair, lifting it high above his head. Tossing his head to the left, and bending himself in the middle, Ralph stood tall, his body bending and contorting unnaturally as he put on his best animation, unwilling to break character, to direct the others toward the would-be assailants. Bullets began to pop off above their heads, zinging past them all, each narrowly missing their marks, but still causing havoc among the motley-dressed roustabouts.

Arriving late to the party, but still willing to dance, Posh knew he had to do something to help his friend even if he couldn't keep a straight face while doing it. *"You ain't Emmett Kelly, but you're good – you're real good."* He chuckled, *"...you make one helluva clown. You just may have a career after this is over; I'd pay to see it."* Posh laughed while slapping his good friend's back left shoulder, lifting him to his full height.

Giving each other glances of both approval and absolute disapproval for what they had chosen to put themselves through in the name of keeping the law, both men whistled their way back to their respective duty posts; Pauly taking his place just under the nets of the flying trapeze to secure any loosened ropes, and Duke returned to his chosen choice of employment, that of a meandering mechanic, allowing the others to chase the goons to the edge of the field and beyond the river where they understood they'd not be welcomed if they returned.

Drawing on years of law enforcement experience, the two formulated a plan on the fly – divide and conquer should the interlopers take another shot at whatever it was they wanted in the first place. Duke would approach the men again once his fellow roustabouts had returned with their report of just how far they had chased the trio off premises, and Pauly if he needed to, would then slip away undetected to gather intel linking the troublemakers to the crimes both men knew were perpetrated back in Illinois.

Thirty feet above his head Nick could make out the form of Delilah Eli; her perfected athletic body beginning her routine upon the swinging trapeze far above the crowd. Delilah's net had been anchored on six separate posts. The one he watched had been fitted last and carried the heaviest of rope loads. Standing impossibly balanced upon her high-perched platform, Delilah was introduced by Restani, now in costume being called by one name only, Rashnell the Ringmaster.

"Her daring feats of perfectly balanced art will thrill you to the core as she creates such death-defying aerial displays of grace! Poised as she is, she'll soon leap from her stand, grabbing the swing into both hands and creating a memorable air dance to thrill and impress as she openly and defiantly cheats death with every swing.

"The net you see if for our peace of mind folks, not hers! In all the many months I've had the pleasure to watch with such amazement as I do, and as you will, I have never once seen Ms. Delilah fall into it; but yet, we want to be sure she is safe to return to repeat her performance as masterfully, and as delicately smooth as she will tonight!" he called, turning to the audience, walking from one side of the Big Top to the other, a large white spotlight following his every move.

Rashnell stood erect and at full attention, thrusting his right hand into the air while simultaneously removing his tall black lacquered hat with his left to proclaim, *"...and now, ladies – and – gentlemen, children of all ages - cast your eyes to the skies to see one of The Bollen Group circuses most delightfully daring and death-defying performances – Delilah Eli on her flying trapeze!"*

With that, every light in the tent ceased immediately, throwing everyone into pitch darkness without any hope or glimmer of light. Their eyes trying to adjust to the new obscurity, each person squinted with hopes of catching the first glimpse of whatever was to be expected. Surely, it would be as promised; a spectacle to behold and remember for the rest of their lives.

After a few seconds several lamps were lit and several flaming torches as well with men and women clad in darker-colored clown attire carrying each torch in a makeshift pattern of intertwining points of light until finally they made their way to the six posts holding the giant rectangular net; Nick being asked to handle the ropes rather than to hold a flaming torch. A burning torch could be dropped, but an accident in the air would require every inch of the woven safety mesh to be intact.

Despite the dangers inherent in her craft, there was something almost serene about Delilah's movements – a sense of freedom that spoke volumes about her life's journey thus far. Her routine began slowly, deliberately as she climbed from the bottom of the ladder where she had positioned herself when the lights were shut off. With each rung of the three-story ladder, she climbed higher and higher, oftentimes removing one of her hands to lean delicately and dangerously to one side or the other.

Once at the top, she paused for dramatic effect before deliberately launching herself forward into space with both of her long arms stretched fully wildly as if she had wings before reaching for the first swinging bar being sent to her by her quiet assistant hidden from the crowd.

Jude Stringfellow

For several heart-stopping seconds, she hung suspended mid-air, then suddenly snapped into motion again, spinning wildly along the central bar. Delilah performed her act skillfully, calculating each move, every second, every thrust, every swing, every smile she cast to the crowd. She performed five, six, and now seven turns, leaping from one swinging bar to the next, each time seamlessly into the next. By the end of the act, she had transformed from a mere mortal into an ethereal creature of flight; leaving the awestruck crowd breathless with amazement. Nick Posh had never seen anything like it before in his life.

Once their evening duties were over, they planned to get out from under their costumes and wash off their faces to reveal their true identities again to the world. Having thought about it long enough to understand the concept, Nick understood fully how it is that any man dressed the way they did could be seen but not recognized.

He could virtually walk around in plain sight with an entirely separate persona, while all the while keeping his dark secrets to himself or sharing with anyone willing to join him in some underhanded enterprise; such as the men he knew had robbed several banks in just this fashion in and out of smaller rural towns dotting the southwestern vistas from the Grand Canyon down to the border of Mexico. Ingenious, simply ingenious.

To his knowledge, not one of the businessmen in Chicago who had been murdered was done so by men dressed as clowns. That fact hadn't stood out to him until that moment. It didn't mean that the killers weren't the same men has had robbed the bank; it's just that murdering investors while dressed in robes would have been the reason for someone to notice; these men wouldn't

Mesa

have been hiding in plain sight at that time. They would have stood out; the paradox was fascinating, to say the least.

EIGHTEEN

Her heart began to pound, and her hands began to sweat. She began to envision all of the people who could be hurt by her actions if she confessed; she wasn't ready to do it. She needed time to think. Maudine wasn't emotionally involved in Rushby's murder, he wasn't the center of her passion, just the target of her rage and her action. She planned his murder to stop the free fall; it wasn't about moving forward. She had to stop the bleeding in her soul.

Leaning on the door jamb she shifted her weight, giving her time to think of what she would say to Aldo Restani, the older brother of the senior ringmaster, and owner of The Bollen Group, a thug the world called "*Buster*". For two years the man had followed her, almost worshipped her and for all the good it did him, she treated him with less attention than an alley cat. There he was, she told herself, Aldo Restani, a man of men, so powerful in many ways.

Why on God's green Earth had he fallen for her? She couldn't convince herself that it was true; not after the things she had said to him, not after the way she walked away so many times. "*You love me don't you, Buster?*" she calmly asked, her head nearly buried in her chest. "*You love me, and that's why you never told anyone what I did...what I did to Titus.*" She waited. "*You hated him as much as you loved me, didn't you? I saved you the trouble of putting a bullet in his head. At least this way no one can say you did it. Fire is a woman's revenge ain't it?*" she asked.

Mesa

His silence was heard. Several quiet minutes passed before the rugged man lifted his head and began to speak in lower tones, drawing her ears intentionally. As Buster spoke she listened; his face turning pale. He knew she was right; he did hate Titus Rushby. He hated him with every hot-blooded pumping vein in his body. He would have taken Rushby out himself if he didn't need the man to bring in what he did; money from investors; money for the cause.

There was no future for anyone hoping to invest in The Bollen Group. Anyone who did so suddenly found themselves breathing their last at the hard edge of Rushby's single blade, or at the end of his revolver when their money ran out or when they began to figure out what was happening; sometimes it was immediate, but others could take longer. Rushby meant money to Buster; that's all.

Hearing what she said about Titus made the situation that much more irrefutably confusing; he knew Rushby meant nothing to the woman he desired. Why did she have to throw herself at such an underling; was it to shove it in his face that she couldn't care less about his operations, about his money, about himself, or his power with the Las Vegas crime syndicate?

He was a developer in that organization; he was a made man. With him she could have anything and everything she wanted; why would she do what she did? It wasn't that she killed the man; no, he understood that her conundrum was her own. He couldn't get it out of his head that she had slept with the man – or that he would take the one woman he knew belonged to his boss. That was the bullet shot straight into his heart.

Jude Stringfellow

Understanding and clarification became paramount to Restani now as he listened to Maudine's words while she explained. It wasn't about the killing itself, he told himself; it was about betrayal. All along, Maudine had played him, she had played him hard and ruthlessly at that. The thought of his lover sharing herself intimately with another man, and a man he had full command over, that was the last of it.

That was the pain he knew he could never overcome. His once-passionate feelings for Maudine morphed suddenly into deep-rooted anger and disillusionment, something that had been stewing for several long months. How could she have been so cruel? Allowing his mind to fill with images of unspeakable sensual acts. He at first, writhed with anger, until for a moment he managed to shake it off; giving into the pleasure of watching even if only in his imagination; where he still controlled her.

Standing up, the man took a few steps toward her before realizing his approach brought on yet another refusal. She stepped away, moving backward into the foyer of her small wood frame cabin, hoping he'd remain where he was. He watched her. He watched her slowly retreat; he knew he had reached an end.

Maudine, seeing the man turn from her let out a sigh of relief. She hadn't expected him to react so strongly to the news about Rushby, but she knew after the few months of silence she would have to give him something when he returned to the area. His reprieve had taken a lot longer than either of them had expected, but business is business and the winters in Chicago were harder than those in the southwest; driving through the storms was something Buster had never been too comfortable doing.

Mesa

Though now, without Rushby to bring in a few investors, it was going to take a while to find a replacement for him. "*Hey,*" he said, turning back toward her again, this time with a renewed spirit of enterprise rather than desire; "*Do you think maybe you could do me a solid on this one since I did get you this place, and the land for your horses?*" he asked. "*I did what Rushby promised. I made good for you.*"

"*Can you at least think about keeping your eyes out for a few folks who may have a bit to give, tourists or some who won't be missed if they don't show up for a while?*" he asked thinking perhaps she'd have a sense of loyalty considering all he had done for her. "*You don't have to do what Ty did; you don't have to advertise or go looking for anyone, but if you meet them on the golf courses or you come across them in the cities...*" his words shortened as he remembered just exactly who it was he was talking to. Maudine was never one to socialize. If she could hole up in the canyons taming wild beasts from sun up to way past sundown, she was content to do so.

Her answer wasn't lost on the man, murder may have been her solution for Rushby, but he deserved to die. She couldn't see herself bringing unsuspecting people to the end of the line for money. When she told him she couldn't do it, he nearly collapsed from the weight of her words. He knew when to cut bait; it's just that he knew it years before and chose to continue the struggle. This time, he told himself, would be the last time he laid eyes on Maudine Faye Cooke; one way or the other, it would be the last time – he would never let her know.

"*I'll come by next week. I'll ask you something; you can think about it.*" His words were short, his tone flat.

Jude Stringfellow

Maudine closed the heavy door behind him. Retreating to the stone walled fireplace, she shifted through the burnt ashes creating a new bed for kindling. She knew one way or the other she'd pay a heavy price for her words, for her actions. Restani would never turn her in for murdering the dog she knew he hated, but he may just put an end to her life for not showing an ounce of remorse for her sexual misconduct; at least her feelings for Rushby never entered the picture.

Rushby wasn't anything to her, only a means to an end. Titus had promised her over and over again that with the next good investor that came along, he would give the money to her without telling Restani; she'd have the cottage she'd have the land. Until recently she hadn't known Titus or Restani were murdering the would-be investors; she believed them both when they told her she would be hired by the various smaller circuits to train their horses for future shows.

Their words were empty, she knew that now. Before, they had allowed her dreams to run wild and rampant within her spirit; they manipulated her life and took every thought of hope from her. It was everything to the woman; everything. She could isolate herself from society to raise and train the Mustangs in the hills away from sight, away from everyone. She would never have to coexist with anything walking upright again.

Rushby's death didn't stop that hope; one request to her most devoted benefactor was all it took. If a few nights of rough and rumbled sex was all it took to have what she needed, she wasn't above that. She wasn't about to say no. In some way, in the back of his mind, Buster Restani had to know it wasn't about love. He had to know. She paid her price, he paid his. If nothing else, to her it was a business arrangement. Let the people talk; she wouldn't be around to hear it or to care about it either way.

It was too late now, she thought to herself. What she did wasn't going to go away. She knew she hadn't made any promises to Buster, and she knew he realized this as well. It was too late for second-guessing. All she could do was to move forward, put her wits back where they belonged, and hope for the best that somehow, someway, she could find an inkling of redemption amidst the bedlam in her life she had so brutally created; one beautiful disaster. She knew she would have to either kowtow to Restani or find a way to never see him again; it would have to be one or the other with him. He wasn't a man to give her too many choices.

As the sun began to set over the western horizon, Maudine Cooke considered the distance between herself and Restani. Living in the heart of Las Vegas, with herself being about thirty miles west of the Grand Canyon, this put her about one hundred miles due east of where the bright lights blared both day and night, day in, day out. She could do the math; with his car and the way he drove, Restani could be on her land and through her front door in just under two hours if he had a mind to do something to ease his heart where she was concerned.

He may not return that night, she told herself, but he would return. He wouldn't trust the job to anyone else, she knew that. He's come with one question; the same one he had asked two years before. He'd want to know if she'd marry him, and if she agreed, he'd be sure to spare her any trouble – but what is trouble, exactly? Marrying a mobster meant understanding and accepting his ways, his means, and his business. She could perhaps go on as she had, training and working wild horses with or without any real companionship; but when he wanted her, whenever he wanted her, she'd have to be both willing and able to give him anything he wanted; and it didn't matter what that was. She would be permanently bound. Her options were slim; she knew that.

As dusk fell over the canyons surrounding her modest home, Maudine collected a few things that meant something to her, and she loaded up the Ford, aged as it was, she could count on it. Driving slowly through the winding roads, she navigated the rocky dusty terrain as she had for weeks, knowing every twist and every turn until she reached a hidden clearing where she parked just beneath a grove of pines that seemingly guarded the ridge.

Exiting the car, she walked briskly for a while toward a billowing nearby stream; one she often took solace in with the sound of it echoing in her mind, a peace and an understanding she knew only through its song. Reaching into her purse, she retrieved a handkerchief given to her by Buster; she couldn't understand for the life of her why she had kept it, or why it meant so much to her.

Walking another a quarter mile to a small general store up the road from the stream, Maudine wiped the perspiration forming on her brow before pulling out a small crumpled piece of paper from the pocket of her breeches; a paper bearing the name and telephone number to Jerry Jeff Dickerson, lawman of the west. Taking a deep breath before forcing her fingers to dial the numbers, praying silently that this desperate gamble she now attempted would somehow pay off.

Mesa

NINETEEN

The same smooth evading sun careened across the desert skies into an abyss of solitude bringing the same evening tides to Nick and Ralph; who having worked another weekday with The Bollen Group, had been given the rest of the night off. Wednesdays had been routinely sparse for entertainment considering it was a valid church day for those citizens who were more devout.

The mid-week reprise was welcomed not only by the two undercover law enforcers but everyone connected to the Big Top. If The Bollen Group was known for having more clowns than any other circus, it was also known for its more compassionate terms, allowing the performers a bit of a break. Only the matinee was performed between the hours of three and five o'clock on a given Wednesday, and of course, the same was true for Sundays as well.

As the golden orb continued her descent she cast long shadows across the dry and dusty landscape, Nick and Ralph pulled into the parking lot of an obscure bed and breakfast boarding home to give off the appearance that they too were workers, somewhat transient perhaps, but not apt to be holding up at a fine three or four-star hotel on the income they were purporting to make. While most roustabouts chose to save every penny they had, sleeping with the performers and sideshow freaks, Posh and Ferguson needed their time away to plan, regroup, and organize their next moves.

Jude Stringfellow

An associate of Jeff Dickerson, a man by the name of Cedric Fauer met up with the two, posing as another roustabout when asked by the matron of the house as to who he may be. *"I'm not too keen on having visitors staying past supper, and if you do eat I'll need a dollar from you."* She told the man. *"Food ain't cheap around here, but it's good."* She added.

Excusing themselves from the table just after the meal and before dessert, Ralph asked if he might take a slice of Claire Harroll's thick creamy chocolate pie with him to the rooms. He promised not to spill any of it, swearing that he'd give up his left lung if he did. Because the ol' gal found his smile too irresistible, or perhaps he reminded her of her sweet son who would have been Ralph's age, she allowed the inconvenience.

"My Tommy is about your age I suppose. He was born with a mess of black hair and dark eyes just after midnight on July 1, 1894. I can remember it was a Sunday, one of the longest nights of my life. I think I went into labor in one month and had the baby in the next." She said. *"The same day he was born a Dutch minister of some sort died. I can't remember his name, but it was fancy enough. They say he was seventy-seven, that's two sevens you know; good luck usually. I guess it was meant to be.*

"My Tommy and his wife have two boys of their own – live in Tennessee." She said before telling Ralph the pie was his to take if he wanted to take the entire thing to share it upstairs with the others. He was obliged to do so, carrying off another two forks when he did.

As the men talked, the two outsiders listened to Dickerson's envoy intently as he detailed the loaded information they needed to know regarding the Restani brothers and their involvement not only with The Bollen

Mesa

Group circus, but the enterprise behind it; the coverup was a good one for sure. The circus scheme had come into play a few years back, and was mostly run by his goons; those he could trust. When he finally did put the pencil to the paper he realized he could be losing money to those about as loyal and honest of men as he was. It was after that that Buster became the head of the operation; and later still, when he added Ty Rushby to find investors.

There had to be a way to break the case open far enough to make their move. It seemed to Fauer, after Posh had told him what he had heard from the young trapeze artist, about Buster's connection to the show, her offhand statement had proved to be both credible and incredible. It was quite insightful indeed, revealing a depth of the truth behind the criminal organization that went beyond mere speculation and right up to the threshold of collaboration. There was no way Gino Restani wasn't aware of what was happening right up under his nose. He had to be involved.

With renewed determination, they formulated a plan to trap Restani, Buster anyway, using the intel provided by Fauer. The stakes were certainly high enough, but they knew they had to act fast and they had to act with precision if they wanted to make it happen at all. It had to stick before more innocent lives were taken and more irreparable damage done to the growing city's fragile new social fabric where commerce was concerned.

Another day or so with the troupe and both Ralph and Nick felt that they could find reasonable evidence to encourage the apprehension of at least one of the Chicago-linked murders; that of businessman Julien Leonid, a Russian Jewish immigrant wanted for money laundering

Jude Stringfellow

back East. Anyone involved in the Leonid case knew his penchant for gambling, and they also knew of his personal nearly fetish-like obsession with entertainment of all types. Julian Leonid had to be seen. He had to be in the mix of it and the top of anything was the position he preferred. With Buster, however, there wasn't room enough at the top for the two of them.

Having settled recently in Chicago, Buster had immediately become a favorite of the Moran gang, putting his life in jeopardy with all of the rest; especially with the Italian families in Lincoln Park and River North regions of Chicago. Restani ran hard and fast with the Vegas cartel as well, having been a one-time outcast of Capone's close-knit crew, he didn't fit in. He was a hot-head, a loose screw. When Capone let him go, the rat ran straight across town and right into the graces of the Moran's gang, bringing about a new wrinkle in the old establishment. Restani's disloyal behavior was the first anyone had managed to pull it off and live long enough to do any damage.

When Ralph put the pieces together, he was able to draw himself a vivid enough picture; first Restani gets ousted; the cold-shoulder treatment; it could very well have been at the behest of something Moran had started with Capone to get the man to drop his cards, showing his hand to both sides of the aisle. Restani was good for business; someone was going to pick him up – someone was going to profit from him as long as he was breathing.

Money was involved, and Leonid held the purses. When all accounts were counted, the Italians felt shorted on their cut for giving the Irish more room to operate than they wanted to give. Something had to happen; a message had to be sent. Restani took the hint to mean that anything he could do to help the boss would be appreciated; Leonid breathed his last, and The Bollen Group hit a record low the very same week; coincidence? Restani bought the whole shebang with Irish money.

Fauer listened to Ralph's revealing of material information with bated breath because it was the exact story he had been privileged to know but from the other side. He was in Vegas watching it happen in reverse, while Ferguson was sitting front and center in Chicago listening and observing as the long winter months unfurled slowly becoming increasingly ice-cold for some of the bigger players.

Putting their heads together meant trusting each other; something none of the men were apt to do on their own, but with the new Link, and the way the Dickerson group was fashioned; law enforcement was set to enjoy some of the more technological advances anyone had seen. A man could be in two places at once when the heavy-hitting power of the telegram and telephone were at his fingertips.

"Another year or so and this place will be booming, literally teeming with folks, but the thing is, with the building of the Hoover Dam just outside of town there, we don't have the infrastructure yet to meet the needs of those coming into work. We'll be swamped, and we know it. We're already being told we can't give the work to laborers who have been incarcerated because it'll take thousands of men to finish the job, and no one wants to trust that kind of work to a bunch of felons with records who may cut corners or worse; cause problems.

"The city, county, state, hell, the entire government has already put the kibosh on that one; we have to hire men at full upright wages which is gonna tax

us into the ground but at the same time boom our city to the point of busting at the seams for sure," Fauer said, taking the last bite of his piece of the pie, wiping his mouth and giving a content nod to show his complete satisfaction with the thing.

"You don't mean the building of the dam is going to be a two-edged sword do you Fauer?" asked Ralph, who could only see one side, a good side. How could the multi-million-dollar event be anything less than a miracle for those lucky enough to be stuck out in the middle of nowhere looking for work? This project was touted as being the biggest engineering feat of all time; taking at least four full years to complete which meant the promise of job security for any man on the job.

"Well," replied Nick thoughtfully, leaning back in his chair, pushing his plate from his reach. *"...it's not just about the jobs and the progress it will make or mean to the people around these parts. There's always consequences to the actions people take; intended consequences or not."* He paused, considering his words carefully.

"Take the construction itself, for example. Thousands of workers laboring all day and all night. It's bound to be a work-around-the-clock venture. Where will those thousands live, where will they eat, what will they eat? What will they do when they're not working? Will they blow off all that pent-up steam here in the casinos, at the clubs and bars? Will they shoot off their mouths and brag about what it is that they do to the point it causes trouble?" he asked.

"There's the heat, there's the poor working conditions, the lack of beds, lack of medical care, lack of everything they'll need not to mention they'll take some of

that away from men and women who have lived here for years and take for granted that the food stocked in the stores is more or less meant for them.

"If someone on the backside of the thing, someone in administration, puts in for an order to empty the entire storehouse every week to feed their people, what will the locals do? Where will they go for food or supplies? More and more trucks coming in to feed them probably, but they'll need gasoline and where's that going to come from? More trucks will need more gasoline to bring it.

"Route 66 will have to widen up to four lanes just to keep up with the supply and demand." Nick's comments struck new chords in the minds of both Fauer and Ferguson alike. *"Growing a city too quickly can create any number of problems. One major issue I can think of, and we've discussed is simply the infrastructure getting in place to bring about the endless supply chain that will need to be set up to build the bridges and roads just to get to the dam. That will have to be done first."* Posh mentioned.

Nick turned to Ralph to add, *"People will be displaced. Homes and lives will be destroyed. If they don't do it right the dam can leak; the waters could break through and destroy whatever hoped to thrive in these parts. They can't hire a bunch of dim-witted idiots from jail or detention centers to do the work if they expect it to hold. Big projects like this deserve big if not bigger budgets. Rents will rise, mortgages too, and the price of nearly everything out this way will push through the ceiling in no time."* Nick stated.

Next, it was Cedric's turn to remind them all that with projects like the Hoover Dam another influx of personalities besides those of the heavy hard-working class would soon grace the doorsteps of their growing small town. *"We'll have to build interior roads, stops, add traffic lights, and hire more police, medical personnel, and firemen, not to mention building the stations for each of them to house themselves. The hospitals, schools, and other community services will be busting soon. This place is a hotbed for men like Restani who are already beginning to add up all those dollar signs in their heads even before it starts,"* He added.

Politicians, corporations, gangsters, and more, all vying for a slice of that pie; thick and creamy, good to the last morsel, this is what the city planners of Las Vegas were thinking about; it's what kept them getting out of bed each day, and keeping them up at night all at the same time. *"When they switch all the power over to it from the electric power grid it is today to water power, well..."* his words trailed off, allowing the implications of those thoughts to hang in the air.

"I'll make my way back home now, I guess." Stated Fauer, teasing Ralph with a quick attempt to snatch his plate from his hand. *"I'll let you boys rest tonight, and get to work early as you can tomorrow. Keep an eye on both Gino and Buster Restani. Let me know if you see them talking, and if you can hear anything that would be best.*

"We need to find out who or if anyone from The Bollen Group besides Buster is connected to the other two killings of the local businessmen out in the Greek Delta, out in the north part of Chicago." Fauer's last words stuck deep into Ralph's thoughts; he had made a point in the past to bring up the many fineries of the Grecian eateries in that part of his hometown, remembering the night the two bodies were found outside the bar and grill.

Mesa

The eateries in the Greek Delta had mostly started out as food-preparing groups for others, sometimes peddling their wares to neighboring communities who thought, acted, and believed as they did. Naturally, these actions led the people on a course of ownership to some of the most amazing restaurants in the country. For nearly a century the Greeks were concentrating around Harrison, Blue Island, and Halstead, giving it their unique edge and style; *"Greek Town"* was referred to by the younger set, and by those who lived outside of the area.

After Fauer had driven away, Ralph took out a notebook and began writing down a few things he wanted to be sure and remember. "Nick, *tell me the names again of the performers you watch all day. I'll try to recall the others; the sideshow freaks I've worked with and seen and the mechanics and carpenters I deal with. I know Mike Chandler, Bob Isley, Phil or Phillip Brewster. Those aren't Greek names. They'd stand out if they messed around the city's Delta too long, or after hours."* He said somewhat under his breath.

"All of the murders happened on weekdays, on Tuesdays, and on a Wednesday maybe. Not during the heavier times when a lot of folks would be in the area, but all the men were killed near Halstead; one of them was Greek for sure, and Leonid, was Jewish, but he was also a Russian. He wasn't well-liked or accepted from what I've read." Ralph added.

Taking in a breath or two the man thought hard about the names Posh could remember. Again, not one of them sounded the least bit Greek; maybe they only hit the area but were themselves complete outsiders. The community, Ralph knew from experience, might initially face some skepticism or reserve. They weren't the type of people to instantly shun someone or worse, to use violence; they took a more passive manner when letting outsiders know they weren't exactly welcome. Because hospitality was so deeply ingrained in the Grecian culture, most visitors would at least be tolerated during daylight and in places where they could spend their hard-earned cash.

Still, the thought of outsiders in that close-knit community being able to get that close and gain the trust of the restaurant investors who were killed, it only made sense that they'd be either related to one or the other of them, or they were at least familiar with the setup or maybe the supplies being taken in by the two men. It was going to take more thought, and more thought required more sleep. Both men knew they had a busy and intensely important day ahead of them.

Mesa

TWENTY

An early dawn broke over the eastern cloudless skies of Las Vegas. Nick and Ralph found themselves sitting across from one another at the small diner a few blocks from their boarding house. Hot coffee and bagels had a way of bringing Ralph back to reality, while Nick preferred a full breakfast of thick fluffy pancakes, bacon, eggs, and grits. He'd asked the cook to throw in a cup of baked beans and a grilled slice of tomato to help him connect with the years he'd spent living in Edinburgh; he missed his family.

Breakfast allowed them to come together in the same place. *"That's a lot of food for one man, Nick. You won't mind if I ask you to leave a little, do ya?"* joked his friend, taking another bite from the rounded bread on his plate. The aroma of the food and coffee filled the air around them, providing a welcomed respite from the ever-hovering heat just outside the door of the establishment.

Their faces were etched with exhaustion and not a little worry, reflecting the gravity of the situation they faced. Despite the early hour, the place was already beginning to fill up with locals stopping by for a hearty intake of breakfast before heading out into the fields, some to work the strip. Most of the patrons it seemed were men. Men of all ages ranging from just under twenty years of age to old-timers who still believed they had something to contribute to the working class.

Jude Stringfellow

After finishing their meal, the pair stepped out onto the cracked pavement, squinting against the harsh glare of a rising sun. The town felt different already, it had a sort of tightness that neither man had encountered or felt beforehand. The streets had previously been alive with activities now seemed nearly empty as they made their way across the street and over to the car; they'd need to make their way out of town towards the open fields near Lake Mead soon to work their undercover assignment best they could.

The air began to spin somewhat, lifting a faint heat all around them; encasing them in its fleeting grasp. The sound of distant conversations and laughing were part of the atmosphere, despite their temporary isolation. Driving away both men felt a slight twinge of excitement mixed with perhaps a little anxiety for the moment; anticipation hung just out of their reach but was always present. Whatever adventures the day would bring, it was about to start the process at any second.

As Nick listened on the drive, Ralph had set down the morning papers and had begun discussing the topics from the night before. It was something Delilah Eli had mentioned to Nick that held his attention. "*She said Restani, Gino Restani, was going to pay them soon. How would she know that? Is she with him? Is she connected too? Posh, if she is, you gotta get even closer to her than you are. Make her trust you enough to go on about when he's going to pay the performers more. She said, or you said she said, that they hadn't had a raise in over a year. They work for peanuts, you said she told you...like the elephants.*" Ralph started.

Mesa

As Ferguson went on about the intelligence they had received regarding exactly who the Restanis were and how they were connected to both the Chicago and Vegas crime families, Posh understood that the events unfolding in the Big Top had a lot more to do with those events unfolding in the gambling houses dotted around the western states but also connected to the very road that brought them to the Lake Mead streets. It was Route 66 that seemingly tied it all together.

"It sounds like things are getting pretty tense if you ask me," Posh said, rubbing his jawline with his thumb thoughtfully. *"I hope it all works out for the performers, but I'd hate to think that people have to die before the others are given a raise, that seems like a very volatile situation. Imagine how many people, how many investors would have to be rubbed out to keep The Bollen Group in the black over and over again, month after month, year after year.*

"I'm thinking it's more than ticket sales that keep the thing going. It has to be. When I put a pencil to it as we did with Cedric Fauer last night, it only makes sense that ticket sales keep the wheels greased and rolling down the road, but if they're gonna make any sort of money and live the way I know the Restani brothers live, it's more than just good investments. It's a lot more than that" Nick added. *"There's gotta be a power operation going on to make it make sense; they need more money than what they're bringing in."*

When they arrived at the tents, Posh and Ferguson found Gino Restani out of costume, dressed as if he was either about to go to town on official business or perhaps he had just returned. Ferguson, using his delectable

Midwestern charm began to pour it on thickly when approaching the ringmaster to speak with him, using an open-ended questioning method to keep the man talking. Socrates had used the same method; Ralph remembers his Staff Sergeant's method seemed to mimic the philosopher to the tee. If he could keep him talking he might just let something spill out of the bag without realizing what he had said; and to whom.

"Papers say we may get a little rain today, Boss." Started Duke, as the man pulled his two-toned clown's gear over his denim dungarees, pretending to have a little trouble pulling his left shoe through the pant leg. *"Say Boss, I've been meaning to ask you something. You said I may have a place here with the circus if you had an opening – I'm not sure what you mean by that, so I wanted to fix in on something I was hopin' to hear you say. If you think I can stay on for a while I'd be apt to follow the troupe up around Route 66 as far up as Chicago if you think the wind will take us that far up the road."*

Not finishing his sentences, but leaving room for conversation was the plan. When Restani realized he was being addressed, he turned from what had previously held his attention; something he was reading – a telegram. Addressing the hapless smiling mechanic, Gino waved his right hand still clutching the thin yellow paper to exclaim non-verbally that he hadn't much time to talk at the moment, but would catch up to the man another time.

"Can we discuss it later, Duke?" he asked. *"I don't know how much longer we'll be here in Lake Mead, but it looks like we'll be taking off in the other direction, could be sooner than we thought."* Gino managed to say quickly

Mesa

before making his exit through a private hanging entrance on the tent leading to his office quarters.

Gino had been ever-present, nearly everyone had seen the man nearly every morning, and afternoon, and certainly, he was present at every show. Not many if any, however, had seen his brother Buster for quite some time. Some put his absence at just over two days, while others swore it was longer. No one in the camp had needed the owner, and in fact, the last to see him had been Jewel or since he was out of costume at the time, Joe Whitfield; the two had discussed a private matter.

The news of Buster's disappearance seemed to have spread very quickly through the town of Lake Mead as well. The striped and colored tents lining the city's open-air fields were still being written about in the local papers every morning, bringing enterprise and commerce by the scores. Radio shows about the circus and sideshows used to captivate audiences were used nationwide. Folks saw themselves sitting by the radio, being transported to a world of magic where anything can happen with just a little imagination.

Everywhere they turned, crowds of interested people stopped in Lake Mead to offer their assistance if they could, to be seen, to be a part of whatever it was they could find to be a part of. The circus was quite the draw. Those outside the tents may not realize the essentiality of finding Buster, but the troupe knew – they all knew. He was the man behind the curtain; he was the puppet master of them all. If the people of the city-of-the-week couldn't understand that, every member of the cast and crew knew too well what a missing fund man could mean for them and their immediate future.

Some whispered about foul play, knowing the erratic fickle relationship between Buster and Maudine. Most knew and understood their roles and would never have mentioned anything to anyone other than to themselves in hushed conversations when they were sure no one else could hear them talking. Everyone knew about the affair Titus Rushby had carried on with "*Buster's gal*", but no one said a word about it, not giving an opinion or a word of advice.

Most kept secrets and kept them to themselves while others found it particularly unusual that the rumors of how Rushby had met his end had similar beginnings to how they knew Buster had been behaving toward Maudine over the past few months since Rushby's death; since he'd returned from Chicago everything seemed tense, dark, so unknown.

They couldn't read his mood or his expressions when he was around; it became obvious any word from Buster would need to come from his younger brother. If folks were expected to walk on eggshells - eggshells it was! No one wanted to say anything off-putting or bring undue stress to them all by opening up that can of worms. If Gino had something to tell them; they believed he would tell them.

Business was business, some told themselves. It wasn't unlike Buster Restani to simply pack up his car and take off down Route 66 on his way to meet up with friends and business acquaintances from Vegas to Chicago; after all, they speculated, the road does lead to both places and since he'd provided for The Bollen Group in the past, they expected he was off doing the same now. Maybe, they told themselves, his absence was a good thing – he was only thinking of them.

Either way, foul play or not, it was clear that without Buster at the helm, things were bound to change drastically in their little world. The circus was everything they had; it wasn't permanent, and no one thought so, but it was what they clung to now. Performers began their day; usually stretching, exercising, and getting loose enough to do the most amazing things possible with their bodies. Alongside them several small monkeys chased one another, clinging to ropes, and crates, and climbing atop the many trailers while their two handlers called each to their side using their names.

For many of them, this traveling roadshow was their only hope to work or earn enough to sustain themselves. A nomadic existence yes; filled with thrills, excitement, and the unknown; a fleeting paradise of sorts where dreams come true if you let them, and reality can be put off as long as you allow it to be.

The day wore on, with each passing hour bringing more intelligence regarding both the relationship between Cooke and the older Restani, but also that of the entwined goings on under and outside the Big Top. Performers continued to practice, animal handlers caged their charges to prepare them for their meals before the show, while the folks of the sideshow made it very clear that without another stipend to deposit for the upcoming week, they would consider leaving the Restani brothers for a more lucrative offer being made to them by another roving circuit group more in line with their particular and unique acts.

William Baros and Marcus Drakos were two of the world's most intimidating personal performers, having gained notoriety from their ability to create flame from seemingly nowhere, controlling it and even swallowing it right before the eyes of onlookers who the two men allowed to stand close enough to investigate whatever scheme anyone believed the men were capable of pulling off. With several years of experience between the two, they had worked side by side, sometimes as individual acts, but usually in tandem with one another, creating such grand illusion, and discombobulation of foolery for their audience, theirs was a heavier draw to any company than most could boast. As far as sideshow draws were concerned, they were kings.

When the men emerge from behind the heavy canvas curtains draped before the audiences, their painted bodies dance through smoke and mist being poured out onto the stages; dry ice working its magic. Baros's long black hair pulled severely back from his face in complete opposition to that of his partner Drakos, with his mop of unruly auburn curls loosely falling over his eyes covering any hint of his identity from the crowds.

Their movements were liquid, fluid, and precise as they dance and glide from one corner of the stage to the next. Lifting his hands in an almost hypnotic fashion, Baros brings his hands above his head and releases a torrent of flames that climbs higher and still higher the closer he approaches the audience; fear and astonishment are immediately seen upon their faces.

The other figure, his flexed strong muscles rippling beneath his bare exposed chest, as he performs feats of strength amidst the blazon chaos; lifting incredibly heavy dumbbell bars with seemingly no effort; their metal ends engulfed with fire. After setting the bar down, he walks around it purposely. Taking one of the flames into his hard hands, the man seemingly rolls it into a dizzying ball of fire, thrusting it into his throat with the quickness and the agility of a daring bird of prey clasping an unsuspecting fish.

Pulling the blaze inward rapidly, before spitting it evenly out across both of his arms creating wings of flame, he becomes a living phoenix. With each thrust of his body, sparks fly, as burning embers scatter around his entire body leaving spectators spellbound in the act itself. The powerful display and control over such primal base forces of nature captivate everyone who sees it – it is truly a testament to the raw talent of the two men willing to perform so intimately close for so few to see.

"Did you know it takes four of those metal soda acid fire extinguishers, 'Automatics' they call them, to put the guy out if something goes wrong?" Ralph asked. *"They're manufactured in Chicago."* He added. *"Something like that could be harnessed I'd think"*, said Ralph to his buddy, as the two men stood just behind the scenes but close enough to understand that some of the act was quite expectedly dangerous indeed.

The crowds were beginning to gather in and around the sideshow tents; it was one of Duke's other assignments when he wasn't working on a motor or putting something together, to seat the audience when they poked through the flaps in the tents between the different acts. After escorting a few to their rightful spots, the man whispered to his friend regarding the fire eaters and their particularly dangerous act.

Jude Stringfellow

"They could take that to the films and make a lot more money, and from what I'm told neither of them is going to do it. They live here, they work the circuit, and they have for quite some time. I've asked around a little and no one has ever seen either of them without the other one being fairly close by.

"The older one, Baros, he's going on fifty they say, and either he taught the other guy or they've been around each other long enough that neither of them has ever had a normal family to speak of. They aren't married of course, but they live together, and they have been billed as a team for most of their careers. It's like they can't be apart from one another." Ralph mentioned the last detail about the men was given to him by another mechanic, the one they call Les or Lester.

Lester Burkhardt was the only black man in the company, though he wasn't the only man of color. Several of the animal trainers as well as the long-time roustabouts were either Indian, South American, or Persian; they, like Lester, had been adopted or accepted by The Bollen Group several years back. It was almost as if the team itself was one big family moving around nomadically from town to town without anything other than the sky and its clouds or stars in common.

"Most don't have anything to do with banks, I'm told." Mentioned Posh. *"When they are paid they store it together, feeding one another off the lot of it, pulling all their resources into one kitty to make themselves as comfortable as they can. These guys, the sideshow performers don't do things that way."* Nick said.

"They get paid one at a time, sign for their pay, and negotiate monthly pay based on how much is spent on their side of the gig; not taking in what the Big Top

Mesa

makes. None of them have families to go home to, it's like fingers on a hand; they're separate, but work together.

"The sideshow folk are paid strictly off what they bring in, so they can split any time they want to. They mostly work day to day in some instances; which allows them the freedom to come and go, join back up, make some here, makes some there...and..."

As he spoke Nick realized that even the words forming in his skull were pulling together in such a way to create reasonable motive, opportunity, and means for the connection between the murders in Chicago and The Bollen Group could very well be the sideshow freaks themselves. They have the means, and the freedom to move around when not attached to any group, and if they are, several of them could simply choose not to work any given show.

As Ralph and Nick continued to mentally put the pieces of the puzzle together, another enigma from the sideshow wandered up behind the two men. Cassie *"The Little Wonder"*, a woman of full adult age standing under three feet tall, approached the men by purposely walking up to, and spreading Ralph's legs apart to make way for her entrance onto the stage to follow the fire eaters' performance.

Giggling to herself a little louder than perhaps most would over the delicate tease, Cassie pushed her small chest as high as she could, moving seductively from one side to the other, inviting anyone who cared to see her to view everything she had to offer. What she had to offer was unique if not bizarre; strange and yet familiar. The curious would continue to watch, and the little woman knew this; she used this to her monetary advantage when she could.

"If it's not one thing, it's another with these people." Ralph laughed. *"I know I was somewhat of a horndog back before I met my Stella, but these sideshow kicks, they can't stop themselves. They don't want to stop themselves, I'm sure of that."* He laughed, turning himself away from the open display of genteel womanly play set before him. The pair tipped their imaginary hats to the woman and walked outside the tent where she had taken command.

"If you haven't seen it for yourself Posh, you may not believe it when I tell you what I've seen. They find the smallest tightest little corners to hide themselves in, and then all you hear is two or more of them grunting around, and a scream or two coming out from under the side of a fold in the tent. You see the thing moving, and maybe catch a glimpse of someone's feet or hands sticking out from under it, and God's truth, I'm outta there fast. It's all day too; they have no shame. I don't think I'd be over the top if I said they don't care who or what they do, but they sure do...they...sure...do."

His words muffled into the palm of his hand while trying not to share his intel with anyone other than his friend. Nick's expression said it all; he had been among the hardened elements of human life in his life, but never like those who made their mark and their livelihood like those behind the flaps of the collapsable tents of the sideshow *"freaks"*.

Mesa

TWENTY-ONE

Their conversation with Monty and Eoghan much later that night from the comfort of Cedric Fauer's house was anything but normal. First, because of the time difference between Las Vegas, Nevada in the United States and Edinburgh, Scotland a full eight hours difference, it was decided to make the call around eleven at night to allow the two men on the other side of the big pond to wake up and have at least one cup of coffee before being forced to endure their stream of intelligence and their over the Big Top excitement dealing with the various and quirky lives they were engrossed in presently.

"You can't imagine it for a second Eoghan, you can't. Just when you force your mind to accept the fact that a person aged over forty years can walk around the world being under three feet tall, that's about a meter to you, you start asking yourself if it's even possible for them to...well, you know...live a normal productive life. Heavy on the emphasis so the word 'productive' if you understand me." Ralph laughed.

"I don't mean to be rude or whatever Stella calls me; she calls me 'crass' sometimes. I'm not trying to be that way, but when I saw her, little Cassie, I think I immediately went there. I couldn't stop myself. Then about a day or so later, I see for myself that she's just one normal everyday broad who makes her living by showing off what the good Lord gave her - - right there in front of everyone. She has a hat she passes around and collects a

little something-something for herself, and if they wave the bill a little, she shows a little more." He added.

Eoghan MacRae listened intently to Ralph's story from overseas; he couldn't help but give a bawdy braw laugh at the man's frankness. *"Och! Ralph, yer takin' the piss right out ya know that! Always speaking your mind no matter who's listening or who may be listening. Some of these things cannae be fit for work ya know; I don't want old Monty here tae keel over on me an' make me the Chief by default!"* he said.

"But seriously now, I do understand where you're coming from, mate. It's hard not tae be curious about such things an' tae be amazed at the same time. Tell me more about these sideshow folk an' why youse say they're different from the circus folk." He asked.

Ralph passively paused for a few seconds before continuing to say, *"OK, obviously everyone every living being deserves our respect. They can't help how they were born, or what happened to them, I know that. I also know that every one of them is truly amazing in and of themselves or if they couldn't stay in the club, they'd be thrown out if they didn't bring audiences to their shows.*

"Most of the folks who come to see them also stay for the Big Top performance; don't get me wrong, but you could just make a day of it staying at the sideshows and taking in their oddities, their uniqueness...well, their strangeness too; let's be honest. If anyone is going to spend their money wisely it won't be at the circus or the sideshow." Ralph said.

Describing the sideshow people took time, it took energy to use proper words so as not to seem callous or disrespectful; still, it was inherently impossible to accurately describe them without defaulting to language much baser than was common in civilized communication.

"*I'll read the article I read this morning in the paper about last night and last week's shows here in Lake Mead. It's from the Journal Review. It reads, 'As the lights dimmed, the crowd hushed in anticipation. Suddenly, a shrill scream pierced the air, followed by loud almost thunderous applause.*

"*Out from the backstage and onto the small wooden stage stepped Elena Hauge, a petite woman with large imposing wings sprouting from her shoulders. She glided effortlessly around the open-topped canvas encasement making her way from one pointed corner to the next, and back again several times before making a quiet and calm remarkable landing, so gracefully and without the use of a trapeze swing.*

"*Next up was the Human Torch himself, a man whose entire body seemed to be engulfed in flames yet he didn't appear to feel a thing.' It's gotta hurt, you know it does.*" Said Ralph, adding that this man was actually part of a pair of fire eaters who often performed separately during the actual acts indoors, and in unison when performing outdoors to draw crowds to them. Ralph read on, as Nick and Cedric listened to him; it was almost as if Ralph was performing considering he knew he had a captive audience with Monty and Eoghan both glued to his every word.

"*Again, we have acts like the bearded lady, but you can imagine she's merely wearing a fake mask of some sort, but I do think they use cement or loose type of glue to hold it in place. I don't think she keeps the costume intact when the show isn't active.*

"There's the Siamese Twins, and they are the real McCoy. I've met them, and I have to say I like them both. It would be really hard for one or other of them to be vastly different from his brother. They've had to pull together to get...well, that was a bad choice of words, I apologize for that...they had to learn to get along.

"Part of their story on stage is what type of life they had before the sideshow gigs came along when they were about the age of your oldest Eoghan. They were fourteen when their parents sold them to a circus but after a while their act was considered harsh for a family-oriented audience and they were handed over to the sideshow.

"Then again, now that I think about it, they have a better opportunity with the sideshow when it comes to being paid out of the hat. They keep their act pretty clean actually, and if anyone in the group is the least bit religious it's these fellas. I've been with them when they pray over their meals and for the other people in the show."

Ralph finished the article explaining that the conjoined twins were born in Minneapolis, Minnesota, not in some far-away foreign country, but that some of the acts are in fact from remote corners of the world. *"Wolfman comes from Costa Rico, I think. He's covered head to toe in hair. It's a body disorder that runs throughout his family he told me.*

"Even his sisters and mother are mostly just as hairy. You can only imagine they have a very close-knit family; they aren't seen much and he sends his money home to them somehow. The others tend to take care of

Mesa

him because of it. They love him like he's their own son." Ralph ended by asking Eoghan if he had ever taken the girls to a real circus before, to which he enjoyed the answer.

"Nick kens more about my life I suppose, an' how I was raised literally by one of the world's more famous actresses an' stage performers. Mum wasn't in the circus, but the makeup, the smells, the lights, the costumes, all of it was part of my formative years for sure. I went tae an' saw every last stage an' off-stage performer from the time I was born tae about the time Jane an' I had the girls I think.

"I dinnae want them tae see what I saw, an' I have tae admit I've never taken them tae see such live performances where they could be tempted tae try some of the things they'd see." He stated openly. *"I dinnae mind them seeing clowns, horses, an' those who do the contests, but I think I'd like tae keep them a little protected from the way some performers act, dress, an' talk. You cannae wallow with the pigs an' not get muddy, ya know."* He said, while nodding over at Monty to take the next round of questions.

"This particular line of work isn't ever easy you know." Monty started his end of the conversation, describing how the more senseless and barbaric murders were at the time, taking place about fifty miles south of their fair city of Edinburgh, and among those who called Glasgow, Scotland their home. As Monty continued to give more details about the gruesome events taking place at an unprecedented pace, Nick and Ralph, along with Cedric Fauer who had been listening in on their call, exchanged glances and somber looks.

Jude Stringfellow

Despite the vast differences in time and space separating the five of them, they were all in the same boat when it came to choosing their careers; they enforced the laws. Sometimes that meant watching and hoping, while other times it meant getting into the mix and making something happen to stop the madness.

As they continued to talk, Nick couldn't help but reflect upon his own life experiences as a lawman. As a private investigator or detective, which oftentimes gave him freedom to explore. At the same time, the likes of Chief Montgomery and Cedric Fauer, a plain-clothed officer of the law, had clear-cut boundaries they were forced to maintain. The harder it was to toe the line, the more men like Fauer and Montgomery thanked their lucky stars for men like Posh and Ferguson, who even though they knew they weren't given carte blanche when it came to recovering what they hoped to recover, they were allowed to poke around a lot deeper and in a much fluid way than most.

"This line of work has never been easy" Monty repeated. *"...but it is necessary, and it is needed. We protect the innocent and those who just want to have peace in their lives. It's a military of sorts when you think about it. We're bound by oaths and honor; we step in and we step up when others can't or won't. We work, so they can sleep. It's who we are."* He finished.

With determination etched into their hearts and souls, each man knew his place and each man knew the others as well. Both sides of the ocean had good men who vowed to do everything they could, everything in their collective power to bring justice to those affected by tragic and unnecessary incidents. It didn't matter where the clues may end up leading them; each man was prepared or preparing himself to go.

"Monty, Eoghan, have you ever heard the name Justin Zane? He's an author. He's written at least two dozen books I know of; most of which deal with the Old West, murder, and mayhem on the frontier. Have you heard of him?" asked Nick, knowing the two had already discussed Dennis Rockford in the past. When Monty stated that he had read a book he believed was written by an American calling himself Zane and that he may have been lucky enough to have seen the man in London a few years back when he was on a world book tour.

"That man, Justin Zane is no other than our good friend and now our connection, Dennis Rockford. They're one in the same Eoghan. I'm damned sure now going to ask him to bring you over to this side of the world to play at his barn and maybe get you some churches lined up to play in so you can make a little money when you do come over. I know you'll miss your family while you're here, but I think I can fill your time up to the point you'll be just a little too busy to think too much about them." Nick said.

"Nick, are you going to tell them about the body ranch too?" Ralph teased, knowing the sound of it, and going into too much detail could cause Eoghan to toss the phone's receiver like a hot potato. When it came to working the cases, Eoghan's mind was his nemesis, he could be his own worst enemy. He could think things on his own, causing himself to work his heart and mind into a tangled anxious frenzy without any help from the peanut section, as he called Ralph and Posh the instant he felt he was about to be assaulted with inherently grotesque and macabre

details certain to send him over the top with concern and disquiet apprehension.

"*Och! Are ya tryin' tae send me into the heavens lad? You'll give me the heebie-jeebies if ya start that! No, don't do it. Just the sound of it, a body ranch. I think I can guess the outcome of it; Rockford youse said has a big place, big enough tae hide a few bodies being exposed tae whatever elements there are so he can what...write about them later in one of his books? Is that it?*" asked the squeamish receptionist turned private investigator.

"*Aye! You've got it mate!*" exclaimed Ralph at the top of his lungs. "*He has more than a few mind you. He's got at least several dozen and they're all in various states and stages of decomposition. You'd have to see it, I'm told.* Ralph stated, "*But I can only imagine you'd smell it long before you could put your eyes on anything or anyone. Which of course, as you can guess, is something I'm really looking forward to doing on our way back to Oklahoma.*" Ralph added. "*One of the bodies he has is the very woman Posh was hired to find, or asked to apprehend her murderer anyway; at least we think it's her.*

"*I'll let him tell you more about that end of it, but we can make a stop on the way back home I'm sure, and make arrangements to return the girl's remains to her family...well, that is, if she's ....still got...you know, remains.*" His voice purposely becoming eerie and supernatural at the end, adding a touch of his best ghostly hoots and hollering. Halloween was still a few months off, but any opportunity to be a little haunting had to be taken.

"*Another one...*" Ralph explained, "*...was strangled to death; another woman. She must have been in the water when it happened because the medical examiner said her skin had to dry out good enough to see* *the bruising patterns. Doc said it would take a full day to see them show up all purple and dark. He even said veins in her eyes would show the way she was killed. They pop – the veins, not the eyes."* He quickly corrected himself.

When Eoghan caught his breath over the matter, he flinched. His lips turned inward, protecting himself from saying what he wanted to say. His mind hadn't toughened as quickly as he had hoped it would in these matters. His stomach tightened, reacting to the details being given. Ralph continued, somehow realizing his duty in Eoghan's training. Leave it to Ferguson, Posh thought, to be the teacher, trainer, mentor, whatever he thought he needed to be to bring up the images he thought Eoghan needed to handle.

"Two weeks in the water," Ralph added, *"and the body won't decompose like it would out in the open air. Depending on how cold the water is, the longer the body takes to deteriorate. Keep that in mind if you find one and want to know when the person actually died."* His voice was about to rise as he remembered to mention the lack of soft flesh around the face, neck, and limbs would indicate the nibbling of fish, turtles, or some other wildlife. *"They gotta eat too, you know,"* Ralph mentioned almost off-the-cuff.

Monty shook his head, thinking of what Nick must feel knowing that the man who hired him to find his niece would have been told the terrible grim news about his family member. She wasn't only murdered needlessly, and from what Nick described, quite brutally, the young woman's body had been unclaimed and therefore able to find itself being used and studied for both medical and seemingly entertainment purposes. On one hand, it seemed incredibly unfortunate, but on the other, it meant she could be returned and given a proper burial in a family plot.

Though he knew Rockford, or Justin Zane, would never exploit the name or reputation of an unknown person he had in his custody at the site where he was doing his research, he felt a sense of sorrow and even deep sadness thinking about how the young girl merely hoped to become a part of something thrilling and stimulating; something fascinating to its core that could bring about delightful feelings of ownership.

She wanted to use what she had in this world to move in it, to make choices about what she found mysterious and wonderful. Her death was exceptionally sad because of the innocence of her mind, and this created more hurt in the lawman's heart because of his own son's hope to make the world a better and safer place, before he was killed in action only a few days after his military graduation.

"Well, OK then, enough of this death-school business; it's time to introduce the two of you to our new cohort. You'll find him in the yellow pages under plumbing because he's so full of shit – but for the most part we think of him as being one of us; just not as good looking, or as smart, and to be damn sure, he's got no skills on the dance floor – it's as if he were raised by a pack of wolves. I'll let him tell you more." With that, Ralph Ferguson handed the telephone headset to their new friend.

"My name is Cedric Fauer, that's F-A-U-E-R." the man stated into the phone. *"I was told to spell it out for someone named Gabe Hanshaw, just in case he wanted to*

write a personal article about me, and if he ever wanted to interview me about how real lawmen enforce the rules and regs over on this side of the world." He laughed.

"I'm devilishly handsome, and I guess I'm a little like Posh in that I know the truth can be difficult, but in some ways, I'm a lot more like Ralph when it comes to putting it to the bad guy – Nick has this thing about keeping it all too moral and above board; me, I wouldn't cry if some of these men found their way off the side of a cliff or if they were fed to the alligators down in the swamps of Louisiana." He said.

It was a full half second before Ferguson piped up behind Fauer to add, *"Be careful about talking about being thrown over cliffs now Fauer, one of us has had that happen to him, and he ended up being pissed on by Nick's little terrier before the damn thing chose to live with him!"*

The five men laughed equally hard at the hard cold facts being displayed so candidly and so dead-level honest; it was the perfect segue to yet another line of banter that would keep Ralph Ferguson up past midnight giving as much as he received from his big bearded counterpart in the middle of the city of Edinburgh.

TWENTY-TWO

The activities of a new day began to stir amongst the rows of brightly colored temporary tents and trailers. Early risers emerged from their humble abodes, rubbing sleep from their eyes and stretching each limb. The unmistakable scent of fresh coffee buzzed through the air simultaneously with that of hot grease, toast, and scrambled eggs.

A sense of belonging throbbed in every chest of those calling themselves a family; a family on the move making their living and their memories the way they do. A call to breakfast hits the air, drawing men and women from every nook and corner of the place to the main meal tent where performers, staff, and roustabouts eat together; no one is more important than the next.

Laughter fills the space after breakfast. Everyone instinctively takes their places to stretch their limbs, practice their craft, mend whatever may need mending, and nearly everyone at some point during this time will take a gentle pass to and through the animal trailers to throw a bit of unfinished breakfast to those less likely to join them around the portable tables. "*Eat up children.*"

The animal trainers call as they push through the mounds of leftover meats and meal pieces thrown together for the carnivores; and pick through piles of hay for the rest. Gentle giants begin to emerge; chained of course, walking in unison with their handlers trumpeting their way across the field to meet their own at the eastern edge of the lake. Allowing the elephants to bathe takes hours, but hours are well spent for anyone who has seen the spectacle in person.

Nick considered what he was witnessing; he thought long and hard about the smells, the sights, and even the separate language these folk seemed to use when speaking amongst themselves. He couldn't wait to tell Alistair and Elaine everything he could recall from this very different and memorable experience. He'd heard of people running away from the safety of their homes to join the circus; everyone had heard such tales. Here; here he saw it firsthand. It was so much more than he had ever encountered, and so much more than he believed he could retell.

He watched with a sense of awe – the extravagance of it seemed overwhelming at times, and yet, this was simply just another day, another morning for the performers and The Bollen Group. If they were as tight as they seemed, it may be difficult for Nick or Ralph to pick up on any wrongdoing; especially if everyone condoned everything, refusing to seep even the slightest innuendo of malfeasant behavior. Despite his many adventures throughout his life, nothing quite compared to the unique familial camaraderie and energy present within a traveling circus. While he took in the sights, sounds, and majesty of it all he had to pinch himself to prove it wasn't a dream.

Ralph slowly approached Nick from behind, checking twice over his shoulder to be sure that what he had to say to his friend would be said in private. *"You're thinking what I thought yesterday when I watched this; this is not an act. This is how these people live Nick.*

"This is their whole life. They'd rather keep a deadly secret and take it to their grave then to rat on one

of their own – even if it means suffering through whatever it is with the fiend. Fiend or not, this is family." He stated flatly. *"I'm thinking we'd have more luck talking to the sideshow people considering where they know everything there is to know about everyone they aren't connected like the circus people seem to be.*

"They take their money separately. They sleep separately. They eat separately. Theirs is a true business. I think we'll get more dirt on whoever it is in the circus doing the dirty work by poking a little over that way. Bring a few dollars with you if you do.

"Maybe say you gotta know what's goin' on so you can feel safe enough to do your job for the next few days. Maybe suggest that one of the Restanis isn't particularly happy with you. Let them think it's Buster, not Gino. I think the fire boys are up and out soon if I had to guess. Gino hasn't paid them, but they know Gino gets his orders from his brother where that's concerned."

Ralph's suggestion was taken with careful consideration. It made sense to seek answers from outsiders rather than those with family ties; hadn't his mother repeatedly defended her older son adamantly claiming his actions were brought about by being raised in the tribe when she married Nick's father so many years ago?

Whenever Nick reminded his mother of the way his half-brother conducted himself her answers were usually softened by some form of excuse before she could bring herself to admit the illegal activities were as vile as they were where her older son Charles Yargee was concerned.

Stepping into and through the velvet curtains draped loosely over the opening of the main sideshow tent, Nick found himself face-to-face with some of the most unusual specimens able to consider themselves human. Having stood to the side of the stage with Ralph a few times, he had encountered the likes of the men who drew, danced with, and seemly ate fire.

He had met Little Cassie, the Bearded Lady, and her good friend the Human Werewolf; but before him now stretched a figure far darker and quite sinister indeed. Hooded in robes covering her body from head to toe, it was obvious to anyone daring to see, that the woman was covered in hundreds if not thousands of fleshy growths.

Were they tumors Nick wondered to himself. Was this woman capable of speaking, could she be made up somehow to seem so hideous, so cast from social norms? Without a doubt, this world he had stepped into so nonchalantly, had turned his mind upside down with questions and information, intelligence he had never considered or had reason to contemplate. It took his mind by storm, leaving far more questions than he had answers.

Pushing back the heavily drawn curtain Nick approached. *"Excuse me, can I speak to you for a minute?"* he asked quietly, blinking to adjust his eyes to the dim lighting. Before she spoke, the woman turned slightly toward the intruder, perhaps instinctively believing that once he could see her fully he would simply walk away without receiving an answer from her. Approaching ever so cautiously, Nick continued his desire to inquire what he could.

"I know I'm not part of the sideshow per se, but I'm here you know, with the group anyway. I...I've been here the whole week with Duke." He said. *"My name is Paul, most call me Pauly. I've...I've seen a few acts on this side of it, and to be honest with you I'm quite intrigued by*

it all. You have to admit..." he started to say before catching her eyes; darkness burned within her.

"I don't know, I don't really know how to say this, but I can't quite figure it out. I can't seem to figure out how the sideshow continues to make ends meet and pay you folk when the lion's share of the audience I see coming to the Big Top every night hardly makes their way over this way to see you do what all it is that you do. I mean...I don't want to be nosey or anything." He continued.

"My old man, he was a caller, a barker now and again, so I have seen a few shows and performances in my lifetime. I even helped set up a gig in London when King George had a sideshow as part of his birthday celebration." He lied, hoping the woman would raise an eyebrow to show interest. It was about this time another woman entered the small closed-off area where they stood to take the *Warted Wonder* by the shoulders to direct her through to still yet another draped-off area of the larger tent.

"She's not an American, fella." Said the other woman. *"She's from Syria, and she doesn't speak any English. I can help you with your inquiry though. You seem to be one of those who gives a damn about nomads; we're not all freaks of nature, but for most of us living a normal existence isn't possible."* She said.

"Take me for example. I seem normal to you, right? I mean, you look at me and I look OK. You think I should be working in an office somewhere; I should be married. Maybe I should have children. Maybe I should be a nurse, right?" she asked Nick, who had by this time taken a seat on the edge of the wooden stage to face his singular audience of one; to hear her, to listen to her before

asking her what it was that he wanted to know. She must have overheard him; she all but admitted to having been listening from the other side of the smaller curtain.

Stepping out to face Posh, a sizeable stout woman perhaps of German decent herself, made it very clear by the way she protected her fellow showman, that Posh's questions would need to be addressed perhaps, but only if she knew them first.

"We have a lot of people coming into the tents when they think it's allowed. These curtains represent the same type of boundaries you'd find in a home, in a house somewhere. Just because they're made of cloth and we don't have locks on them doesn't mean you can just step inside and start asking people questions. I hope you understand – I hope you're not offended when I ask you to either state your business or leave." She said.

She waited a few long silent seconds, and when Posh crossed his leg she knew he wasn't taking the hint as she had offered it. He wanted more, and the woman allowed his presence. He didn't offend her. In the distance they could hear the rumbling of the tents and the tent people; they could take their conversation elsewhere if they wanted to be more private with it.

"We aren't like everyone else you know. We are a collective set of misfits, all unique or bizarre you might say. Some have physical conditions that led them here, while others have talents and gifts beyond what most people can imagine. Take Zhoe; the Rubber Lady she's called. If you were to walk up to her on the streets or see her in a church somewhere you'd think nothing was very special about her, but when she's on stage and puts herself to it, she can wrap her entire body around a pole so

tightly, and in reverse mind you; you'd question if your eyes were seeing what they were seeing.

"She's an act alright; something you'll not ever witness outside of the show. We had a man once, it's been a few years now, and he was just over two feet tall. He's gone on to bigger shows, more pay, more everything. They called him General Tom – as you can imagine, he was never in the military but it was our owner's idea to put a tiny uniform on the man and have him give orders while the barker called people to the front of the decks to pay their admissions.

"We get a few good ones, we really do." Her words seemed to pack a punch with Posh; he wanted to know more. Silently seated before her, the woman escorted her Syrian friend to another location within the folds of the tents, to return to her captive audience of one. Sitting close to the man she only knew as a common everyday roustabout, a local from just beyond the Lake Mead boundary, the woman settled herself into a comfortable position so she could spend a little time explaining what she felt needed to be explained.

"I'm a lesbian. I'm not a weirdo or something out of a horror movie. I don't fit into this world, that's all. When people found out who and what I was I couldn't find a decent job to save my life. I couldn't go my church anymore. I was ostracized by my family; I wasn't even being called their daughter anymore. I wasn't anybody. I was thrown out; and berated, and one way or the other I had to face the hard cold facts that whatever happened I had to make it happen.

"What's that they say, 'If you want something done you have to be the one to do it' or something like that." She asked with purpose in her voice. *"I found these*

Mesa

people to be the least judgmental people on the face of the earth; and you know what, they think I'm pretty awesome too. I do the books for them. I find cities for them to perform in, and I find money where we can't get it anywhere else." Now, she was talking; and this is exactly what Posh wanted to ask about.

"What's your name?" he asked, hoping it wouldn't be too much of an ask to ask. *"My name? Oh, well, like nearly everyone else on the circuit, I go by something other than what my good ol' mom called me when I was born. I guess legally I'm Patricia Whitaker. I hail from Philadelphia, Pennsylvania; the city of brotherly love. To be honest with you, no one has called me Pat, Patti, Patricia, Patsy, or anything other than Penny for about eleven years. It's Penny for Pennsylvania."* She said, extending her right hand to shake his, revealing the fact that she was one of the rare exceptions of nature's choice to gift a person with two very distinctly different colored eyes.

"Pauly. Pauly from just about fifteen miles that way," he said, gesturing to the west with one hand while reaching for a smoke with the other. *"Your eyes?"* he questioned, realizing immediately that she had quite an enchanting spell over him; *"I assume you were born with this...well, they're different."* He said, not being able to pull out of his stare.

"Heterochromia iridium. Born that way" She stated. *"You can't smoke in the tents, but I'll walk out with you. I'll even answer your question."* She said. *"Buster Restani is the reason we have food in our mouths this month, but he's not been around much, and he's not made plans for next month either.*

"We're looking at needing to look somewhere else because the week's about to end and without a promise to continue, this show may need to break up and split into what's called a disbursement. We break up for a time, work where we can, and then down the line somewhere we find each other again. That's what happened about six months ago when The Bollen Group found us all; well, they found me and I made a few calls to bring us back together." She stated.

"I have to be honest with you Pauly, I don't think Buster is coming back. He's been talking about making a permanent thing outside of Las Vegas with his other line of business; I think you know what that is, right? I don't care much for it, but I'm not gonna look a gift horse in the mouth." She said, but just as she said it, she found herself checking over her right shoulder to be sure she was quiet enough for her words not to be heard. *"...and speaking of horses, that's where you'll probably find Buster Restani. He's been twisted up with Maudine Cooke for some time now.*

"She's got a little ranchero thanks to him, it's somewhere up around Grand Canyon Park. She's got some beautiful views if you have to know. I've been up there with Gino once; once when he was helping Maudine settle in; Buster asked him to help her get settled. It's been a while, several months or so, it was after our head coordinator found himself being killed by the woman herself." She said without blinking.

"If you ask me, and believe me, no one has," she added somewhat sarcastically, *"Buster could do a helluva lot better for himself considering the line of work he's in. If you're gonna be in that line of work you'll need someone a helluva lot more diplomatic. That woman Maudine*

Mesa

hasn't a diplomatic bone in her body. Living among the rattlesnakes; like her, venomous and deadly." The woman complained.

"Wait, I take it back, she's a lot more Latrodectus than that; she's a damned black widow spider that one is. If it's not her way, it ain't no way. Buster seems to think she walks on water more often than the dirt beneath us. He's more or less threatened any of us with out-and-out violence if we so much as say a crossword to her. She's never been mistreated here; I'll give you that." She said. *"We know who spreads the butter on our biscuits."*

After their open discussion regarding Buster's blind love and trust for a woman who seemingly had no intention of being loyal to him or anyone else, Penny made it clear that for all the gold in Sierra California hills, Maudine wouldn't give up a single wild horse once she'd coaxed it over the imaginary threshold from what it knew was a wild safe zone to that of sharing living space with her out there in the neverlands.

The woman, Penny said, may not have a single need for another human, but she was breathtakingly amazing when it came to coaching horses. *"I've seen it with my own eyes."* She said. *"I've watched her sit and wait a horse out for hours; when it's ready, she approaches it, stands a little sideways, and bends her leg at the knee to show it that she's relaxed and won't threaten it any. Then...the damn thing just couples up to her like he was best friend and they go on to making introductions with sounds and the like. I'm telling you, there's nothing like it. Not nowhere."*

Nick thanked Penny for her frank and open attitude with him, and explained to her that he wasn't asking to be in anyone's business; he just couldn't put the math to it when he thought about how everything in the world seemed to be depreciating, but still inflation was taking them all by storm.

At every turn, he told her, the cost of living was rising but no one seemed to be making another dollar to keep up with it. *"Buster finds dollars, Mister. He comes back with money every time he takes that road up to Chicago. It's like a thing with him. He could find investors closer, I'm sure, but he has some sort of an axe to grind up that way, and doing the things he does, well, he thinks Chicago can afford to lose a few more men like the ones he finds to...well, like he says, to 'invest' in the future of entertainment."* Her words hit hard. Asta Pate had merely wanted to invest in something worthwhile and it cost her everything – her very life.

Mesa

TWENTY-THREE

Once Ralph and Nick mapped out their route to where they believed Maudine Cooke lived, their plan had to be implemented and coordinated through means of explaining their absence from the circus set. Cedric Fauer stepped in to make the decoy, allowing himself to be seen first by a few roaming roustabouts set on finding out just exactly who he was; and what he wanted.

"*I'm looking for two men, both in their mid-forties, they call themselves Duke and Pauly I think. I'm looking for Duke really, but I hear Pauly has the car, so if I take one I'll have to take them both I reckon.*" Stated Cedric to two men who pointed in the direction he should go. Finishing up his rouse, he told the men in the tents that Duke's wife had called the Western Union office and he was standing in it at the time. She said she was having their baby on the other side of the vista just west of Lake Mead. She's asked for someone to fetch Duke so he could come home and watch the other children while she stays a day or so up at the midwife's home.

Understanding almost anything related to family obligation, the men continued to point and send Fauer on his way. When the news of his imaginary wife's need for him reached his ears, an act of sheer ecstatic joy breeched Ralph's face. "*Oh boy! I hope it's a boy this time, dammit. I've got seven girls at home, and I swear to God, if I have to do it all over again with Carrie, we're gonna have a boy*

Jude Stringfellow

damn it! This one better be a damn boy! That's all I have to say about that."

As Ralph whooped and hollered his way out of the sideshow tents, he seemingly dragged Posh by the arm forcing him to drive to his otherwise fake home just beyond the ridge where they were standing. Nick could barely contain himself; needing to keep his head lowered so no one would see him laugh. There were times, he told himself, that Ralph Emerson Ferguson could take the cake with that mind of his, and then there were times when he baked it all from scratch and you never knew what could come out of that man's head.

Once the Buick pulled out of sight and was far enough away, the two men pulled over to the side of the road to have a belly laugh over their covert accomplishment. Slapping his good friend on the shoulder, Nick could only add that he too hoped the damn kid turned out to be a boy this time as well. He asked Duke to name it after him, *"Name the kid Pauly. I don't care if it's a boy or a girl, just name it Pauly – that'll make me smile for the rest of my days."*

The heat of the afternoon sun had not quite made its climax before Nick and Ralph made their way toward Maudine's small frame cabin nestled among towering red rock formations. A cooler breeze teased them as they climbed higher into a higher elevation. Cedric sat behind Posh so he could angle himself just right to carry on a conversation with Ferguson, who had all but wrestled the man for the shotgun position, claiming he got motion sickness if he had to ride in the backseats. Arriving at their destination, they quietly approached a weathered wooden door, hard and sturdy, art imitating the woman they knew was behind it.

Mesa

Peering through a small window, they caught sight of movement within- flickering candlelight dancing across the walls where shadows had formed, hiding much of the interior of the house. Drawing closer still, they listened intently for any sign of life. Just then, a low murmur drifted from out of the afternoon winds, punctuated by the unmistakable sound of the cocking of a shotgun. Nick and Ralph steeled themselves simultaneously, each reaching for their pistols; drawing them at virtually the same instant.

"Maudine Cooke? I'm Detective Nick Posh, I don't mean you any harm at all ma'am. I'm here with police officer Ralph Ferguson of Chicago, and county officer Cedric Fauer from Las Vegas; we're here to talk, and that's all." Nick shouted at what he knew wasn't an empty front room.

"Fauer here, tells us that you've been talking to Jeff Dickerson about what's going on in Chicago, and about what's happening here as well. We know you're trying to do the right thing, and we're here to see that you make that happen." He continued, waiting cautiously for her answer.

The men remained calm, waiting for the still air to be breached by some sort of sound, a lowly whistle made its way through the window and seemingly past them. Its echo repeated more than a few times before the sound of thunderous hooves could be heard behind them, and the vibrations coming from the wooden deck wrapping around the home all but buckled each man to his knees.

A woman's voice called out abruptly. Without hesitation, she cried, *"You boys need to drop your weapons and get inside this house if you know what's good for ya, that herd won't stop if I don't stop them, and I won't have you coming into my house loaded for bear. I ain't gonna say it again, you have seconds to make up your minds. If you want me to open this door, you need to set those guns down now.*" She said, knowing her words were heard.

In no time, all three men had holstered their guns reaching for the door; a door only capable of being opened from the inside. "*Don't make me bury your asses, don't be stupid.*" She called, as she unbolted the door to allow them a safe entrance only seconds before the horses reached her porch; each stomping, ready to trample anything and anyone between themselves and their goddess.

Nick and Cedric exchanged excited glances knowing all too well the dangers posed by a stampeding herd of wild horses. The fact that these horses would obey Maudine's command spoke volumes about who she was, what she could do, and how she could accomplish it. It wasn't fear that entered his heart that day, but sheer respect and admiration for the hardened woman standing alongside them.

Setting down her weapon, leaning it against the corner of the stone fireplace, Maudine gave out a few quick sharp sounds to indicate her appreciation to the herd; at the same moment, dismissed them of their duties. Like the softening of butter over hot cornbread muffins, the horses relaxed themselves as quickly as they had erupted into their collective fury. The gentle beasts whinnied softly to one another, exchanging nuzzles, one or two of them lightly pawing at the hardened ground beneath their strong imposing hooves.

Mesa

"I've never seen anything like that, ma'am. I'll be completely honest with you. I thought for a second you'd lured us here to end us. It wouldn't take too many of those brutes to do us all in; not the way they looked, and not the way they obeyed you.

"If no one else is willing to say it, I'll say it; you have a way with animals like I've never known." Nick's compliment turned to a question. *"Would I be too far-fetched to think that maybe you had once worked with Buster and his brother either with The Bollen Group or maybe some other circus circuit they were involved with?"* he asked.

Seemingly lost in her thoughts, Maudine began drawing simple patterns with her fingertips on the coffee table before her. Her mind raced from one thought to the other. Some thoughts were memories while others were more fearful; she avoided his question, her answers would be permanent and she knew that. *"Yeah, I know Jeff Dickerson. You said something about him before you came into the house.*

"He and I met about a year ago when he knew I was about to pull out of The Bollen Group; I didn't want any more of it. I hadn't been a part of any of it, but if you sleep with the man people think he's told you things. I guess to some extent he did, and I guess if I'm made to be honest with myself I count my stars that he told me enough to get me the pardon I need for things I've done." She admitted.

Hot coffee was poured and everyone settled down, Maudine explained more about how Buster had been behind the investors' scheme, and how Titus Rushby was more or less the muscle, but he had made a few advances toward working the angles himself; Titus wanted a partnership. She informed the men that though she knew very little about the two women Rushby had swindled, she knew enough to know that if they had taken the time to drive out to Lake Mead to meet with him once they withdrew their funds from the local banks, through warrants on their accounts. She knew they'd live only long enough for the payoff to be given.

It was Dorothy Eischer she told Posh, who figured out that the two of them had been taken and that they weren't going to become true investors. "*I don't think either of the women thought they'd be hurt. Maybe they just thought they'd lost all they had and they'd be set out on the side of the road to walk their way home. I never met them, and didn't talk to either of them. What I'm telling you about those girls I got from Buster the other night when he came up here to get what he wanted and found I wasn't in a bargaining mood.*

"*I don't know. I do know that after I took my revenge on that man, I heard about the taller one – your governor's niece, was probably the one they let the rancher have for his studies.*" She said, before adding. "*I can't know or even imagine what evil they endured before they were killed. Titus had a mean streak in him. Hell, he was one big mean streak if I had to tell the full truth about him.*

"*When you do find out, if you find out, just know that that man got every last thing that was coming to him. If it hadn't been me it would have been Buster. Titus Rushby was a dead man walking once he lied to me and took my money. It was Buster's money when you come right down to it. He gave it to me to buy the land here, but when Titus told me he could turn a few thousand into*

Mesa

thirty nearly overnight, I guess something in me believed him.

"When I found out he took my money I thought maybe he had done the same with those two girls – I asked a few questions after the fact. Ty didn't tell me too much about either of them, just that they were from Oklahoma; Red Man's land he called it." She said, without an ounce of remorse, "...so, after what he did, I lit up his world; instantly. I wasn't scared really. I guess deep down I had known all along that things weren't going to end well for me seeing how I'd hooked up with Titus in the first place. Still, taking my body is one thing, but taking my money is another thing altogether. That's what got him killed."

Nick waited a few moments before leaning back into the sofa beside Cedric Fauer, giving a silent nod and signal to Ralph, who had been watching the front door. It was another reticent gesture from one soldier to the next. "*Maudine,*" he began slowly, holding her attention with his eyes as he spoke. "*You're being given full immunity for helping us. It won't do anyone any good if you hold back on us now. Are you saying you know without any doubt that it was Titus Rushby who possibly kidnapped and who definitely killed both Dorothy Eischer and Asta Pate of Oklahoma City just after the first of the year? Is that right?*" Nick asked.

Maudine sighed before answering. "*I know enough to know Titus wasn't the only one involved. He couldn't do anything without being told to do it, and he worked for Buster. I also know, that Buster is not a man to be crossed. I'm crossing him now; I know that, but I'm also hoping...no, I'm praying, that you boys will catch up with him and end him before he has a chance to kill anyone else; anyone here, or anyone in Chicago."*

Her last words hit hardest with Ralph Ferguson, who had often pondered if the connection had been higher up than the circus clowns; but there again, no one did anything without being told to do it, and they too, were paid by Buster Restani.

"Before he came to talk to me, the last time I saw him, he had been acting strangely, sort of more melancholy I guess you'd say. He kept repeating how much he loved me, how long he's loved me, what love meant to him, and things I didn't want to hear. I wasn't in love with Buster. He knew that.

"I couldn't love anyone after what I've been through. People hurt others. People use others. People never truly trust; which is why, as you know, I have chosen the Mustangs to commune with and to join up with. I'm part of that herd, not the human herds I see twisting and lying to one another. No, thank you. If a horse has a problem with another horse, it's made obvious and every other horse knows about it. They settle their matters right then and go back to living. It's perfect. We could all learn from it." She said.

"That might work," Ralph said, *"If it wasn't for all the laws we put in place to keep us civil you know. It has to be that way. I do hope you at least appreciate that. I also hope you appreciate that we're willing to put our own lives at risk to bring in a man you know is a serial murderer, whose very existence is fueled by mayhem and criminal activities.*

"He's not only a menace, he's a monster. Helping us nab him will absolve you of what you did and how you did it; don't think for a second that any one of us condones

what you did and we don't think it was justified either. We're not horses. We're human, and we have to live among all the other humans. We have laws to protect us from people like you – people who take matters into their own hands. We know that you're willing to help get this maniac off the streets, and some say it takes one to know one, so we're hoping whatever you can give us will help us get to know Buster enough to bring him in before he kills you or anyone else."

With that explanation off his chest, Ralph walked from the open front door jamb to the edge of the hall, telling everyone in the room he was going to the fridge for something cold. Maudine all but shook inside herself laughing at the manner Ralph Ferguson spoke to her. She wasn't used to being handled, and to be so in her own house by a man who so willingly decided to stand up and get whatever he wanted from her was nearly enough to send her over the top.

Leaning forward she turned in her seat, glancing over to the spot where she knew she had rested her shotgun. It was gone. When he had passed behind her on his way to the kitchen, Posh had managed to retain her attention; it was the way he stared back at her, coaxing her, calling her to keep herself focused just long enough for Ralph to take what he needed to take.

As she began to straighten herself, she locked eyes with the barrel of a .38 revolver being aimed directly at her. Posh hadn't needed much time to ready himself or to protect his friend. *"You bastards!"* she cried. With nowhere else to go and no way to call for help, Maudine Cooke's heart began to pound within her. She waited for whatever fate awaited.

Jude Stringfellow

Posh and Fauer stood to their feet, communicating to the woman it would be best if she sat still exactly where she was. "*It's going to be a long evening Maudine.*" Fauer said, "*We're here to get all the i's dotted and the t's crossed. Your deal with Dickerson, and of course with us, is contingent on us being able to arrest or stop the Restanis. We'll start with Buster, but we want to hear about Gino as well.*

"*We want to know all the ins and outs of their enterprise if you know it. The papers today said another man had been shot cold dead on the streets of East Chicago this past weekend; the same time we heard Buster Restani was making his way up that way. Do you know who he was going to see? Do you have names or any places he may be?*" he asked. Fauer let the woman know she was in good hands, but she was indeed in their hands for good.

The three men took turns sleeping that night, making sure one of them was awake in case anything or anyone intruded upon them. Maudine, for her part, commanded the herd to once more take their place around the front, side, and back of the cabin to stand watch. No one would get through their guarded posts without her knowing. She'd been fooled once, and one was enough. She couldn't let them bully her into doing what she was already planning to do; she needed them to understand. It was a rare moment of weakness she recognized in herself.

"*Throw a few wild donkeys out there with that herd of yours and you've got yourself an army that no one would chance to fight. I've seen what a wild burro can do to a coyote. I can only imagine he'd not be too easy on a man if he didn't know him.*" Nick commented, knowing any talk of horses would achieve his goal of earning a bit more trust from their home-bound captive.

Posh and Ferguson took a minute to clear any sharp objects or what could be used as weapons from Maudine's bedroom. Before she retired for the night, leaving the door open at everyone's insistence, Maudine gave a glance in the direction of Cedric Fauer; noticing he hadn't left the front room as quickly as the others had. She being disarmed, he hadn't much to worry about when the time came for him to keep watch.

"Good night Fauer." The woman called a little after midnight; and only to Fauer. The gesture hadn't gone unnoticed. *"She's taken with you Cedric, my friend."* Came the tease from Ralph Ferguson, who had helped himself to a heaping of cornbread and beans he found stored in the ice box. Heating his late supper on the open fire, the Chicago police officer gave a jester's smile to his country counterpart before scooping up the first spoonful from his bowl.

Throughout the night and early into the next morning, Maudine recounted facts and what she believed to be facts in both chronological order as well as things that simply came to her mind as she unveiled everything she could. Wanting to be exonerated of course, she tried her best to convince the lawmen that she may not have acted in the most civil of ways, but that what she had to offer them now would be enough to let her simply walk away and ride off further into the canyons where no man would have the nerve or fortitude to find her ever again.

"I got a call the night before you boys came up. I don't have a phone myself, so when the call came through at the general store down by the creek about three miles

to the west southwest of the edge of my land, Harry Morton took the information and had his wife write it down good so I could read it. Harry has a limited education; so he don't trust himself to write anything down if it means something." She said.

"What he told me was a call came from someone in Las Vegas asking if Buster had made it this way before going to Chicago to meet up with his newest investor. He didn't give a name, nothing like that, but he did say that whoever called was either related to Buster or claimed to be. It must have been Gino, and he may have said 'my brother' since Harry thought they were related.

I'm thinking Gino don't know where Buster is either, and if Gino don't know, then Buster didn't want him to know." She ended that sentence and walked into her kitchen to put on a pot of hot coffee. Her bare feet were silent on the cold stone floor of her kitchen, she reached up into a narrow pantry to withdraw a canister of rough whole beans she had roasted herself some time back. *"Can you get the grinder for me there Cedric?"* she asked, pointing to a cabinet behind the man.

As Maudine spoke she swept several locks of her thick dark red tresses up over her forehead, allowing it to land hapless on the left side of her face. Ralph listened; his brow furrowed in concentration. *"So, basically, we're dealing with a few crooks who don't trust one another, is that it?"* he mused aloud, rubbing his chin thoughtfully. Up at Stateville, there's an order to all that come into the place. Just because you're a don when you were on the outside don't mean you'll run the show on the inside. I think maybe that's the way it is across the board with crooks – if they're out and free to walk around they have a helluva lot more moxie; but when they're trapped they're easier to deal with.

"That makes our job a lot harder, but it also gives us an opening. If these guys are operating independently from one another, but all of them listening to the same boss, there might be some cracks in their armor that we can find, and when we do find them we can exploit them," He said, glancing back over at Nick, who nodded grimly in agreement. *"Keep digging, Maudine,"* he said urging her, *"Anything you can come up with now will be that much better for you in the long run."*

Nick pulled out his gold pocket watch to reveal the time. *"We should start making plans to get to where we're going. We won't be able to take Maudine with us, but you can see to it that she makes her way to Carson City tonight, can't you Cedric?"* He asked. *"Carson City?"* exclaimed the woman, *"There's nothing there but a prison!"* As the words left her mouth she knew instantly where this conversation was headed. *"You can't take me there. You said I was going to be exonerated, not incarcerated."* She asked with no little bit of worry in her voice.

Cedric explained to her how holing her up in the prison made the most sense. *"You're not going as an inmate, but we have to have a way to keep you locked away so you don't escape before we pull the curtain down on the Restanis. You're a material witness at this point and we can't afford to lose you. We've decided to work out a deal with the warden at Carson to make the others think you're a new worker, that's all.*

"You'll wash the bedding and do light janitorial work for a few days to keep you busy and give you

Jude Stringfellow

something to do until we can release you. When we do, you'll need to find another cabin to stay in if Gino or some other person connected to Buster thinks you had anything to do with the sting. I know you understand that much of it. I heard you telling Dickerson that you had another place down in Grand Canyon where you could etch out a living taking tours of the place on the backs of the horses that you wrangle.

"I've gotta hand it to you lady, you're tougher than an old pair of boots, and I admire your backbone." His words finding her in a particularly weakened moment, Maudine's eyes began to well up under the stress of the past few days. At the end of every day she was a woman. She turned to the man and began to weep. Her body quivering under the pressure of it all; she managed to stand a little longer before nearly collapsing on the slate floor beneath her.

Lifting, and holding her in his arms, he chanced everything he believed in when he took her trembling form into his hands. He felt a strange mix of emotions coursing through him. On one hand, he was doing his duty as a law enforcement officer – protecting innocents from any harm. But on the other hand, there was something undeniably human and vulnerable about Maudine Cooke.

He knew her backstory, where she had come from, some of what she had encountered. He knew she faced fear, unmeasurable loneliness, abandonment, and even being cast from the general society as a whole. Perhaps it was because they shared some similarities that he felt a twinge of empathy rising through him – both having experienced betrayal and violence in the past.

Maybe it was simply the bond between a lonely man and a woman who had chosen to be alone and who

Mesa

knew in her soul she could never fully be accepted by another person. Whatever the reason, Fauer knew that his mind would need to regroup and refrain from giving away too much of himself all at once. There may be another time, some other time, when he could address more fully what he thought could be a connection between the two of them.

TWENTY-FOUR

When they met with Dickerson just outside the general store, who had driven out to the canyons to meet with the two men, Nick couldn't help but tease Ralph regarding a conversation he had overheard between his best friend and the woman they had in their custody waiting to be exonerated for her misconduct.

"*Seems Ralph admitted to Maudine Cooke, a woman you know, can outwit, out-train, and outsmart any wild roaming Mustang she ever sets her mind to find, that he has never actually been on the back of a horse long enough to consider himself a rider. He's had his picture taken on one; even as a Sergeant with the Chicago Police Department, they have a long tradition of photographing men on handsomely decorated steeds to appear brave and commanding.*

"*Fergy tells her he wouldn't know the end of the animal from its head if he had to be honest, and you couldn't help but hear the woman cackling from inside her kitchen. She's about to pour the hot coffee right out of the pot and onto the floor. I had to put my cup underneath the spout to save it from happening.*" Nick joked.

At the story's end, Ralph took the opportunity to defend himself stating, "*Well now son, let me tell you how it is.*" He said using the most obnoxious southern accent his Yankee tongue could muster up before reciting the tale.

"*You see, I was raised and brought up in the big city. I never had much use for anything with four legs, not even a dog until I was old enough to take care of one*

Mesa

myself. We lived in the hardest of areas in the middle of the downtown ghettos where the only horses you'll see are hooked up to carriages for tourists to be pulled around in. I hopped on top of one of them once, but got my tail beat for it both by the horse's owner and then by my mom once she heard about it.

"And because we were such good Catholics, when we got to mass the next weekend I got myself whooped again by the clergy who had a few words for me about discipline, respect and generally just being a better person. I learned my ways around the streets, not a horse," Ralph continued.

"Guess you could say I'm more of a got-my-own-legs man than to trust myself on the back of something capable of taking off and running me into a tree or worse. I've seen my fair share of death without a horse being involved, I don't need to add one to make the odds that much worse for myself." He laughed. *"Oh don't worry, Ralph, they probably feel the same way."* Teased Jeff in only a slightly condescending manner.

Dickerson filled the boys in on what it was that he and the others were hoping could be done with and to Buster Restani. Knowing that he had been spotted a few times in Chicago over the past forty-eight hours made it clear enough that the man simply had business on his mind before he decided to seal himself off from Maudine Cooke permanently.

Intel from some of the men Ferguson was connected with, put Restani both on the east and west sides of Chicago dining and carrying on with the two most opposing families in the city. Breaking bread with sworn enemies was a dangerous game to play; both men were no doubt completely unaware that the two-timer had been milking them both not only for money but possibly for intelligence that could lead them to an advantage over the other. It was a dangerous game indeed; one Ralph was all too happy to hear much more about if he could.

Never one to shy away from anything considered too hot to carry, Ralph Ferguson let out a long slow whistle, "*Sounds like we've got ourselves quite the slippery fish with this one,*" he muttered under his breath. Turning back to Posh, he continued, "*So we take Route 66 right up to Chicago, we head into town knowing what we know, and we play nice with the local authorities because once I get back that way I may not be able to accompany you if they want me to stay and finish the job from where it all began.*" He said.

Nick picked it back up to add, "*Until we figure out which side Buster Restani is playing we can only hope we don't end up in some sort of crossfire. I hear you about them wanting you to stay up north; maybe we should find the man in Chicago, and we can arrest him and get names from him maybe if he thinks it'll do something to save his skin by telling us, but he's got to know it won't go down like that. He's got to know he'll never see the light of day once we clap a pair of braces on his wrists.*" Nick assured his friend.

Nick reached into his jacket's pocket to find a many-times folded map of Route 66, having somewhat memorized it from the trip out west in the first place. "*If we play it right we can end up in virtually the same locations, but only in reverse. I don't think we've left anything of value out west, so we'll not need to call the boarding house to have anything sent back to us. I'll make the call however to let Mrs. Harroll know we'll be checking out immediately; she can keep the money we put down for the following few days' stay.*

"When I think about it, I think maybe my mom could rent out her place for a little extra cash," Nick said. "Her cooking is out of this world, and anyone would feel safe and comfortable with her, not to mention learning so much about Oklahoma, its native history, as well as being brought a good healthy dose of the gospel if she had her way with them...then again, I don't want her ending up with a few Dukes and Paulys either."

Nick's chuckling caught up in his throat somewhat, and he had to cough through the last part of his statement. *"You better be careful what you ask for Posh, your momma could straighten out the best or the worst of them."* Laughed Ralph, knowing all too well the love Nick had for his mother Ama, and the love she returned to her younger son; the love and heart of her life.

The day wore on slowly, the heat increasing with every mile they covered. Without warning the skies above them turned a deep shade of gray, and the winds seemed to come out of all sides at once with alarming force and speed. Within minutes, the world around them all but disappeared into a wall of dust and dirty debris. The treeless frontier seemed to groan within itself; something resembling thunder without the effects of rain or lightning pounded the atmosphere encasing them in its wake. Time itself seemed to stand halted as multiple waves of dust clouds swarmed up and around the car, tearing at the two men with everything it had to thrust.

Through squinted eyes, they could barely make out each other's forms, illuminated only by tiny respites of

Jude Stringfellow

light between the swirling and the whirling winds and silt blowing harder and still harder by the second. For what seemed like hours, they hunkered in place, weathering as best they could, taking their places as far off the car seats and as close to the ground as possible. Nick managed to grab one of the blankets tossed haplessly in the backseat to cover them both. From the noise of it all, neither man dared to try and speak, knowing if they did their mouths would be covered in loose red sand, what had to be the top soil or surface of the entire desert behind them.

As suddenly as it had started, the tempest subsided on its own; leaving behind a world coated in a fine layer of the earth. Cautiously, they emerged from the car, dusting themselves, and blinking away the last remaining remnants of the sandstorm. Panting heavily, they took in the muted dusty scene around them; it had taken only minutes, but the storm had left everything in front, behind, and around them saturated in its uniform blanket of silt.

Looking around they saw the path of what should have been a paved road. It was impossible to make out for quite a ways; still visible to some degree they forged best they could until they reached a gasoline station to try and shake loose any debris that had invaded the car's engine and to try and mop out the interior as well. Shaking their heads in disbelief the two men shook the hands of the young attendants who somehow knew they'd be busier in the next few hours; thanking nature for the tips they'd soon receive.

Tugging at his clothes, Ralph let the rest of the silty mess that had accumulated in every crevice of his clothes fall to the ground. After pulling out his wallet to retrieve the necessary bills to fill up and clean the car, Posh quickly asked the first attendant he saw where they may find a

Mesa

suitable place to rest within the next hour or so of driving Route 66's paved roads. Considering they had made the earlier mistake of not spending that extra fifteen minutes it would have taken to find a roadside hotel, the men made sure to ask where the next rest stop may be.

When they were satisfied that the next boarding house was only a few miles up the road, they made their plans to stay overnight, and to place calls to their families, filling them in as much as they could; Ralph decided not to be too specific as he knew Stella's mother's house was part of a party-line telephone connection. He wasn't about to give away any of his secrets that close to Restani or any of his men if he could help it.

"Your wife is what, eight hours away by time and mine is about twenty hours away by car. Time and space, buddy, it just seems so odd to think about." Ralph started, while the two men retired to their rooms, *"I can't wait to hold her. I can't wait to just stand there and wrap my arms around her big ol' belly and squeeze as…well, not too hard, but I'm gonna squeeze that woman when I see her."* He laughed. *"I'm gonna squeeze little Pauly too. He or she is gonna want to know how her favorite uncle is faring, and I'll be the one to say he's a dandy that one – he's a dandy."*

"When you do call your wife, let her in on the secret that she's just had your eighth child, and that she finally gave me that son you've been harping on about. I'll tell Stella all about the Rubber Lady and how she liked to contort herself all around you just to see if you could get out from under her." Nick joked.

"I didn't think you saw that, buddy. Yeah, I guess you did; I saw you hogging time with Little Cassie

though; that one just blows my mind, Posh. Can you imagine first being born so small but then going through school not being able to climb up into the seat or being able to use normal furniture the way we use it? I remember being so little that my feet didn't hit the ground in the outhouse – I hated that. I clearly remember the day my feet...you know, touched when I was...you know." Ralph stammered.

As they approached the Texas border, the air became thicker with a humidity they had not felt in any of the desert states; there it was an unbearable heat, but at least it was a dry heat. The skies opened suddenly, drenching them and everything in sight. *"God has a sense of humor now doesn't He?"* asked Ralph, referring to the way they had ended up covered in dust one day and having it all washed away the next day in torrential downpours. *"Still can't see the roads or the ground outside this window, so I guess it all works out to be about the same."* He laughed. *"One minute I'm so dry I'm spittin' cotton!"* he complained, *"The next it's rainin' thick enough to choke a toad."*

Heavy raindrops continuously fell upon the roof of the Buick when they made their way back onto the road. Their ears filled with thunder and the crack of strong lightning creating a cacophony of noise that threatened to drown out their conversation. Despite the intermittent inclement weather for the next several hundreds of miles, the city of Chicago, Illinois loomed large before them, a testament to human ingenuity and ambition.

Skyscrapers towered above the low-lying buildings, their steel frames reaching toward the heavens. Honking horns and shouting vendors filled the air, adding to the chaotic symphony of urban life that was Chicago. Traffic

Mesa

moved slowly along the congested streets, cars jostling for their position like eager contestants vying for a prize.

Pedestrians, not willing to be outdone by any of the others, dashed between parked cars, making their way from one side of a busy thoroughfare to the next, their umbrellas held tightly overhead to shield them from the relentless downpour. In front of their car, about to find herself crossing the street, an elderly woman with a walking stick leaned heavily forward as if she were going to take a step. When she did, Nick quickly twisted the steering wheel to the left, before severely straightening it again to maintain some semblance of control.

Navigating their way through the crowded streets, they caught glimpses of the stoic Lake Michigan sparkling in the distance, its serene surface contrasting sharply with the frenetic energy of the city around them. Eventually, they reached Lake Shore Drive sporting the ever-impressive Navy Pier with its circus-like atmosphere and somewhat tough reputation among locals. Eventually, they found their destination, taking Lake Shore Drive cutting like a serpent on its path along the shore of the lake itself.

Here the rain began to let up and lift a little, allowing them to breathe in the hearty tang of the shore mixed with the sweet-scented flora and freshly cut grass. Palatial estates stood proudly along the drive, their ornate facades boasting of their grandeur status, reflecting years of social prestige. An ornate section of town known as The Gold Coast held everyone's imaginations captive with its unique blend of opulence and its gritty sense of style. Sidewalks teemed with well-heeled socialites clustered together beneath colorful umbrellas, no doubt reminiscing about their last conquest in either love or finance.

Jude Stringfellow

Despite the gloomier weather, there was an undeniable magic about the place, a pulsing energy that seemed to burst from every cell of the body of the city of Chicago; veins pumping, blood flowing, this was the place to be. Amidst the glitz and glamour of it all, lay a hidden underbelly of sinfully wicked corruption and violence stretching its long sharp tentacles from the city's politics, and civil servants, and even into the many houses of worship lining the endless concrete streets; Chicago, where dreams go to die, and legends still lived.

Mesa

TWENTY-FIVE

It had been three days since their friends and fellow roustabouts Duke and Pauly had left them. Juliette the snake tamer had collected quite the little kitty of coins, as the teams lined up to bet which sex would win out; would Duke finally have his son, or would eight girls be enough to call it quits? Among the rumors of Duke and Pauly having found work elsewhere, another more sinister buzz was threading its way through the flapping folds of the tent just east of the city at Lake Mead.

Little more than his name was known to most of the performers and crew of The Bollen Group, however, when Lucian Alvarez pulled out of the temporary back gate set up to fence in and protect the animals, everyone knew something was afoot. Something didn't seem set completely straight; the people of the circus could sense it, almost smell and taste it. Lucian never really cottoned to the rest of them; he was an insider of course, but with a mind of his own. Him being out of character meant he wasn't working, and if he wasn't planning on working, the people of the circus wanted to know what he was planning to do.

Within an hour of his departure, sixteen open-bed trucks pulling flatbed trailers arrived on the scene. They seemed like serious business. Anyone with the sense to see it for what it was realized that the final curtain had been drawn on The Bollen Group; the last evening's performance would be their last; but it came without warning to anyone.

Jude Stringfellow

This man, this lanky quiet man, certainly the tallest member of the troupe, Lucian, had towered some nine to twelve inches over the ringmaster Gino Restani. The fact that more than one carnie had seen Alvarez speaking with several members of the evening audience the night before, and again the day and night before that, brought about a few rumors perhaps, but nothing like this was expected.

Rumor had it he had hailed from somewhere deep in the South; where images of voodoo and black magic still held sway. Whatever secrets Lucian Alvarez may have conjured between himself and the owner of the circus itself, no man knew. Despite his quiet and unassuming demeanor, Lucian was anything but ordinary; nearly seven feet tall in his boots, he was an imposing character on stilts. Young, strong, lanky, even gangly if the angle was just right, the man created in himself a reason for all the stares he received from children and adults alike.

Stepping from one of the trucks parked in front of the Big Top, another man, a surly barrel-chested man in thick leather boots purposely walked straight across the parking area and over toward the main pavilions. The man whistled as he strolled toward the Big Top tent, calling for Gino Restani to make himself known. When Buster's younger brother stepped out of his private quarters, the bigger man greeted him shortly before handing the ring leader a large envelope carrying what most suspected was their last pay for quite some time. Gino never blinked – he merely turned, stuffing the folded mass into the pocket of his double-breasted suit.

Gino neither confirmed nor denied the contents of the package to anyone. With a smoothness borne of practice, Gino Restani casually walked away from everyone's sight before turning on his heel and disappearing into the shadows cast by the morning sun beating down on everyone from her perch in the cloudless blue sky. Their last great hope then strolled almost nonchalantly towards an exit; heads turned of course, but no one followed him. He simply disappeared without so much as an attempt to explain.

Another hour passed on the skids of the hardened grounds before a call was made to one of the lawmen most of the transients had come to trust; Jerry Jeff Dickerson spoke openly about what he knew to the caller stating that not only had Buster Restani betrayed his brother by selling the circus right out from under them all, he had let down the lives and incomes of literally dozens of men and women who had grown to rely on their leaders for more than just employment.

As if sensing the impending storm about to seize them, the cast and crew of the sideshow began packing what they could before it was stripped from them. Loading their trucks and campers with all they could carry they also disappeared like scattering rats at night when a bright light had been shone from above. As soon as they had managed to load their wares they too disappeared, dipping their wheels onto the streets leading them to other cities with other faces; with other opportunities.

Selling The Bollen Group meant disbursement for those of the circus set; they all knew it. It wasn't something they could hide away or simply not talk about. When crafting skills so unique as they had, there was truly only one profession even capable of maintaining them or for that matter, accepting them. God only knew where or when they'd find another nomadic caravan of entertainment to sustain them. Would the new owners pay them what they had expected? Would they even be offered employment? No one knew; not one word from Restani. Somewhere in the distance, the mighty lion roared cracking the silence of their thoughts.

The streets and alleyways of Lake Mead were teeming with talk, alive with whispered conversations and furtive glances, each person trying so desperately to gauge the mood of those around them. Jeff Dickerson found a phone inside the local Western Union Telegraph office where he placed a person-to-person call to Detective Nick Posh at the Chicago Michigan Arms Hotel. A few minutes passed before the man could be found, but when he was, there was a deeply saddened exchange between the two men.

"*He's gotta be up that way Posh,*" Dickerson's Southwestern drawl heavier that afternoon than usual. "*He's sent money to his brother; some sort of payoff or buyout. I'm here at the Western Union where the money came in and where the clerk walked the recipient to the bank to cash the warrant. We're not sure if Gino is splitting what he got with anyone or if he's just going to take off and leave whatever isn't hauled away. We know the money came from Chicago – from Roosevelt Street.*

"*Buster had it planned I guess for a while;* Dickerson said. " *He had a mole in the midst of them for months. I think you may have met him. He was that tall one; the man they called 'Tiny' I think. He was the stilt-walking clown or I guess he dressed more in a top hat with long tails. You remember him.*" Jeff said.

"*Jewel the Clown, or you know, Joe, called me to say he didn't know what else to do, or who else to call. Some folks thought you and Ralph - or you know, Duke*

Mesa

and Pauly had something to do with it since you took off right after Buster did. I let him know.

"I let Joe know, that the two of you weren't actually part of the town folk, that Duke's wife was from that way and needed to get back as soon as she could with her new baby and all. I had that much clout. They believed me. Posh, you drove him out this way, so you had to leave too. They'll not be blaming you, or looking for either one of you, but let me tell you this; if you think you won't see trouble over this up that way you'd be mistaken.

"I put myself right in the middle of it, asking questions and taking as many statements as I could. These people are right furious right now, and no one is gonna stop some of them from taking the Route up to Chicago to have a face-down with Restani. Let me tell you who's already headed out that way. You know those sideshow boys, the fire eaters?" Dickerson asked.

"Those boys were some of if not the first to throw it all to the wind and head out without so much as seeing if any of that money was coming their way." He stated. *"Baros and Drakos,"* he said. *"Those Greeks are hotter than hell right now over all this...by the way, I told them Duke's wife Carrie had a son."*

Pondering what Dickerson had told him, Posh raised his chin, allowing the phone's receiver to dangle just under his jaw, catching it in his hand as it fell. *"Well now, ain't' that something' A real tall drink of water like Alvarez; yeah, I remember him,"* Posh said. *"I wonder what he saw that gave him the idea that he needed to cotton up to Buster. I wonder if he knew more than most, or if he knew how the circus got their payroll in the first place. He knew something or maybe he just figured it out,*

Jude Stringfellow

and he put a plan in motion with Buster to clear the place out fast." Posh thought another minute. *"Did you say...did you say those Greeks?"* he asked Dickerson; suddenly realizing the implication.

Looking over to his friend, Nick sized Ralph up knowing he grasped the same idea Posh was thinking; Buster Restani played the wrong tune once too often, and the Greeks who had worked so hard to help him bring the circus into play were now feeling blindsided by the backstabbing, two-timing Italian man they'd almost put their full trust in. They'd murdered men for him, hadn't they?

On the word of Buster Restani, they'd donned clown attire rather than their skin-tight fire-retardant outfits, and they'd mingled among the others so as not to be a distraction while the sideshow's performance waned, allowing the Big Top to lure in the audiences. Night after night, and day after day, visitors spent six to eight times more standing in line at the concessions and buying up souvenirs than they ever did under the velvet tarps of the odd and unusual.

"What do you think of that, Ralph? Do you remember Lucian Alvarez? He must have come out your way a time or two." Nick asked, thinking maybe the taller gangly man had been someone his good friend could put a name or face to from another year back or so. *"He had to come from somewhere, most people who have been in the circus any time at all, from what I've been told, either have a connection or they're act is too good to pass up. Being freakishly tall can help a man, but it's not a good reason alone to hire him."*

Ralph shook his head, clearing his throat. *"Yeah, I remember him alright; we had a game we'd play when*

Mesa

the folks were coming up to the tents. I'm just thinking about how quickly things can change for those people. They can't trust anyone; every turn they make another dart or another tidal wave of sorrow hits them. If it's not the weather it's their people hurting them. You never know what secrets are told, what rumors are real, or who to believe." Ralph said.

"No wonder Delilah wasn't happy about you watching the main corner of her net. You and I were thinking it was no big deal, but to her, it meant the difference between living and dying every time she climbed the ladder!" his words catching. Nick hadn't seen Ralph become so inwardly empathic about much in the many years he had known him.

Nick nodded in agreement, taking a heavy drag from his last Chesterfield. *"You usually let life roll right off your back, Ferg. You're not one to get too wrapped up in it. I can see this one's got you bad."* Nick stated.

"Well, I guess that's why we do what we do, right?" asked Ralph. *"We care and we sometimes care too much, but we do try to keep it all in check. Folks like the circus crowd they're even more vulnerable than the sideshow artists because they're more of a unit; they don't want to split up. It's a take-us-all-or-leave-us-all sort of thing for them. I hate to think about it Posh.*

"Those men, they took the tents! Those folk don't have another choice; they'll either go with the new owners if the new owners even offer to take them, or they'll walk to the next circus they can find. Who does that to good hard-working people?" he asked, not truly expecting an answer.

Jude Stringfellow

"I'll tell you who does that, Ralph. A man whose already killed himself twice over by crossing men like Capone and Moran. A man who has ordered hit after hit and collected money for them without paying his debts or keeping up with payroll. A man who lied to a woman about helping her start her life over only to shove her into the arms of a man who crossed her a second time; but she fought back. That's who does this sort of thing Ralph, a damned fool."

Posh set the phone's receiver back on its hook, turned to his friend, and looked him in the eyes to say, *"Sounds like those fire boys, those Greek fire boys are on their way to Chicago now. They'll be here by morning if they drive like I think they will. We made it in 37 hours including our stayover, they'll do it in less time if they drive through the night and don't stop for anything but gasoline and food.*

"They won't stop for much other than fuel, but they will have to stop for that, so we'll need to see if we can head them off along the way; maybe catch them and hold them up at Rockford's ranch until we can make an official arrest." He said, smiling allowing his cigarette to bounce off his lower lip. Posh motioned with his wrist, with the back of his hand, for Ferguson to take a seat. He had something else to tell him.

"Delilah Eli told me something else; maybe she trusted me or maybe she knew who we were. One night after the opening show, maybe the third night, she came up to me in the red tent, the one they used to change clothes and gear. She mentioned that Buster's name was Aldo Restani and that he'd been on the lam for a while from both the law and the gangsters he'd double-crossed

back East." Posh stated, thinking about it for a minute before continuing.

"To her I guess, Chicago is back East, not up North. Delilah, if you remember, is from the deep South, somewhere by the bayou, either Mississippi or maybe Alabama; her twang was hard to pin down, but I could tell from what she said about alligators that she'd skinned a few. She talked about the tougher side of Gino; having been with the man for quite a while. Gino wasn't like his brother; he wasn't an angel by any means, but he wasn't a killer either. They weren't lovers, they were confidantes.

"She told me there was a hoodlum named Jimmy...Jimmy something, I don't remember if she told me his last name. What I do remember is this Jimmy wanted a man called Dom 'Knuckles' Masciulli dead; so he could move up in the Italian organization. Jimmy was the one to put Buster in line to make investors pay their last dollar to the circuses; they're nomadic by design. Investors, audiences, and even the concessions were calculated. Money was washing through there from all sides; legally and illegally. I doubt anyone in that world bothers to pay a penny's tax on whatever it is they make."

Nick had to pause and take another look at his watch to calculate the possibilities being played out at that exact moment somewhere between the mesas and vistas of the Southwest, and the thick heavy panhandle of Texas. When he did the calculations in his head he saw diagrams, figures, numbers, and the way they danced around one another until they made the sense he needed them to make.

"Delilah also mentioned that Buster would one day put Gino in charge of The Bollen Group after buying it for pennies on the dollar from a man Jimmy...it has to be the same man. When Jimmy let the cat out of the bag about needing Dom out of the way, Buster took that to mean that if both Jimmy and Dom were dead he'd have a better shot at the top. He wouldn't have to pay Jimmy what he owed.

"It happened; they took their last, but when Capone's boys found out how it happened and why it happened, it all but threw Restani to the wolves; meaning toward Moran. Moran's outfit used him for a while, but with a last name like Restani, no good Irishman could fully put his trust in the man; you can understand being a Ferguson, right? No red-blooded Italian is gonna trust an Irishman, especially an Irish cop; not in that world. You'd be dead if you didn't play ball. Nick postured.

"No one gets to the level of an Aldo 'Buster' Restani, or for that matter of a Jimmy or a Dom Masciulli without first having lined their pockets with a few cops of their own; those willing to turn their heads when asked or when paid to do so. Jimmy and Dom were made men in the Capone faction; Moran's gang knew them well. Moran had a cop or two on his payroll; Ian Kilpatrick and his brother-in-law Jameson Finley were two of them..." Nick continued to think, to force his mind to muster what it could on the matter in the most precise manner possible; they had very little time to do what needed to be done – and not much intel to go on.

Ralph picked up the conversation. *"Both of those cops, those men had put in their applications for a Stateville position where they could be used to no end by the mobsters, but no one on the force could ever prove their intimate connections; no one willing to talk anyway. If twenty bucks will get you five extra minutes in a joint, a couple of hundred would buy a lot more time than that.*

Nick thought for a minute in silence and then spoke, *"Both Masciulli and whoever the Jimmy guy is, were killed in the Greek Delta; where Drakos' mother owns a small bar with a side grill for a few things. Drakos and Baros were eating there that night when Restani showed up with his plan. Drakos had just kissed his mother goodbye when the fury started back. That's what Delilah was saying, but I didn't know she was talking about the fire boys. I didn't know their names.*

"I'm spit-ballin' now. Three on two is not exactly fair, but it's the gang world, so almost anything goes. Drakos and Baros could say they were threatened in the restaurant and Buster came to assist. There is no loyalty among thugs, we know that, but Capone's people do it by the book; their book anyway. Say what you want to say about the man, but he was organized and in many ways, he had a code he stuck to." He pointedly told Ralph.

Ralph picked up right where his good friend and partner had left off. *" I remember the killings quite well; it was all over the papers. The bodies were found in the grease tank out back of the place. Someone set it on fire after killing them and the fire erupted, spreading quickly to the bar. The thing went up instantly, killing everyone in the damn restaurant; there were eleven souls murdered that night, including the owner.*

"It had to be Restani. He set the fire to cover up the single gunshot wounds to each of their heads. You don't dump bodies into a dumpster of grease alive, now do you? The authorities didn't realize the men were

missing until they found them floating to the top of that thing a day or so later." Ralph grimaced at the thought of seeing the bodies; of having to come across a sight like that.

"If Rockford hasn't done so yet, he may want to set up a similar experiment at his place to see the effects grease or petrol-based fires could have on a freshly obtained corpse. Maybe we could bring him Restani and see if he'll volunteer for the job." Nick questioned. *"You don't dump dead or live bodies in grease if you don't expect to light it up. Restani murdered his own man's mother! You know Drakos wants Buster's head on a pike, maybe he figured out what we figured out. He'll drive to Hell to pick him off."* Nick stated.

Ferguson, recalled the incident at the tents when he had assisted Baros and Drakos by pointing out a covey of outsiders making their way through the sideshow tents in search of something or someone; it made more sense the longer he thought about it,

"Those other boys, they looked familiar to me Nick. The one did anyway. Those had to be the same men we put down in Gallup at the bar; do you remember anything about any of them? Size, color, maybe some tattoos, anything?" He asked.

"They must have been tailing the sideshow to find Baros and Drakos; maybe others too, but they had to be from Chicagoland on a mission. We stumbled onto them, set them back a few days behind bars for disturbing the peace only until they found the tents and pushed their way through to find the Greeks; who they must have been hoping would lead them straight to Buster." Ralph said, thinking longer and deeper about it still.

Mesa

"They didn't want anyone dead that night; they needed us alive. Those thick-jawed asses had a plan. That's why the bullets missed us. They wanted us to take them to Restani; all of them did. All I did was put those fire eaters with their new accomplices, some of Moran's gang I'd bet...yeah, I'd bet my hat on it." Ralph said.

Both men thought about it a little longer. The Chicago cop responded with no little bit of sarcasm in his voice. *"You make a compelling argument, my friend. Perhaps we can turn our heads a while and maybe take a leisurely stroll down Lake Shore Drive, maybe spill a couple of coins at the slot machines on Navy Pier over the next day or so. We don't need to protect this man from anyone; let the trash take itself out for once."*

He laughed, knowing all the while the seriousness of the situation warranted a steady mind and his best efforts to keep and uphold the oath they had both taken regarding the protection of the innocent. *"Do you know where he might be; I mean specifically? I don't want to chase the wind here; we need to get some help maybe before heading out in the wrong direction. We won't get two shots at this guy."* Ralph implicated; knowing he was all but preaching to the choir.

"Most doctors have doctors who take care of them when they're sick. Most lawyers have other lawyers to take up the battle for them in court since as they say 'a man who represents himself has a fool for a client'. I'd bet Restani has a lawyer too. Why wouldn't he? He's smart enough to know he's gonna need one. He's been in and out of the system too long not to have one in his pocket just waiting to pull out and keep himself company.

Jude Stringfellow

"I bet his first call when he felt trapped was to his lawyer and he told him exactly where he'd be and maybe exactly what all he had done so there could be a plan to escape somewhere fast enough and maybe under the cover of night so when the whole thing comes down around him he'll be off on some island beachfront down past the Florida keys where the cops can't reach him and even if they did they couldn't bring him back." Nick declared.

"This isn't the end of it anyhow, no way, I'm not letting that man step foot on some getaway train where he can take his show on the road in another jurisdiction. His road stops right here!" Ralph stated boldly. Whether he was casting words to the air, or sizing them up to make some sort of plan, Ferguson found it easier to talk through his thoughts so they'd be right in front of his eyes and he could read them to himself if he needed to. The air seemed thick with anticipation, and he felt every inch of it compressing in around him while he thought.

As the skirts of the later hours of dusk began to dance, bringing the evening to an end, time forced herself into a semi-fresh twilight. Admittedly, the men knew their window of opportunity was about to close, and it was about to close permanently. For some reason, the name Zachary Visser crept into Nick's mind when the word lawyer was said out loud. It was something Amos Hartman mentioned, but he saw the name in writing; where was that, he wondered.

Perhaps it was something else Deliliah had told him, something else she merely stated as if it was everyday knowledge or something understood. They had carried on several small intimate conversations between acts while the shows were in progress, and oftentimes in the mess tent when everyone took their meals. She mentioned the circus had an insurance policy that could be offered to the community in case someone or something caused damage to the persons or property; something beyond their control, something akin to an accident.

Zachary Visser, a junior partner of the Las Vegas firm of DeYoung, Patullo, and Visser. Arthur Patullo! There it was again; the name meant something after all. The first man's name and number were written in magenta lipstick liner on the side of the makeup tent outside Delilah's vanity booth where she changed and applied her cosmetics. *"It's gotta be him, Ralph. It has to be Patullo. He'd know where to find Restani, but we can't just ask him. Maybe we can get someone in the area to place a call to his office, it's a couple of hours behind us; they haven't shuttered for the day yet. It could work."*

Nick pondered for a moment, knowing he couldn't reach Delilah to ask her about Visser or his partner Arthur Patullo, but he could look them up in the book. Posh had another thought as well, he hoped he could reach Maudine at Carson City to convince her to pretend to be a trapeze artist over the telephone, to call Visser or Patullo. She could tell them she was seeking part-time or temporary employment until she could find another gig to join. She'd tell them about the woes Buster had caused her and the troupe, maybe get some intel of where he may be so she could ask him for a short-term loan. He knew he could count on her to be sensually persuasive and he knew she'd take the bait; he knew she'd give it her best efforts if it meant being free from Restani for the rest of her life.

"I'll make those calls Ralph. I'll set that in motion. I have an idea I know a certain horsewoman who may

know exactly where Restani would be. Dickerson will do what he can, and maybe if we're lucky our ol' cowboy-turned-writer friend of ours can head the Greeks off at the pass.

There are only a few good places to gas up between Gallup and Albuquerque – we know that for sure. You get your command on the phone from your room, and we'll see what we can do to hole up Buster Restani either for his protection or so we can have the first swing at him." Nick said. *"If we can't arrest him outright we'll have to take him under custody somehow before anyone else does.*

"He may hold more information that we can use to send on to Dickerson and Fauer about the money laundering he's been able to muster through the circus routine. He'll maybe rat on whomever else is in the troupe that may have known more or what they should have caught on to; we know Alvarez knew more than most." Posh finished.

"It sounds like a plan to me brother, it sounds like a damned good plan," Ralph stated, his expression growing more serious with each passing second. *"We need to approach this thing carefully Nick. There's no telling what kind of dangerous game these guys are willing to play, or who else might get caught up in their nets."*

It was clear that things were changing rather rapidly, and nobody wanted to be left holding the bag on this one. Being one step ahead was imperative; being three or four steps ahead was on the menu. Even if they had to pull an all-nighter, Posh felt that using every man and every tool in his bag of tricks would prove to be their only hope if they wanted to catch Buster at his own game.

Mesa

A sense of dread seemed to settle in among the gambling crowd out west over the abrupt disappearance of Buster Restani, the man who had until very recently been considered untouchable in Vegas. A man they all believed to be one of their own was now quite obviously leading a double life as both a crime boss in Vegas where he was definitely on the fast track to making an infamous name for himself and what he seemed to be now; a double-crossing independent whose greed and troubled mind was destined to get the man killed. The only question was, who would be caught up in the wake of his deceit and dark violent chaotic behavior?

With his sudden absence leaving a gaping hole in the tapestry of the criminal underworld, rival factions were already beginning to circle like vultures, waiting for the perfect opportunity to strike. It hadn't taken more than a few hours after the sale of The Bollen Group before every corner of the small thriving town saw the likes of gunslingers lurking in every possible dark corner, their fingers hovering nervously above trigger guards as they waited for their chance to even the playing field for themselves. Someone would have to take Buster's slot; every man believed he deserved the chance to do so.

Old scores were tallied up, and new alliances were made within minutes of another shoot-out on Freemont Street; several had occurred during the day and would continue to do so into the night. It was a volatile mix to be sure; primed to explode at any given moment. If he lived through the night in Chicago, it would be a miracle; but it was a damned sure fact that Buster Restani would never see another sunset over the Sierra Mountains again. That much was certain. They couldn't let this thing go to court; they'd seen it too often in the past.

Every time a man like Capone was brought to trial for crimes accredited to himself, the courts were forced to withdraw their efforts for lack of evidence. It was amazing how many family emergencies forced prospective witnesses to recant their stories; grandmothers in foreign countries seemed to drop off like flies – jurors couldn't be persuaded to show up; not if they were going to be seen by these mobsters in open court, their faces on display along with their names, addresses, and other personal information about themselves being put into public records.

"We can't change the facts that just because the laws are written saying he's innocent until he's proven guilty don't mean he can't come after one of these men or women on the jury who stood brave and defiant in the matter." Said one of the bailiffs when asked why the jury pool had dwindled to only three from a required twelve-person panel. *"Even picking the jury, took too long."* The bailiff was reported to have stated.

The papers ran the stories for days when it happened, too. People who were called chose not to show up, preferring to pay the fine for not doing their civic duty. It could have been a real money maker if the courts played their cards right. They could make the announcement that a dozen or more thugs were being tried and prepped, asking hundreds of jurors to show or pay a ten-dollar fine for abandonment. The thought of it hit hard with Posh who told himself if even one dirty judge in the state had decided to implement such a plan he could retire in a month on the amount of money the people would eagerly give up on their behalf. No jury; no trial. Simple facts.

Mesa

TWENTY-SIX

The next conversation Nick had with Chief Montgomery was a mixed bag of solemn respect for a man who had put in his retirement papers after over forty-five years of service to the city of Edinburgh and Scotland, as well as Britain on the whole of it.

Starting the chat with a few bantering jabs intended to needle Posh over his choice to leave such a splendid city as Edinburgh, Scotland to take up his mantle in such a dusty, heated place like Oklahoma City, where neither a castle could be found nor his choice of not one or two, but several volcanic mountainsides to climb to his heart's desire.

With only a few returning quips, Posh knew the air on both sides of the ocean was heavier for them both; it wasn't easy choosing to stop the one thing that kept you going for so long. It wouldn't be easy for either of them since the one thing they had in common was upholding everything the laws stood for.

"I'll give you a big story to take home with you tonight Monty. I'll tell it to you just as it was unfolding, and how it was told me to; that way you'll be right here with us when I call you back later and tell you how it ends." Said Posh. *"Are you ready?"* he asked, almost laughing himself silly from what he was about to say.

Monty listened intently as usual, as Nick filled him in on the latest developments in the combined cases he and Ralph Ferguson were working on. By hook and by crook, the two cases blended almost as independently and as intertwined as the circus group had mixed with the sideshow freaks.

One couldn't stand alone without the other, but together they couldn't really make ends meet and everything seemed to come undone at the seams before it imploded, or maybe it imploded and then fell apart. It would depend heavily on who did the telling of the tale.

"The Greek boys, the fire eaters, were first to fly off the handle when it all hit the proverbial fan. You can't not pay a man for weeks on end, then tell that man he's got another two weeks of work and more to come only to snatch it out from under him hours before he readies himself to perform two shows a day; it's not done in the corporate world and it's not done in this grassroots world they got goin' on either." Nick said.

Posh went on to tell Monty how the fire eaters were on their way to Chicago, driving whatever they had; one witness saw them changing cars in town to take a Ford with better tires. This would make a lot of sense considering the distance they'd need to cover to reach Chicago from Lake Mead, a few minutes outside of Las Vegas.

What these hellbent boys didn't realize is that Dickerson, Fauer, Posh, Ferguson, Rockford, and others in the know had been putting the pieces of the two cases together from the day they met with Posh and Ralph at the Rockford Ranch.

There had been three murders, now four at least, in Chicago, and another two men just outside of Chicagoland who had all been silent or quiet investors. Each man had from about the day up to a week before their deaths, drawn large sums of money out of their bank accounts to give to

Mesa

The Bollen Group accountants and advisors; both with Greek names. You don't walk the streets of the Greek Delta without being one of them; not if you want to live long enough to order your next meal anyway.

They had it in for Buster alright, Nick told Monty, but they didn't know if he'd be waiting for them with open arms or if they'd have to kill him to get what they needed to get out of him. Killing Buster for Capone's boys would be a feather in their cap for sure, but it could just as easily put a target on their backs if Moran's outfit figured it was them who had killed their snitch; their informant. Then again, if Buster had two-timed Moran just as he had two-timed the sideshow and the circus; the Greeks could be given a ticker-tape parade for their actions from either side. It was a toss-up! No one knew what to expect.

Baros and Drakos were especially in the dark about what was happening. They had just about cleared the state line leaving Nevada before being intercepted on Route 66 by a festival of insults when right there in front of their new Ford, they witnessed a spectacle any man would have shaken his head at if he had seen it!

An opened-top car pulled right in front of them on the Route, taking them from behind when the car turned around and gave chase. Inside the car were no less than six costumed clowns! Top to tail, head to toe, painted up, gussied up, wearing the best outfits either of the two men had seen; it was nothing like the budget-ridden costumes everyone from The Bollen Group was apt to wear. These boys were riding in style!

When the clowns leaned over the seats to wave the Greeks over to the side of the road, both men chatted eagerly to themselves saying these clowns must be with another traveling circus and they'd either have recognized the Greeks for who they were, or it was one helluva coincidence, that's for sure. Nick paused for dramatic effect to see if Nicholas Montgomery was keeping up.

"Monty, the rouse was too strong! The Greeks had been conditioned for several months to dress as clowns to enter towns and make themselves as comfortable as they could by meeting folks, chatting them up, getting information from them so they could walk into fully loaded banks, and taking them by storm without being caught.

" The clowns in the open car were none other than one of Dickerson's best, Dennis Rockford, or you may know him as Justin Zane, and four of his ranch hands! Of course, they had the best outfits money could buy - - Rockford paid for it all. He loved the show. He's like that; He does things so much bigger than anyone I've ever seen!" Nick continued.

"Rockford's boys, two of them anyway, took the Ford and drove it back to the ranch in Amarillo, while the rest squeezed the Greeks into their car as best they could. Once the fire eaters were safely detained, everyone got themselves back onto Route 66 and headed to the Ranch; where I'm all but sure Rockford is going to hole them up on the part of the ranch that hosts the biggest body research farm you've never heard about.

"I think we mentioned it last time we talked, but you were doing something or the other, and Eoghan said he'd fill you in if he could get his head around it," Posh stated. Waiting on Monty's response he braced himself for what he knew would be a very important life lesson, but he wasn't sure if he wanted to hear it; Posh couldn't have planned the take better if he had as much time as he

needed. Six or seven heads were proving to be better than just one or two in this crazy case.

"*Well,*" Monty started, replying with a delayed chuckle, "*I guess I'd have to ask myself what could go wrong with a plan like that. You say they're detaining the Greeks until Ralph or someone with jurisdiction to convict them for the Chicago murders can come to the ranch to pick them up and make arrangements for them to be carted off back that way.*" He thought for a minute, "*...what about the ranch itself? I have to assume there's been some sort of OK or vetting going on with a place like that; I wouldn't want an open field of dead bodies being accessible to anyone, that's for sure.*

"*You say the man owns the ranch, and it's guarded I suppose, still – decomposing bodies? The whole thought of it just goes through me. On one level we do need to know how nature works against us, and there's something good-natured about it being so organic too.*

"*I think I read a passage once in a medical paper once that gave me pause; it was about not being cremated or embalmed as it did something to mark or lessen the natural way of things; you know, dust to dust, and all that. I think once a man is dead he may need to be disposed of so he doesn't get others sick from whatever disease his abandoned shell leaves behind.*" Monty so elegantly put it.

"*Who knows what those cops can do to the Greeks out there and no one would be the wiser.*" He said. "*I'm not for vigilante law you know, and I've heard a tale or two from you about the way things are handled in the States. Texas is what they say, a whole other country.*

Jude Stringfellow

Could you guarantee that the Greeks were the ones who killed the men in Chicago?

"Shouldn't a court rule on that and not the people on the ranch? I'm just saying you don't want to be too deep in this if it goes South and you find yourself crawling out a hole too deep to get out of." Monty warned. There was a note of concern lingering in his voice; he thought of Nick like he would his son had he lived to be Nick's age.

When Monty thought about it, he decided to allow Nick another freedom that he knew he wanted to share; he knew because Eoghan couldn't bring himself to explain the body ranch quite the way Monty had imagined it would be. *"Go ahead, Nick. I'll grab another tea and you spill your guts on this ranch thing; tell me everything about it...and did you see what I did there Posh? I used a pun...I told you to spill your guts."* He laughed.

Monty wasn't always a funny man, but when needed humor, he found it. Nick had to take a good deep breath before he described what could only be the most profoundly interesting, and ghastly horrifying phenomenon he had ever witnessed. Somehow talking about it made some of the grizzlier edges dissipate, making his breathing a little easier to handle.

"There are more than a hundred bodies there, Monty. There are more than a hundred men, women, and sadly even a few children who no one had claimed. They were orphans. A special agreement was made regarding the children, in that they would remain dressed at all times, and not one of them would be subjected to any animal contact or chemical contact; you can see why that rule was firmly set in place."

From that point, Nick began describing how a body lying in the sun in the spring was not the same as a body

Mesa

lying in the sun during the summer or the winter. Although he realized he was speaking the obvious, it made sense to start the story off with the understanding that his likely comparisons would ring true to a few cases either he and Monty had worked together in Scotland, or maybe something he knew his good friend would have a recollection of from the past.

"A body in the sun begins to deteriorate at an alarming rate. Its once firm flesh would turn soft and pliant, giving way to touch; something like warm dough being set out to rise. The stench would soon follow, not more than a few days after a body drew its last breath. The putrid smell would be heavy in the air for several feet all around the body, reaching heights of over fifteen feet above it, and about fifty to sixty feet in any direction around it. Temperatures get well over a hundred degrees where I live in Oklahoma; out in the desert, it can reach one hundred and thirty! That's fifty-four degrees in your world.

The ground beneath the body would start to absorb liquids as the corpse released them like some kind of putrid soup, using gravity to assist. The potent acidity and bitterness could make a live man's eyes water while being ever so attractive to insects. Because the bodies go through such various stages of decomposition the study of them became all the more fascinating; details of each were recorded for both medical purposes and simply to satisfy the insatiable curiosity that everyone must admit to having about such matters." Nick continued.

"Insects finding the body would come in a very unique and specific order as well. First, the blowfly, with her curiosity, seeking some refuge for a place to lay her

eggs while feasting on the corpse; a smorgasbord for sure. After a few days of bloating the gas inside of the body would give way, literally exploding leaving the damped skin to succumb to the heat of the next few days and weeks.

"Over time it would harden like leather, drawing in on itself to the point that nearly every ounce of fat or tissue would cling tightly to each bone; causing features of the face to lose any capability from which to be recognized. At this point, a man or woman could only be positively identified by their dental records; if they had been to a dentist while they were alive, that is."

Listening to himself describe the grizzled tales and details of both death and decay created an unexpected emotion of remorse somehow; Nick couldn't put a pin to it, but he felt somehow connected to the information he was relaying to his friend and fellow lawman. Nature had a particular way of dealing with itself; it seemed inevitable, and yet unwelcomed.

He imagined the scene on the ranch vividly while describing it; almost as if he was standing beside a suspended corpse whose flesh had been exposed to the past several seasons there in West Texas, knowing the limits and causation of whatever happened to it would have drastic differences had the same body been hanging off the shores of Niagara Falls or in South Florida with such high levels of humidity.

He imagined the bones cracking after time beneath the weight of desiccated muscle and skin; yet despite the terror and horror of all inherent in such an image, there was also an underlying beauty to it; nearly symphonic in its course. Life as well as death keeps its pace with time. Reducing the details briefly as they did when they reported such circumstances, now seemed trite. "*We don't do it justice Monty,*" Posh said.

"*We just write that he was decapitated or that she was shot in the chest. We see them, and we know the truth when we do, but we glaze over the evidence to be as brief and precise as we can be. But when I think about it from this point forward, I'll ask myself if what I think happened to the body happened or if time, weather, elements, or some animal coming into the mix could have masked the real event somehow.*" Posh explained.

"*I can tell you're enjoying yourself Posh. This sort of thing would play well for those medical geniuses who are writing books about such science these days. I think you're right about Justin Zane. He's been writing really interesting books and now I know why or how it is that he can speak so confidently about the matters. I've seen a lot of dead people in my day, Posh. I'd never want to think about putting a number to it; but then again, most of the ones I've seen have been at the business end of a crime being committed.*" His said.

"*The worst I think either of us has ever seen took place, what about almost two years ago now, out here in Fife. We had the case with the bodies that were fileted and the meat and bones then fed to pigs. You can't get worse than that I don't imagine, but let me just now tell you, that if you can look me in the eye and tell me you saw something more macabre or grotesque than that, then you shut your trap on that one!*" Monty laughed. "*Fifty-four? Are you sure? That seems incredibly hot; reminds me of the books I've read about the horn of Africa.*"

"*I don't want to think about it. I don't want...*" his words trailing off, before saying, "*I think I'll let you and

Ralph talk about it, Nick. I think it's enough for me to know that you'll make sure those police officers out that way don't make up their own rules; you'll see to it that the Greeks get their day in court, and if that means they get a bullet or a jolt from Old Sparky, that's on them as well. Just maybe do me a favor, and let justice be served." He added.

It took Nick a minute of silence before he realized that Monty may have begged off hearing the details relating to the rest of the bodies at the Rockford Ranch because his dear wife of so many years had only been buried less than a few months; everything about life changes when something like that happens.

Nick postured himself, sitting straighter before speaking. *"Monty, I'm sure glad you're in my life man, I can tell you that right now. Since I lost my father, you have been the one man I feel closest to when I need real advice. I kid around with Ralph, Eoghan, and the rest of them. They're all around my age, maybe some younger, maybe some older here and there, but you are the man I look to for that sound and rock-solid advice when I need to know I'm getting the truth."* Nick paused.

"If I've said something, or hurt you..." he stopped. Another few moments of quietness echoed over the line; their parting words so much sweeter than the ones they started their call with; they both knew why.

Mesa

TWENTY-SEVEN

Maudine knew she had been forced into the recent decisions she had made regarding crawling out of the trouble she had caused herself; over the sheer chaos of running with trouble in the first place. Placing the call to Officer Dickerson not only made the most sense from a self-preservation point of view, but it made more sense than living the rest of her life in fear of having to look over her shoulder to see if Buster Restani or one of his cronies was creeping up behind her leveling the barrel of a gun at her face or more likely, to the back of her head.

The anxious woman took a deep breath, steeling herself before making the next call. She knew she had backed herself into a corner, and calling Cedric Fauer was the only truly logical choice. She trusted him; they had a connection. It may have only been for a moment, but there was something in that moment and she was banking on it now. She had kept up her end of the bargain; twice.

Still, the thought of facing more consequences for her actions sent a shock up her spine. She imagined Buster's cold stare, the feel of his meaty hands wrapping themselves around her throat. She tried to put him out of her mind for good; she knew he was gone. It didn't matter if she knew he was more than a thousand miles from her; she needed to feel safe, and her new friendship with Cedric Fauer put her mind at ease.

Jude Stringfellow

With trembling fingers she dialed the first number, listening to the rattle of the phone as it spun back into place to dial the next. She prayed that somehow things would work out – they had to. He'd help her she hoped. He would help her realize that she hadn't gone so far left that she could never return. Not everyone who wanders is lost, she told herself. Some of them are looking for themselves when they venture to the other side of what most people would consider to be civilized.

The mesa was her home now. The towering sandstone formations of rock kept her balanced; she felt a connection to the rugged landscape. Every day Maudine's eyes, ears, and nose were filled with the essence of this reality. Streams of water rushed through the rocks with purpose while birds of prey lived nearby; she saw them take flight from less than a hundred yards away.

When he arrived at the cabin, Cedric Fauer listened to the hardness of her words, how she recounted every detail of what happened to and between the two of them, he understood Restani's role in her life was over; she would never be bothered by him again. It was clear that she had been caught up in the web of deceit and manipulation, only to be trapped further because of circumstances that spun out of her control. A spark of resilience and determination resounded through her confessions; he held her allowing the words to flow without end. She needed the release.

After they'd finished a home-cooked evening meal, a little wine was shared without restrictions of duty or professional expectations. Maudine opened up about another subject; a topic that meant the world to her. It was the reason she woke up every morning before the sun, and why she never bothered to keep a clock of any kind in her house. There was enough time in one day to do a day's work, she told herself. One can only do that much; one can never do more.

At the end of the day, every day, she rested. Her horses saw the most of her most of the days. She wasn't one to dress in fancy clothes, adorn makeup, or wear silly fashions to impress. She worked with horses; there wasn't time in the day for being fancy or frivolous. She would never be anything she wasn't, but she knew she would always be a strong woman with strong needs and even stronger desires.

The following morning the two of them rode through the canyon along ancient trails and barren plains. The wind often whipped through Maudine's auburn locks as she sat astride the robust sorrel stallion she called "*Reno*". There was something about him that stood out to her among the Mustangs roaming the narrow ridge near her home. Neither of them mentioned Restani or her past.

Maudine felt a kinship with the horses understanding their life struggles and small triumphs throughout each surviving day. It was in small moments when progress with the herd through Reno was made. Like anything worth doing, this too would take time; a lot of time.

Explaining her work to Cedric made her feel useful again, wanted even. It made her feel as if there was something she could do that not many had a heart or stomach for. Most people considered the herds of the canyons to be a bothersome nuisance when they grazed on lands others hoped to use for cattle or flocks of sheep a little further up the way. Maudine's explanation to Cedric hit directly where and how she had hoped.

Jude Stringfellow

"They were here first, Cedric. The Mustang; they were here before any of us were. They came sometime in the fifteenth or sixteenth Century and they haven't needed or wanted to fight for their existence up until now. Our own government is trying what it can to drive the herds out of the flats and into the Sierras where some will survive, but they're not burros or goats; they need to run on lengths of long flat plains. They need freedom to be what they are; perhaps one of the only wild things left in this forsaken part of the land that no one needs anyway. They should be left alone!" she told him.

"The Mustang isn't like domesticated horses Cedric. They don't look the same, they don't act the same. They don't think the same." She started, *"...you don't tell a Mustang what you're going to do, or what you think he should do for you. You ask. You wait for a response, and you never disrespect his answer.*

"If he thinks your way might be a good way or that it could help him or his herd in some way, he'll tolerate it. You may not get him to do exactly what you want – he's still free. He's not a puppy or even one of those circus mounts you saw down in Vegas. Those horses are mostly from France or French origin; very smart for sure, but they do exactly what they are conditioned to do. You can't condition a Mustang – you negotiate."

The isolated breed of horse that is the American Mustang is as openly free and wild as the land they share between themselves. With origins dating back several hundreds of years to the Spanish invaders and possibly before that, many of the hooved beasts were orphaned; some escaped, while others were purposely dumped in the expanse when people could not or would not care for them.

Mesa

The hardy strong animals could be found roaming the reaches of the western states; rumors were that there were scattered herds throughout the United States, even some living off small islands on the Atlantic coast. Known for their incredible mannerisms, stamina, and agility, Mustangs maintain a unique blend of intelligence, strength, grace, and determination like no other breed. Maudine knew this to be true; it was apparent from the very first glance on the very first day she saw her first Mustang. She was such a small child at that time.

Her words brought her solace and clarity; her mind relaxed and became capable of deep thought when she worked with Reno and the few mares he allowed to come close enough to her to be touched. Cedric questioned her about the small herd of stallions she had trained as some of the best watchdogs he had ever witnessed in his life; he was simply fascinated by how they came to her aid the second she sent out the signal.

"*Oh that...*" she said, laughing under her breath. "*They aren't part of Reno's bunch, that's for sure. It's a lot like the circus and the sideshow gig. Reno's herd is just that, his. He's the master of it. He calls the shots, and he tells me and them when it's time to come together. He even calculates how long we'll spend in each other's company before he eases them back down the ridge. The boys, well, that's another story.*" She laughed.

"*I found them struggling as yearlings about a year back. They're all quite young, and in some cases, the ones I know about anyway, they were dumped out here when a family out in Jessup County couldn't take the horses with them when they moved back East, and they just set them free. The family let me know so I'd keep a watchful eye on the herd, but they ain't Mustangs. The mares among them may end up joining Reno, but the stallions, like a lot of males in the human world, spend too much time bullying and challenging one another to catch the attention of a good mare. They've become separated because of it, and they had no one to lead them."* She mentioned, taking a little bow. *"That's where I come into the picture. I trained them to watch me too."*

When Cedric thought about it, he knew the animals on the ridge seemed smaller and more densely built. They were compact really; not more than fourteen hands or so. The horses he could see from the edge of the butte overlooking the mesa below were mostly the same colors; sorrel or brighter red than chestnut.

A great deal of them bore striking tri-color coats, like the Indian-painted horses he had seen in magazines; but had never seen one so close or in person. Their manes, upon examining Reno and the mares who dared to step close enough to view, were doubled in thickness, falling both to the right side of the horse's neck as well as to the left. He noticed they bore *"feathers"* just above their heels; heels so hardened and so thick, they made such thunderous noise when freely sprinting across the plains.

Maudine knew she'd never live among the folks she had spent so many years with; she was not a city dweller. She wouldn't be heading back into a world of civility any time soon, but those thoughts never bothered her. If anyone could live alone and live a sustainable life, it would be Maudine Faye Cooke. Instead of planning to spend another night under the stars, which she often did, she decided to take a chance and ask Cedric if he had to be back in town any time soon; she hoped he would tell her he could stay.

Mesa

Cedric walked along the rocky clay drive of the small house Maudine had somehow set up; the place she called home. He couldn't help but feel a sense of isolation even when he was with someone. Being alone wasn't the same as being lonely, he knew that, but he had had just about enough of both. Maudine was a loner, he knew this, but he also knew that she didn't mind his company. He certainly didn't mind hers.

He sometimes missed the camaraderie of fellow officers at the close of the day. Having no one to share his evenings with he often sat beside the fat black stove pipe in the sitting room reading the latest papers he could find in town; reading, eating, and just being alone. Not giving the woman an answer would never do; choosing not to say anything was confirmation enough. Whatever it may turn out to be, Cedric knew one thing for sure; he was tired of walking into an empty house alone.

Jude Stringfellow

TWENTY-EIGHT

As long as there were men like Aldo Restani running around in this world, men like Nick Posh, Ralph Ferguson, Eoghan MacRae, and Chief Montgomery would be there to stomp them out when they got the chance to do so. The Jeff Dickersons, Dennis Rockfords, and Cedric Fauers of the same world would join the other good guys to bring due process and the compliance of law to the forefront of every criminal's mind, and to the minds of every citizen they were charged with protecting. As long as men and women were hell-bent on causing destruction there had to be people willing to sacrifice to mete out justice wherever and however they could.

When they put their minds to do what they knew must be done, they knew they had a very short window of time before Buster Restani made his way to the Union train station before making his getaway a permanent resolution to the wake of devastating and destruction the man had left behind in Chi-town. Years of his felonious behavior had come to a point, a climatic one indeed, where it seemed no one was safe to call the Windy City their home.

Putting out his hand to open the door of the suite they both occupied, Posh realized the operation of taking on Restani would only get one shot at taking Restani alive. They needed him to testify if possible in the case against the deceased Titus Rushby; what Restani knew about the murders of Asta Pate and Dorothy Eischer wouldn't shave a day off his multiple life sentences, but Posh was sure he could talk the authorities at the District Attorney's office to give the man life in prison without the possibility of parole. Life with three meals a day and his cell might be enough to use as a good chip to coax the piece of filth into telling the truth if it was the only time in his life he ever did so.

"Ralph, we can't go up Washington Street and not be seen by someone. We can't be seen or we'll not breach the archway to the office building Maudine said Buster was likely to be holed up in when he needed to think. She said it was the Reliance Building; do you know it?" he asked his friend, a man who knew every inch of the City of Chicago no matter what address spit out at him; Ralph Ferguson knew the place.

The first and basement floors of the Reliance Building had been completed in 1895, just a couple of years after Ralph was born. It stood tall and erect in open defiance of gravity as one of the first skyscrapers of modern times. The building boasted plate glass windows making up the majority of the whole building; a rarity on its own. The lower-level windows opened outward, one of the first of its kind giving a sense of safety to its occupants; thus allowing them to let in the air without fear of accidental falls.

"We'll dress in dark clothes Ralph, head to toe. It's warm enough we don't need any overcoats, nothing to get in our way. Pants, shirt, shoes, a cap if you've got it. I think my Fedora is dark enough, but I'll leave it here. I don't need to draw attention to myself with it being out of sync with the rest of what I'll be wearing." He said. *"I think I can pick up a pair of black brogues cheaply on Washburn, is that where you said the secondhand store was?"*

Ralph picked up the cue quickly enough, adding that smudging a bit of motor oil on their faces, neck, and arms could help conceal them further. *"I can't shoot if I'm wearing gloves, so that's not gonna happen, but at least we can duck in and out of the buildings and around corners or behind the cars if we need to,"* Ralph added. *"We can get the shoes for pennies there; they have quite a few at the Navy Pier surplus as well."*

Several hours passed before they were able to set their plan in motion. Meetings had to be held, dinners had to be eaten. Restani's schedule was nothing if not full. Poking their way through the city just after two o'clock in the morning, Ralph again, knew the route best taken to avoid the occasional passerby who may be coming out of a closing bar or restaurant; the downtown Chicago atmosphere was teeming with activity long into the later hours of the day.

With each cautious step, adrenaline coursed through their veins, heightening the anticipation of what was to come. Despite the late hour, the city buzzed with the hustle and liveliness of a strong and prosperous nightlife. Both men walked on the balls of their feet, lowering themselves to the point of being hidden in plain sight should anyone be of mind to notice.

Inside the older edifice, Restani stood alone in the middle of his third-floor office, he had given strict orders to the two men he'd hired to keep watch not to allow anyone past the elevators; no one meant no one. With the pressures of his most recent decisions bearing down on top of him, Restani stood staring blankly at the wood-paneled walls of the office. Walls covered with framed photos of himself mostly shaking hands with politicians, musicians, entertainers, and other mobsters like himself; made men.

The once brilliant vibrant life he knew had faded like the yellowing edges of the photographs behind their glass. He could hear whispering echoes in his mind; voices accusing him of betrayal and treason. His heart raced faster inside himself as he tried to make any sense of it. How did it get to this point, he asked himself, was it the money? Was it power? Wasn't that the point of it all? He asked himself.

Desperately pondering more and more questions, he paced the floor back and forth, feeling trapped like the rat he was; a rat in a maze he had built all around himself with his own two hands. The reality of it shocked him to the core. Suddenly, a knock from behind him sent shivers down his back – whoever it was, they weren't coming for tea; there would be no one showing sympathy for the man; they were coming for blood. They were coming for his life. He knew it.

It was Tuesday, another Tuesday, nothing special about it. Just another typical day in a very motivated city; a city he had somewhat controlled to some degree for a very long time until he began to think outside the box with the Las Vegas boys. He could do both, he told himself. Why not diversify, split things up, and make money on both ends of Route 66 with nothing between his life and the open road?

Two days tops, and he could be on either side if he drove through the night. There was something graceful about the way he was living; he bought into it hook, line, and sinker – and now, like a snagged carp, he knew his days were numbered. The lures too shiny to resist; the net coming up from all sides to take him.

Dressed entirely in black, their movements were fluid and silent, almost catlike. Making their way through the dimly lit corridors of the building; their every step was silenced and meticulously laid. Quietly they moved into place, a sense of impending danger flooded their hearts and minds. Remaining calm would prove difficult of course, but not something either of them had not faced a hundred times before.

As it was when they dressed in motley attire to blend in with the mayhem around them, tonight's attire had a very similar goal; to not be seen for what they were. As the men drew closer to their target, Buster's breath drew inward, quickened slightly with anticipation. He thought he heard someone; he was certain of it. His blood turned hot, racing through each pulsing vein until finally, he drew his last free breath.

Ralph Ferguson had stepped across the office threshold, his right arm extended fully, holding in his hand the .38 revolver he had kept on his side since the first day it was given to him as a punk private during the war. Beside the dark figure of one stood the other, ready for anything Buster Restani had to offer as a means of defense. As his eyes adjusted to the dimness of the moonlit room, Ferguson's heart thumped wildly in his chest. He took a deep breath, steeling himself for what could happen; nothing was guaranteed.

Without a word, the two lawmen entered the space with a confidence that shook the criminal to his core. He was trapped; the only way out was down. Time seemed to stand still as they sized each other up; motionless, wordless until the caged bird started to sing. *"The window is shut boys. Can you give me a minute so I can at least try to escape, maybe I'll just break my leg or something. I'm not too far up, am I? Maybe I can still make the night train out of town."* Buster laughed the sound of it catching in his throat before trailing off. He knew he had no chance.

Ferguson's face was lit by the moonlight striking through the glass of the third-story window. Silence fell again between them; no one spoke, instead they locked gazes each trying to read the other man's intentions and his abilities in what knew would erupt soon enough. Sweat trickled down Ferguson's back pooling at the top of his hip; he wouldn't let his uncomfortable state be known; this wasn't just another job; this was personal.

Buster hadn't tried to guess who it was that had made it past his guards, he only knew someone had made it past them; and needed to know how. Breaking the silence, the man began to unwind enough to move somewhat freely in front of Ferguson and Posh; both men refusing to take their eyes off the scoundrel for even a split second.

"Well, well," Buster snickered under his breath, trying to find the strength to remain standing on his own. *"If it ain't my favorite Irish cop, Ferguson, right?"* he said bitterly, his voice dripping with sarcasm, running his hand through the thick mop of his dark loose curls. *"What do you want with me, Ferguson?"* he asked, *"I thought you were up at Stateville anyway, whiling away the hours for salary and looking for new meat to throw around. You cops like it up that way I understand. You run the place; not like most prisons in the country. How did you boys get to be the masters of that joint, I wonder?"* he said,

continuing to lose his voice under the pressure of realizing he was finished.

"Who are you?" Asked Buster. *"Don't a man gotta right to know whose coming to kill him?"* he asked. Detective Nick Posh stood in the doorway of the office silent, not giving the man an answer. The room fell silent again except for the ticking of a clock on the wall. The incessant sound began to irritate the man.

"You know Maudine, my sweet sweet Maudine; she doesn't even own a clock. She don't even know what time it is during the day or the night. If it rains and the skies are gray she could think it's noon when it's time for supper, that one. I guess she...I mean, she..." he paused, slowly raising his hands before turning around in what appeared to be retreat.

"Alright. You got me. I'm done. Yeah...I'm...done." He managed to spew from his dry lips, leaning into his desk, and placing his hands behind his back. As Sergeant Ralph Ferguson of the Chicago Police took a step forward to better angle himself on his suspect, his muscles tensed in readiness; the sound of Buster's feet shuffling under his substantial size. Posh took out the cuffs he kept in his belt, opening them with one hand, and using his other to steady Restani's wrist. The sound of metal clinking filled the air around them. In one swift movement, he was caught. Posh couldn't help but feel a sense of closure beginning to muster deep within himself. It was done.

Suddenly yet not too surprisingly, Restani's mind pushed for one last effort to escape; stretching to his right the man lunged toward Ferguson. Reaching with his uncuffed hand Buster desperately tried to plow through the lawman in an attempt to snatch the gun from his hands. Everything seemed to happen all at once. Time slowed as everything seemed to stop in one hard second of movement. Nick saw or rather felt the move unfold before him. Without hesitation, his lightning-quick reflexes were set into motion. Pulling his side piece forward, unholstering it, lifting it, and aiming it all seemingly in the same instant, Posh fired his gun. A single shot hit the vile gangster through the right side of his temple; failing the man instantly.

For a long moment, they stood silently, unable to speak. A heavy quiet descended in the room following the sharp crack of Posh's gun, punctuated only by the heavy breathing of the two men standing. Then, slowly Ralph lowered his arms, holstering his weapon on his side and he sighed.

"Guess that's how it ends for him after all. The man went out the way he wanted to go; not being behind bars for the rest of his miserable life thinking about murdering more people, not thinking about how everyone owed him instead of it being the other way around." Ralph said, keeping his eyes open just in case someone in the building wanted to come see the spectacle for themselves.

Nick grimly nodded in agreement, thinking to himself, that giving the man what he wanted was the last thing Nick wanted to do. Shooting the man took less than one second; the memory of doing it would last a lifetime. The angry detective hadn't wanted to let the man off so easily; he wanted to parade the two-timing bastard through the streets to show both sides of the criminal syndicate what can happen when they least expect it.

He knew such a show would be impossible; it was the driving force behind wearing solid dark colors to make their entrance into the office building at that late hour. Covert operations were by definition to be secretive.

The men waited in quiet solitude for the city authorities to relieve them of their posts. They had started the task knowing the killers could be connected, but to be so connected by one man with such an elaborate plan spanning thousands of miles of concrete roads, involving not two, but three mafia syndicates spoke volumes of the narcissism running every crevice and every cell of Aldo Restani's mind.

They called him *"Buster"* because he had managed to bust his way into the underground world of extreme darkness with equally extreme precision. They needed to stop him; they knew they had to finish what they had started. Making their way down the marbled-floor corridor leading to the thick metal handrail of the banister lining the majestic stairway, they felt a sense of relief washing over themselves; it was over. The dangerous game they'd played, the cat and mouse of it all; finished.

The echoes of their footsteps reverberated off the high arched ceiling; its many elegant curves and crevices proudly displaying the majesty of the place; the two men paused halfway down the stairway to take in the fresh air they had been denying themselves. Outside the sounds of sirens wailed, bursting through the Chicago night; wailing in the distance, signaling the arrival of the backup units Ralph had requested several minutes before they made their final approach. Inside, however, silence reigned supreme, broken only by their occasional breath, and the clearing of their throats.

"Let's see if we can clean this mess up and put a win in the column for the good guys, shall we?" Posh

asked his friend. Ralph gave his approval with a nod as well saying, "*Nick, I'll call Dickerson and let him know, and I'll let the main street station have the honor of talking to the press. I don't need the cameras in my face right now; I gotta think about Stella and our baby.*" He stated plainly. "*She's only about a mile and a half from here, staying at her mother's for a while. If you don't mind…well, I'll be heading out that way since we have tomorrow to fill out the paperwork, Buddy.*"

Posh couldn't stop himself from thinking about the expression on young Stella Ferguson's face when she opened the door of her mother's townhouse to see a blacked mug like that of her wandering lawman of a husband; full of himself and enough bravado to take on a dozen Buster Restanis if he had to. "*You go on, Ralph. Just remember to take a good look at the woman so you can tell me in detail what her eyes do when she takes that first look at you!*" Posh laughed.

"*So, maybe this makes us even?*" Ralph laughed. "*I saved your ass about a dozen times and this makes about a dozen times you've saved mine.*" The words seemed to find a chord in the heart of the stoic Native lawman from Oklahoma. Who himself was missing his wife and son more at that moment than in any moment he had ever lived before it. After thinking about it, and putting his spin on the matter, Posh turned to Ralph with open arms. "*Bring it in pal,*" he said. "*…and no, we're not even. You still owe me.*" He said, "*I introduced you to Stella. Don't you ever forget that.*"

TWENTY-NINE

Posh held the phone with his shoulder while striking a match to light a cigarette before breakfast. He hadn't smoked this much in the past twelve years of his life, but the weight of this particular mission had brought the habit back to him in spades. He was triggered by the looseness of the circus people, the edgy rawness of those in the sideshow, and how each person within both factions could exist, live, thrive, and survive one daunting chaotic experience after the other.

Overhearing his wife's voice, the man smiled. *"You got my sweetheart in that office, Eoghan? I can hear her! Put her on the phone will ya?"* he asked excitedly. Nick smiled faintly, hoping against hope to see the woman when he closed his eyes. There was something undeniably charming about the way she spoke; he couldn't pin it down, but every word she said pricked at him in a way no other person on earth had ever been able to touch his soul.

"Aye, no, she's actually helping Monty right now, he's putting up the banners an' streamers for his retirement party later this afternoon. I wish tae God you were here tae see it Posh. She's got the whole place dolled up with colored paper bobbles an' ribbons. Alistair too; your son is making paper balls out of flat colored paper, an' somehow they turn out round enough tae throw into the air an' be caught without opening up. I dinnae ken how he does it, or where he learned that one, but my girls are all over him trying tae get him tae teach them. It's a

competition ya know. Everything they do is a competition; they live an' breathe each other those three. It's not them by themselves, mind youse, no. That dog of yours; he's a terror when the three of them get riled up."

Eoghan MacRae spoke openly and passionately about his country, about the ways and means of it; he told Posh their plans for the next few days coming up after the party, how he and his wife Alice Ann would take Elaine, Alistair, and the girls up to an old area of the Highlands just north of Skye called "*The End of the World*".

Taking the liberty to laugh, he added, "*It's not the real end ya know, if it were we'd all fall off it.*" Joked MacRae. "*That's how youse know the world ain't flat, Posh. If it were the cats would knock us all over the edge of it; gone!*" Even amid commotion and danger that surrounded them at times, moments like these reminded them all of why they did what they did. Law had its own order about it; making things easier to grasp and understand.

Meanwhile, on the other side of the large precinct, Chief Nicholas Montgomery listened attentively, nodding now and again at whatever he thought Eoghan was conveying to his good friend Nick Posh, a man Chief Montgomery held in the greatest of esteem.

"*If I can't have Nick here, tell him I've got his better half anyway. I'd rather look at her than his ugly mug!*" Monty bantered before adding, "*...and tell him I'm not going to the End of the World because I'm afraid I'll stay there. It's quiet, quite peaceful, and has far too many lures. I'd fish the next part of my life away if I went up there. Tell him I'll make plans to visit the Sooner State soon enough, and he can take me to that Red River he* *keeps talking about. Maybe I'll see a rattlesnake or two. He can make me a pair of those cowboy boots out of its skin!"* Monty laughed.

Hearing Elaine's voice again, Nick took a long drag from the Chesterfield before insisting that she be brought to the phone. Leaning casually against the headboard in his room near the open window, he blew a long trail of smoke into the open morning air, his gaze fixed on the busy streets below.

Despite the enormous distance between them separating them physically, he felt strangely connected to the woman; drawn in by the warmth of her, by her charm. Elaine seemed genuinely excited to speak to her husband, not realizing until she had been spoken to by Eoghan that Nick had even placed the call. Taking the receiver into her hands she gasped loudly with excitement, *"Nick, darling, is that really you?"* she asked.

"Oh sweetheart, it's been three weeks since I've heard your voice. I'm about to die without you. I know Scotland is so dear to me, it is, but my heart is with you wherever you are. You are my home, Nick." She whispered, trying hard to hold back her tears. The two spoke for several moments, both describing their time apart from one another, but with Nick purposely not going into too many lurid details he knew would cause his dear wife to worry about his person and his safety.

"Will you promise to tell me more when I come home?" she asked. *"I want to hear it all, I don't want to have to read about it someday in your memoirs. You know those things are so inflated. I want to know all the real details, even the ones you think are too raw and ugly – just be sure to prepare me for them before you tell me."* She giggled.

Mesa

"That's going to take longer than telling you what all happened!" he laughed. *"I'll say this now, and fill you in later. I'm about to go to a place in Texas where the dead are the stars of the show, and you can't buy a ticket to see it, but once you do see you can't unsee any of it."* He explained. *"I joined the circus for a few days. I don't think I'll ever get the hang of juggling, but I did give it my best. I got a few points for sharpshooting, and I did manage to outride one of the ring leaders during an impromptu horse race. We weren't allowed to use saddle or bridles, but I did get the reins to do what I needed them to do; he came off and I didn't, but neither of us made it to the finish line."* Nick said, trying to recall the lighter moments of his time spent on the mesa.

As she continued to talk to Nick, describing the various activities the families had planned for the remainder of their summer stay, Elaine reminded her husband that in less than a week their son would turn nine, and because they were celebrating his birthday in Scotland there had to be at least one more family member present to make it all very official.

Elaine explained that Pop Donny Posh would be joining the festivities and that Agnes their favorite waitress and Carin the cook and cashier at the Red Door Café were throwing him one heck of a shindig such as the joint had never seen before. Newspaperman Gabe Hanshaw and his new steady were coming, along with Gabe's mother too; she was sure there would be plenty of excitement – maybe even a few clowns!

"Alistair has already been given his first birthday gift from Eoghan's well-meaning sassy mother Maggie

Broonford MacRae; a large suitcase with his very own initials embossed on the top of it as well as on the front lower corner. She told him every young man who was going places would need one; he is in love with it. He has placed everything he's brought with him from the States into the thing, and he walks around the apartment as if he's been traveling around the world. You should see him, Nick. He's just such a little man." Elaine's words stung and soothed at the same time.

He knew someday soon he'd hold his wife again; for now it would be his dreamlife where she took command of their hopes and created something too glorious for words and too ethereal to remember. Until that day, he would focus on his duties, content in knowing that people would always be who and what they were, and if he wanted to keep those he loved safe to be who and what they could become, he would need to remain exactly the man he was made to be.

Before Elaine passed the headset to Chief Montgomery, her husband had a word to add regarding his son's party at the Red Door café'. *"Elaine, sweetheart, you know I love a good party like anyone else - maybe you don't need any clowns; just a thought."* He said, and the two shared an unexpected laugh.

Monty took the receiver from Elaine to have a word with Nick. *"Say, Nick,"* he started. *"I know you can't be here, and that you would be if you could be, so I'll just say this to you now. Men like you, men like men, and well, you know I'm going to say it, men like Oscar Keogh, my partner for over a decade in this hell of a life I chose; we're not like the others.*

"We have a calling and we answered it. We may come off as brash, rude, hard-cased, and formative but in

the end, when the last light is turned off and the folks go home to their families; we will always have each other." He said, his words being met with silence on the other end. Another moment or two passed before Nick could speak, but when he did, he thanked his friend for the time he put into the service of protecting the people he knew and those he would never meet on this side of life.

Monty started to end the call but remembered another bit of information he had run across having read another one of Gabe Hanshaw's piggy-back articles in the evening news. *"Posh, you told me those boys up in Chicago were found floating in the tank full of lard or grease from where the restaurants would dump their leftover fats.*

"You said the market for it was unusual, rather niche, but a necessary evil so to speak. With very few places to dump that stuff most folks around these parts have been finding rivers and lochs closer to the English border to dispose of their wares, sort of a gift if you will for all the centuries of crap that lot has been doling out to us Scots. What I'm telling you is that another body was found in a different type of vat, and Gabe wrote about it saying the murders were using the same type of reasoning as maybe your killers used back in Chicago.

"A bullet hole was discovered only after the man's body came floating to the top of the vat; a Boudreau wine in fact; quite rare. I guess the flavoring of this one would have been even more unique if anyone had been so unlucky to have taste-tested it." Monty stated flatly. *"I bet the French don't throw it out though; they might if it was being distilled in their country, but why not let the Brits have the tainted batch? Saves them the trouble of picking the grapes to replace them.*

Jude Stringfellow

"You can't make these stories up, Posh." He said, *"People find the most curious ways to die these days. I have to be upfront and honest with you, I'm not one hundred percent sure I want to hang up my holster just yet; not when I see stories like that literally floating around me."* He joked, realizing the pun was obvious.

Monty thanked his friend before saying farewell, adding their work was never really finished. *"Oscar, God rest his soul, is here too, Nick. He's with us right now, and if he could speak from his grave, he'd tell you the same thing, Posh. If he had read about what you did there in Chicago and in the West, he'd have something to say to you, that's for sure.*

"He'd tell you we all love a good public service killing when we can get one," Monty tried hard to put on the particularly thick brogue his good friend Chief Inspector Oscar Keogh had to say, *"You know we have to keep this up, right? The bad guys keep it up on their end, we have to fight them the best we can within the boundaries of the law.*

"Sometimes those lines get fuzzy. Sometimes those lines blur a little; but we do what we need to do." Monty turned himself away from earshot of Elaine, from anyone else to say, *"Posh, we may need your ongoing help on this one. You know we do."*

Mesa

AUTHORS NOTES:

It shouldn't have to be said, because the fact that this book is a work of fiction should stand on its own, but I will mention it, because some may either take offense or be offended by the use of names, similar names, traits, or described areas that may resemble them or someone they know.

Any use of names, places, and references is done so in the name of creative writing. This book is a work of FICTION – I do mention real names of real people who lived or died, but they are not in any way key to the plot or narrative of the book. They are merely references.

Scotland is a real place. I will admit to that. Chicago exists, as does Las Vegas. Oklahoma is real too, and it's still sitting on top of Texas, the way God intended it to. Boomer Sooner!

ABOUT THE AUTHOR:

Jude Stringfellow has written more than a dozen books using various genres to do so. She's written several Nick Posh thrillers; *"Mesa"* being the 4th in the series. She hails from the Great State of Oklahoma, just like her main character, though she was born in a completely different time. Nick Posh does, however, have the same birthday as Jude's maternal grandfather Ernest Rivers Edwards; who was born in Indian Territory on November 19, 1890.

Jude is a proud Blue Star Mom. Her son Reuben has served in the United States Army in one capacity or the other for nearly twenty years. He is currently in the Oklahoma National Guard and a member of their elite 45th Infantry. Her daughters hold themselves as Oklahoma State fans rather than rooting for the University of Oklahoma Sooners; God Himself only knows why. Both Laura and Caiti write fanfiction stories, and poetry, and are both published in their own right.

Jude's grandchildren are the joy of her heart for sure. At the time of this book's first publishing, she has three grandchildren, with another one on the way. Life is fun, happy, and exciting in the Stringfellow brood. Between writing, traveling, and spending as much time as she can with her family, Jude also enjoys tuning in to watch Charlie Garrett of The Superior Word in Sarasota, Florida. His teaching and preaching have meant so much to Jude over the past several years. His words of grace and God's truth can be found on YouTube and Rumble.com.

Jude's social media links are:
https://www.instagram.com/judestringfellowauthor
https://www.linkedin.com/in/judestringfellow

Jude Stringfellow

Printed in the USA
CPSIA information can be obtained
at www.ICGtesting.com
LVHW090842090724
784993LV00004B/148